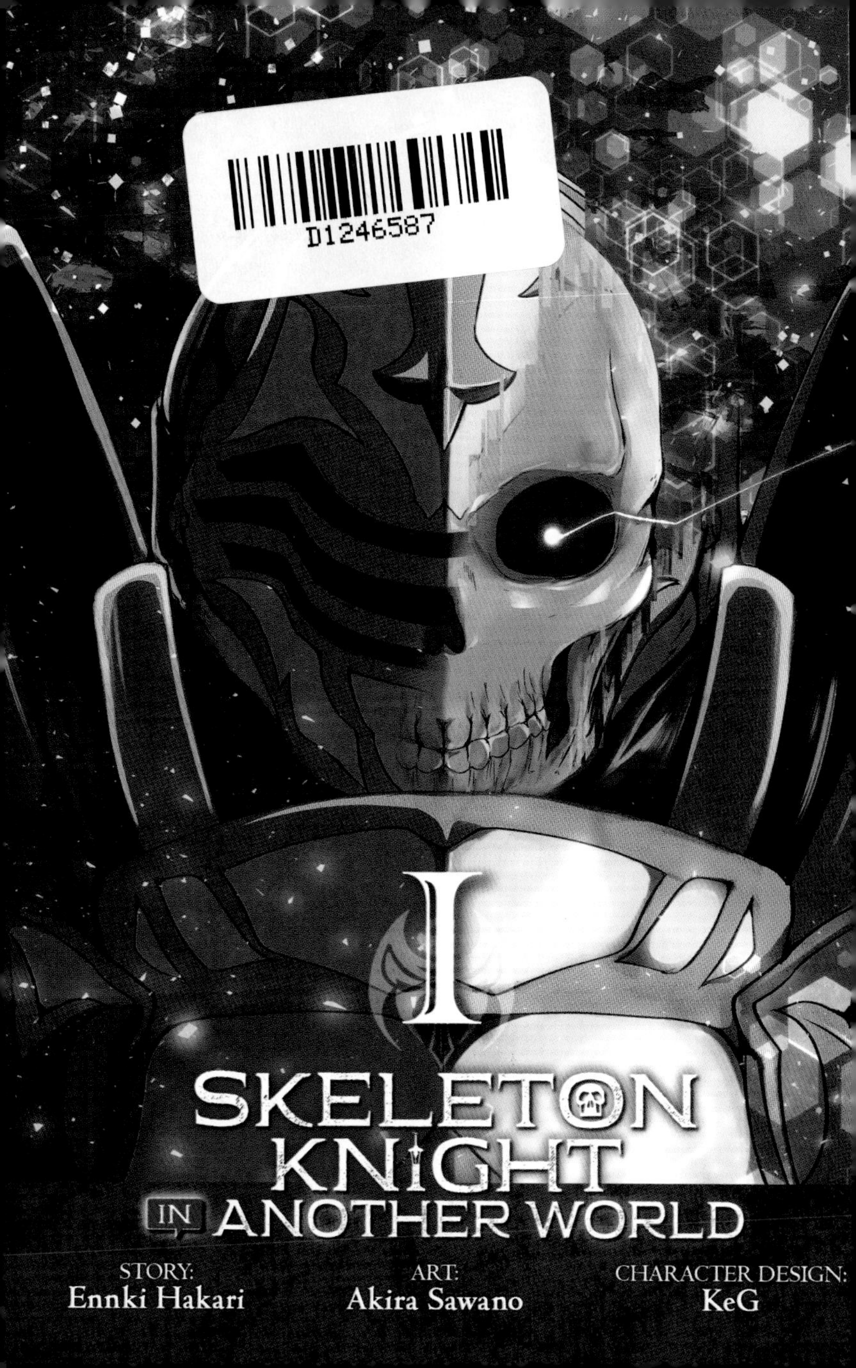

I

SKELETON KNIGHT IN ANOTHER WORLD

STORY: Ennki Hakari

ART: Akira Sawano

CHARACTER DESIGN: KeG

SKELETON KNiGHT in ANOTHER WORLD

❧ CONTENTS ❧

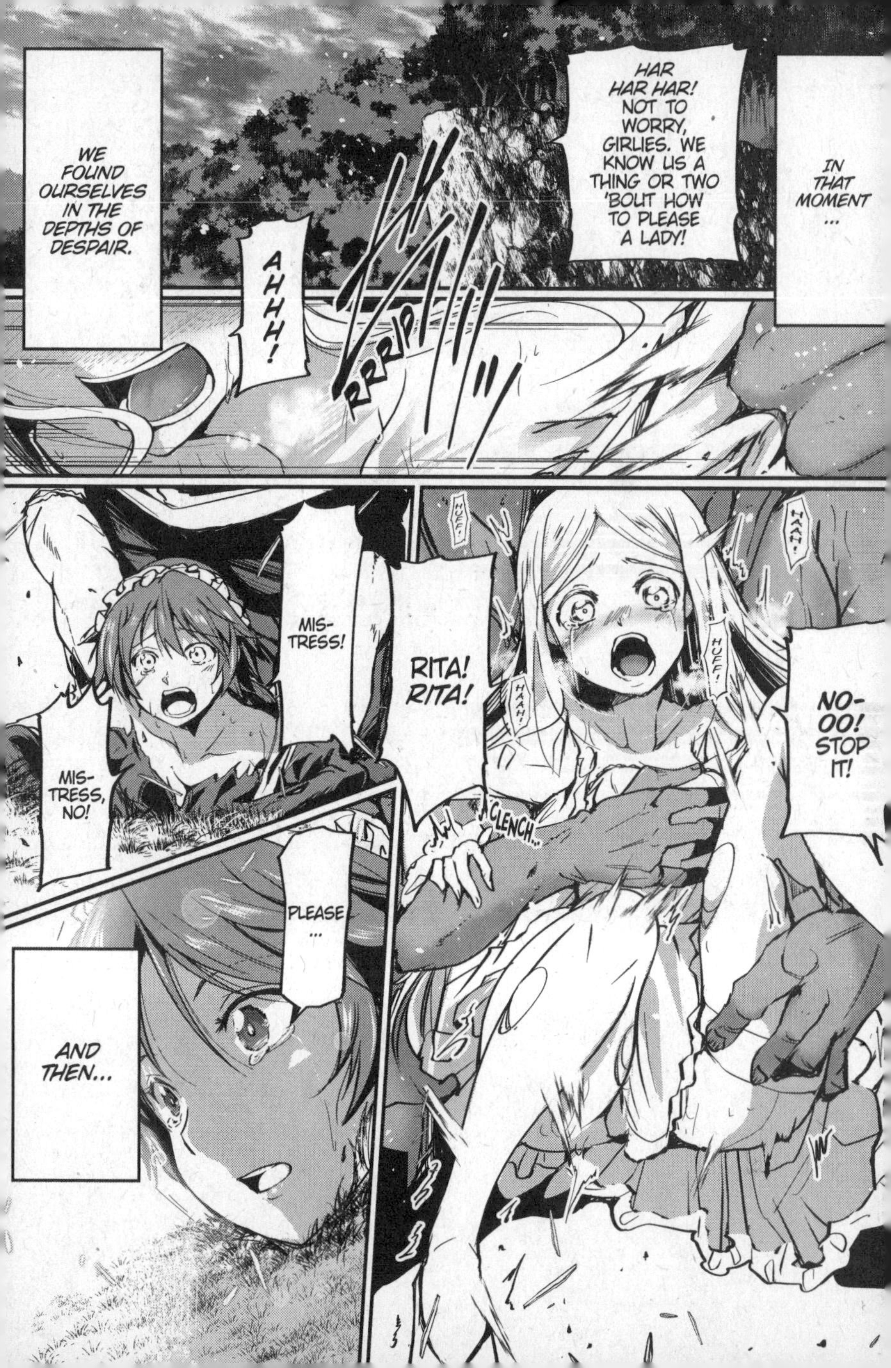
IN THAT MOMENT ...
HAR HAR HAR! NOT TO WORRY, GIRLIES. WE KNOW US A THING OR TWO 'BOUT HOW TO PLEASE A LADY!
RRRIP!!
AHHHH!
WE FOUND OURSELVES IN THE DEPTHS OF DESPAIR.
HAAH!
HUFF!
HUFF!
HAAH!
NO-OO! STOP IT!
CLENCH...
RITA! RITA!
MIS-TRESS!
MIS-TRESS, NO!
PLEASE ...
AND THEN...

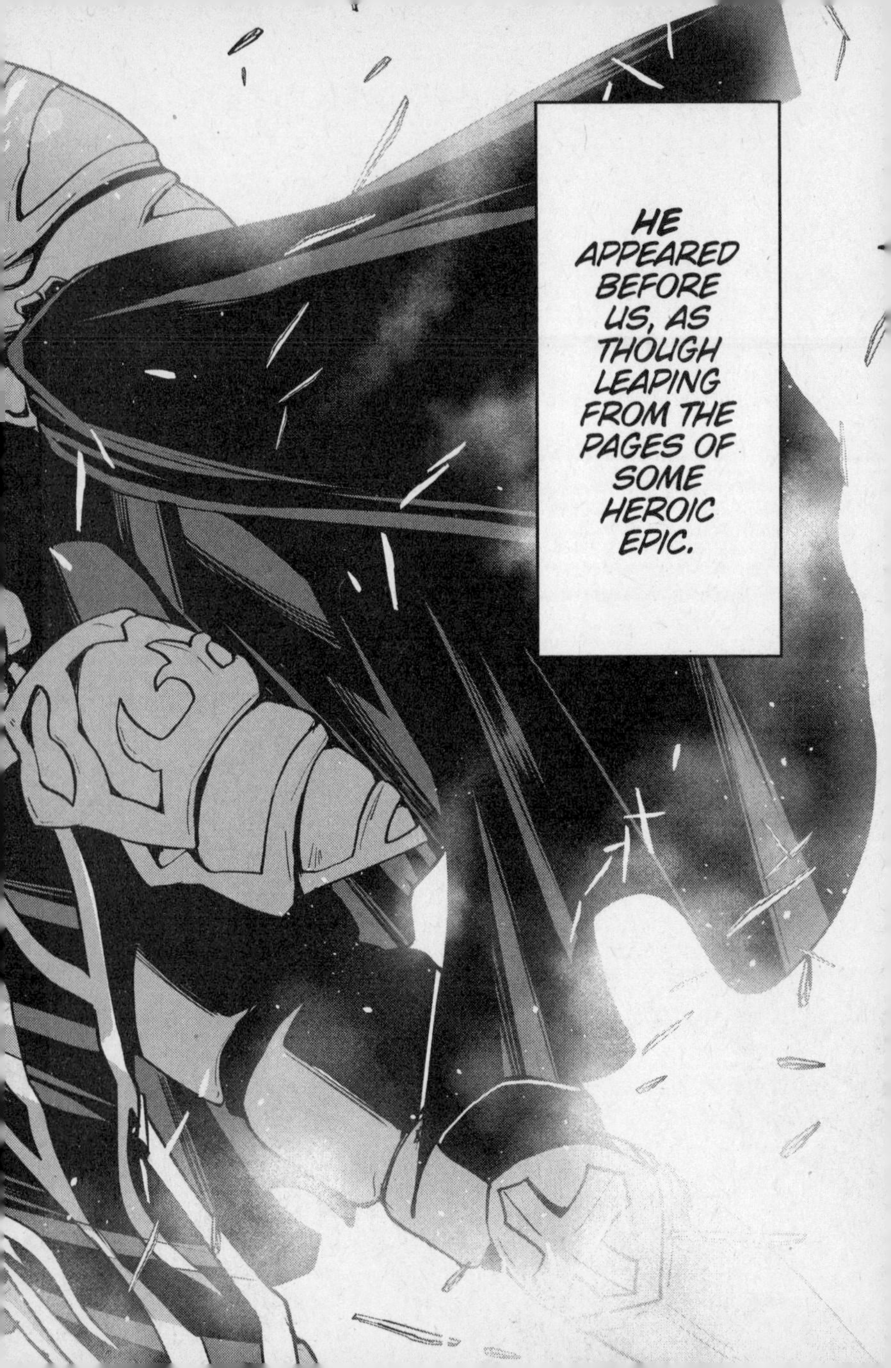
HE APPEARED BEFORE US, AS THOUGH LEAPING FROM THE PAGES OF SOME HEROIC EPIC.

CHAPTER 1:
Journey to a Mysterious World

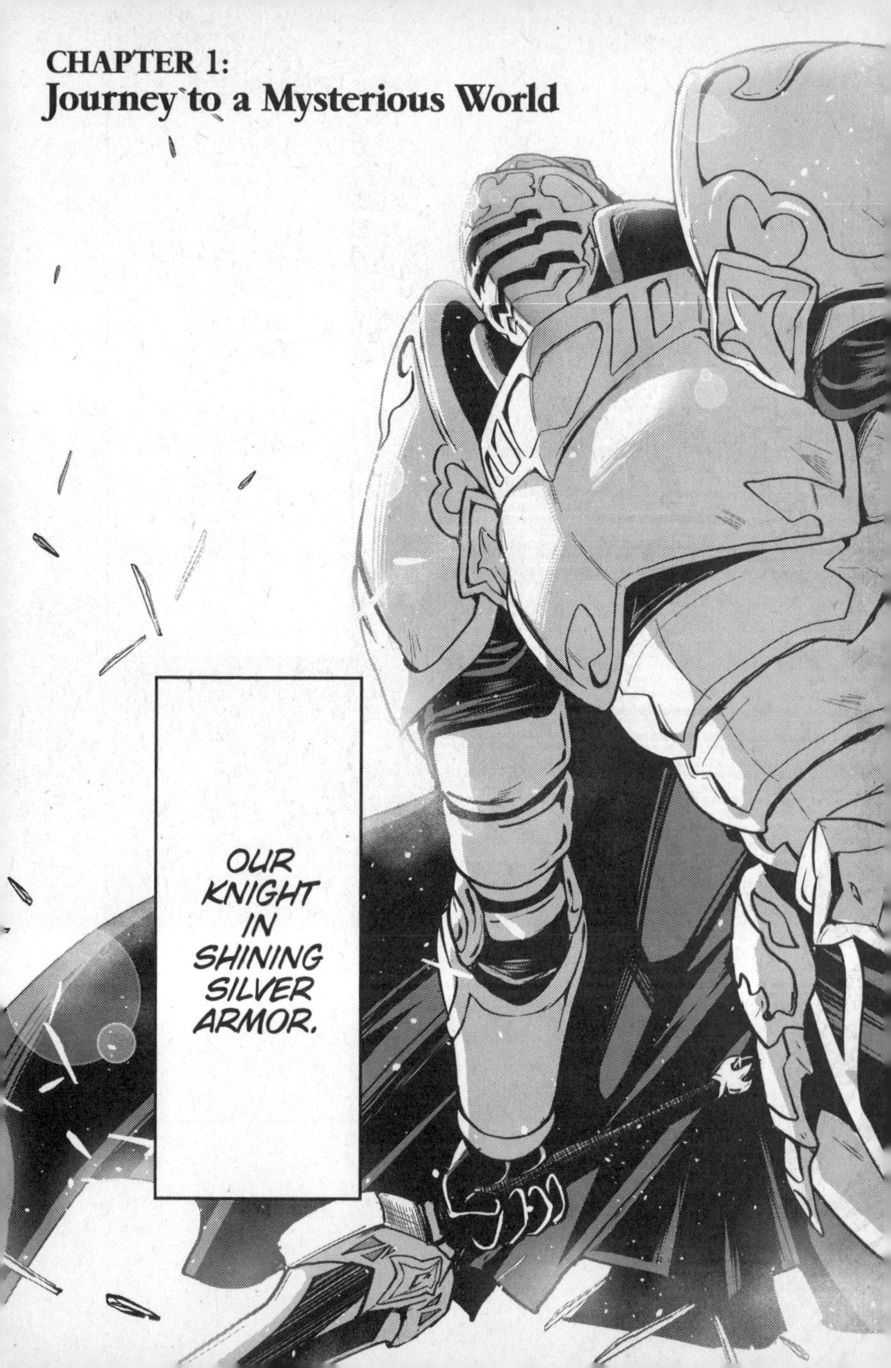
OUR KNIGHT IN SHINING SILVER ARMOR.

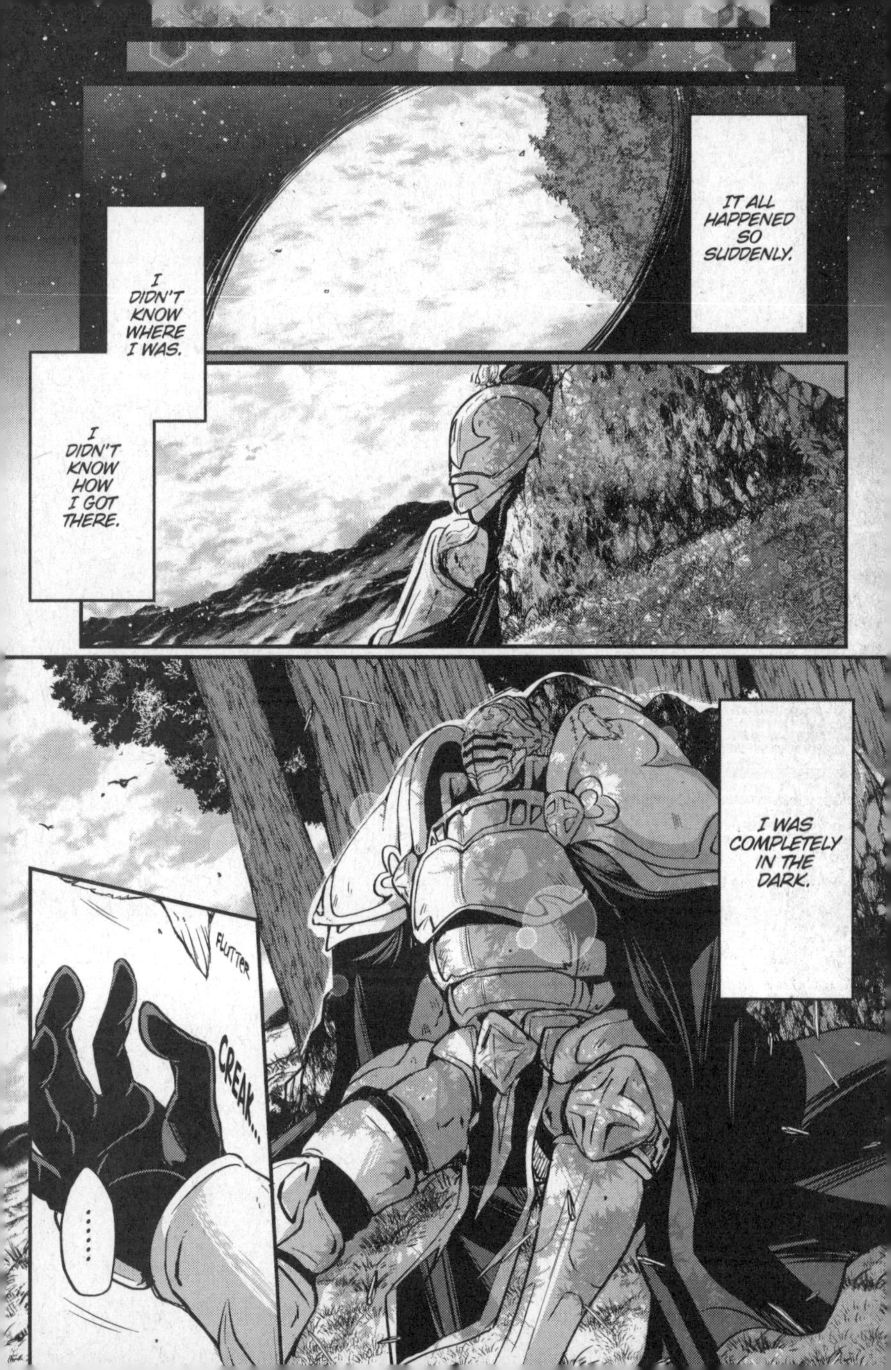
IT ALL HAPPENED SO SUDDENLY.
I DIDN'T KNOW WHERE I WAS.
I DIDN'T KNOW HOW I GOT THERE.
I WAS COMPLETELY IN THE DARK.
FLUTTER
CREAK...
......

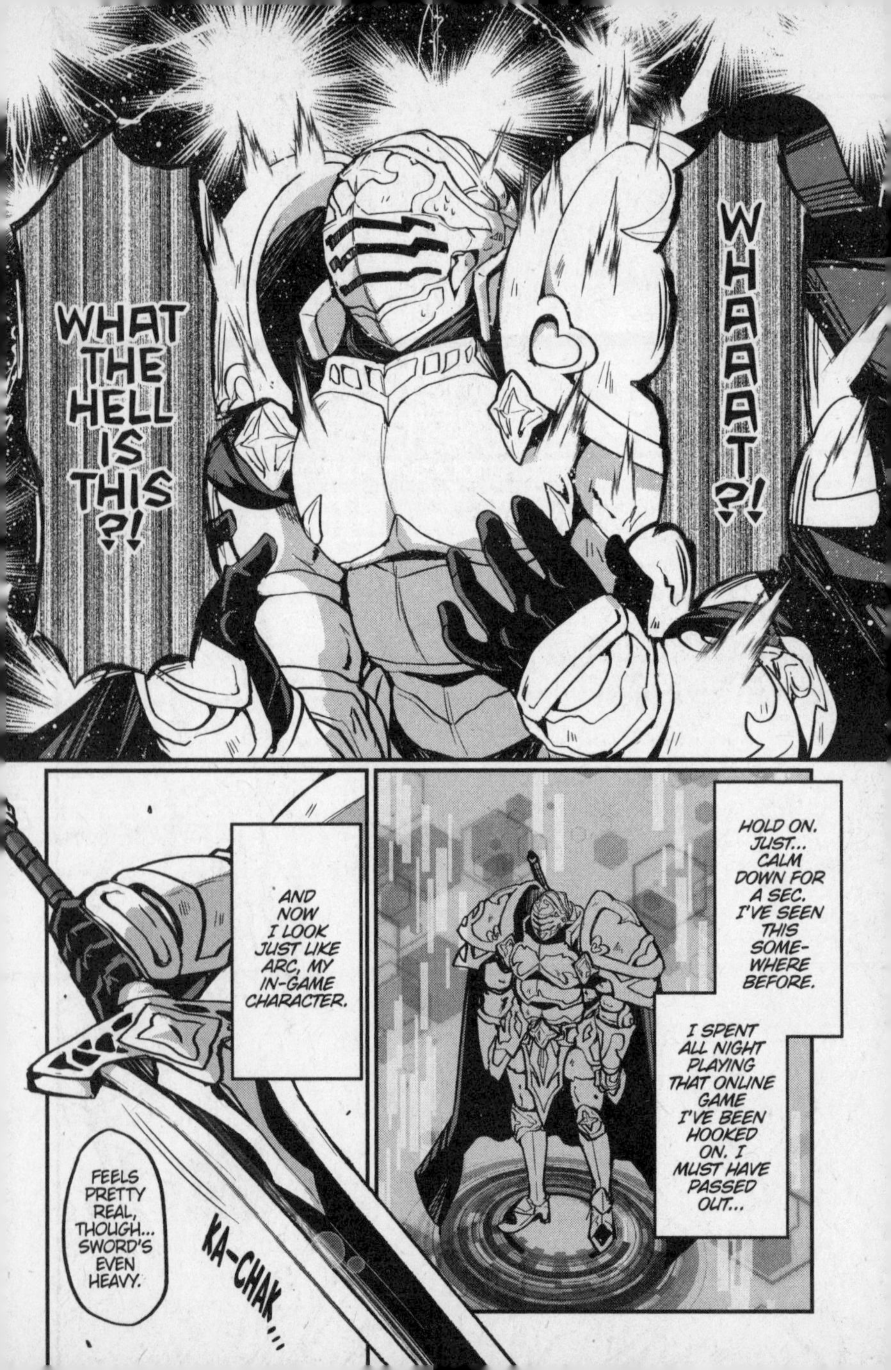
WHAAAT?!
WHAT THE HELL IS THIS?!
HOLD ON. JUST... CALM DOWN FOR A SEC. I'VE SEEN THIS SOMEWHERE BEFORE.
I SPENT ALL NIGHT PLAYING THAT ONLINE GAME I'VE BEEN HOOKED ON. I MUST HAVE PASSED OUT...
AND NOW I LOOK JUST LIKE ARC, MY IN-GAME CHARACTER.
FEELS PRETTY REAL, THOUGH... SWORD'S EVEN HEAVY.
KA-CHAK...

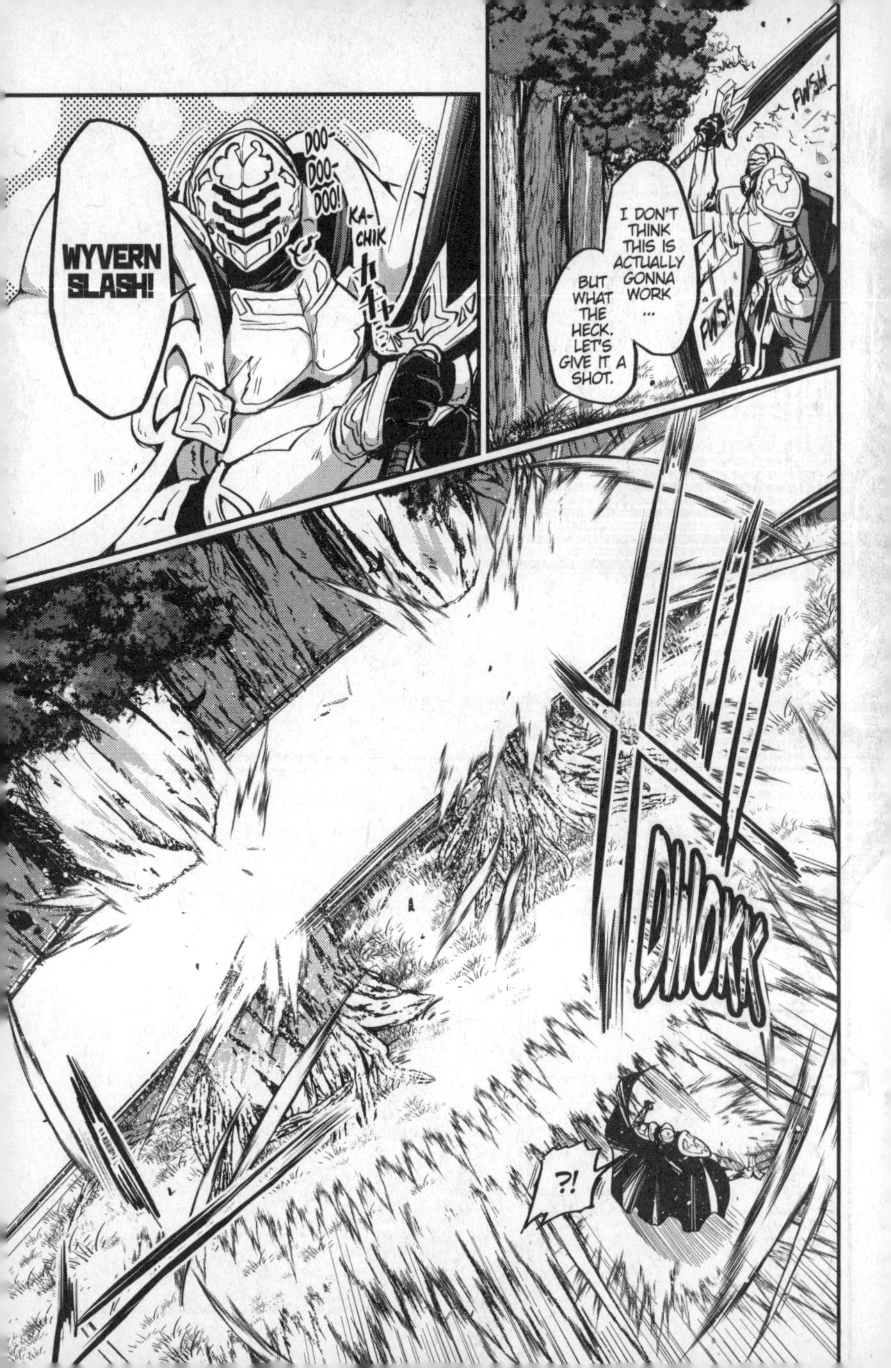
FWSH
I DON'T THINK THIS IS ACTUALLY GONNA WORK ...
BUT WHAT THE HECK. LET'S GIVE IT A SHOT.
FWSH
DOO-DOO-DOO!
KA-CHIK
WYVERN SLASH!
DHOKK
?!

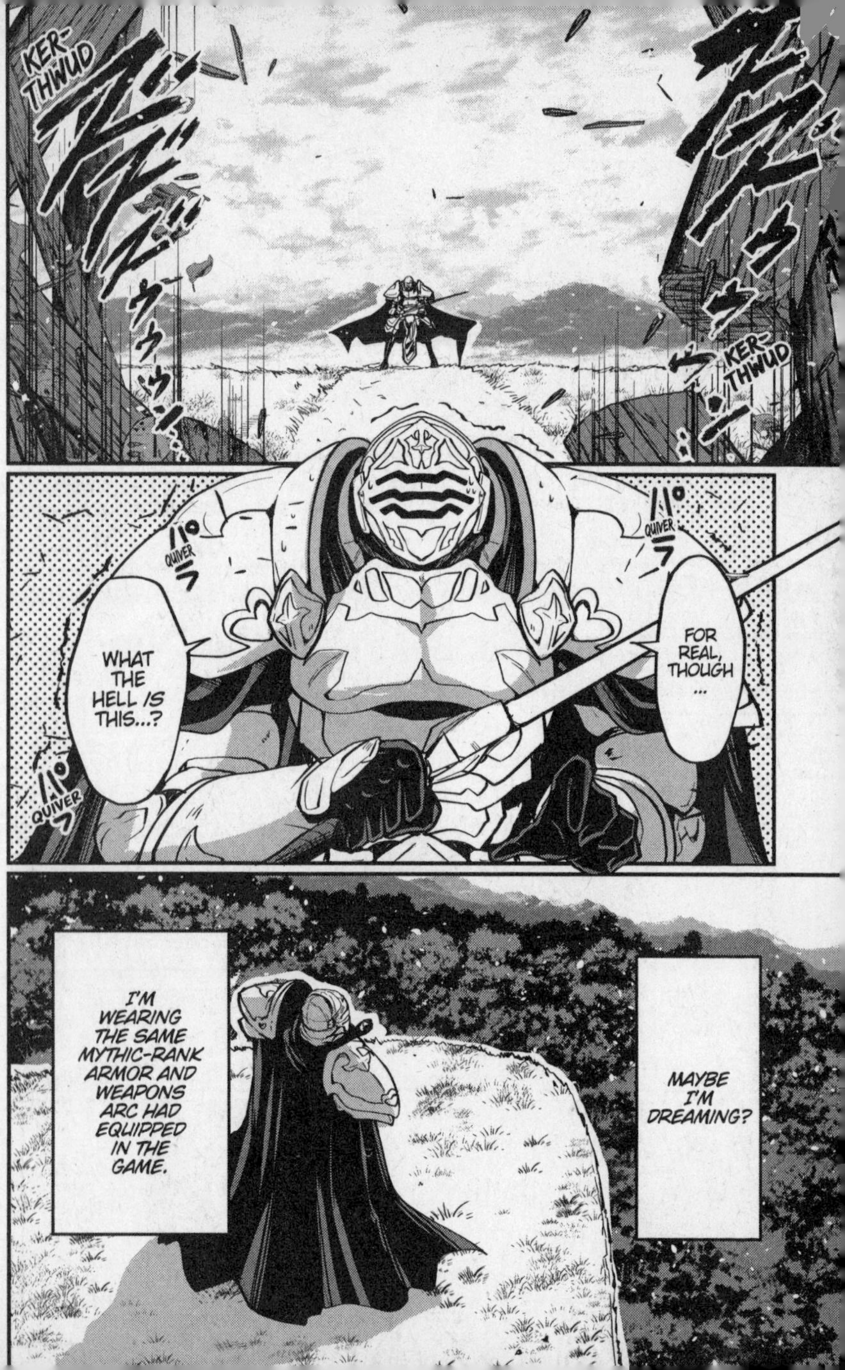

KER-THWUD
KER-THWUD
QUIVER
FOR REAL, THOUGH...
WHAT THE HELL IS THIS...?
QUIVER
QUIVER
MAYBE I'M DREAMING?
I'M WEARING THE SAME MYTHIC-RANK ARMOR AND WEAPONS ARC HAD EQUIPPED IN THE GAME.

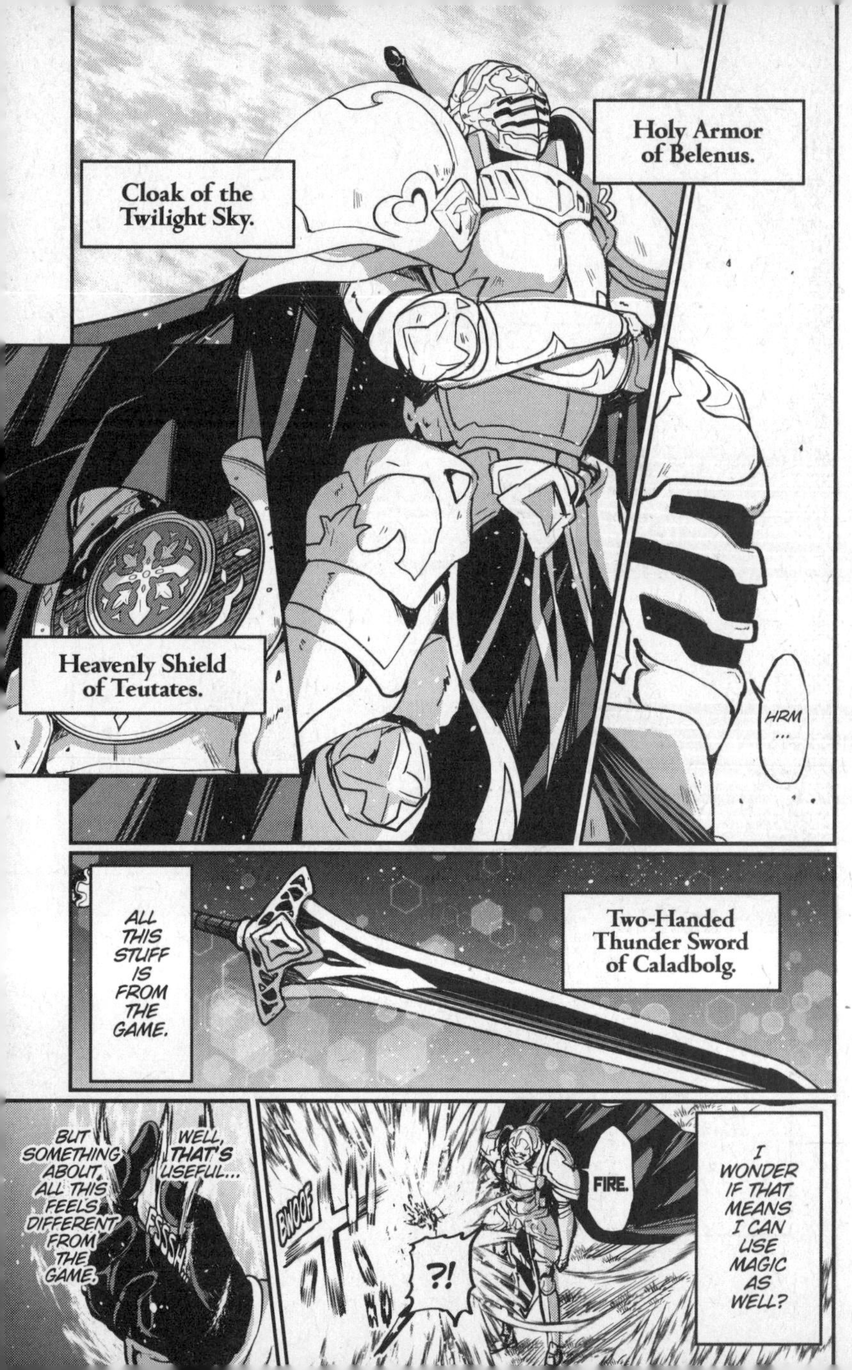
Holy Armor of Belenus.
Cloak of the Twilight Sky.
HRM...
Heavenly Shield of Teutates.
Two-Handed Thunder Sword of Caladbolg.
ALL THIS STUFF IS FROM THE GAME.
I WONDER IF THAT MEANS I CAN USE MAGIC AS WELL?
FIRE.
BWOOF
?!
WELL, THAT'S USEFUL...
FSSSH
BUT SOMETHING ABOUT ALL THIS FEELS DIFFERENT FROM THE GAME.

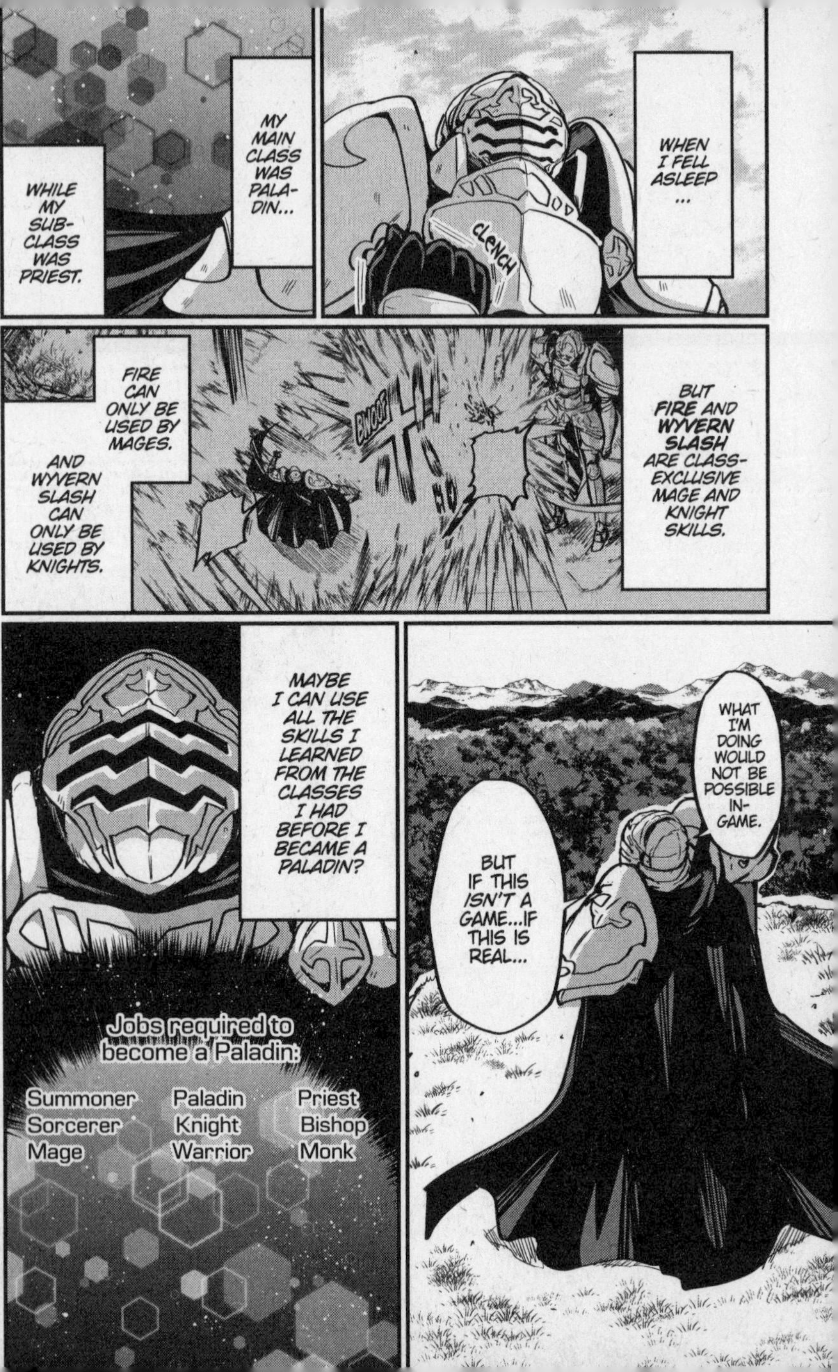
WHEN I FELL ASLEEP...
CLENCH
MY MAIN CLASS WAS PALA-DIN...
WHILE MY SUB-CLASS WAS PRIEST.
BUT FIRE AND WYVERN SLASH ARE CLASS-EXCLUSIVE MAGE AND KNIGHT SKILLS.
FIRE CAN ONLY BE USED BY MAGES.
AND WYVERN SLASH CAN ONLY BE USED BY KNIGHTS.
WHAT I'M DOING WOULD NOT BE POSSIBLE IN-GAME.
BUT IF THIS ISN'T A GAME...IF THIS IS REAL...
MAYBE I CAN USE ALL THE SKILLS I LEARNED FROM THE CLASSES I HAD BEFORE I BECAME A PALADIN?
Jobs required to become a Paladin:
Summoner
Sorcerer
Mage
Paladin
Knight
Warrior
Priest
Bishop
Monk

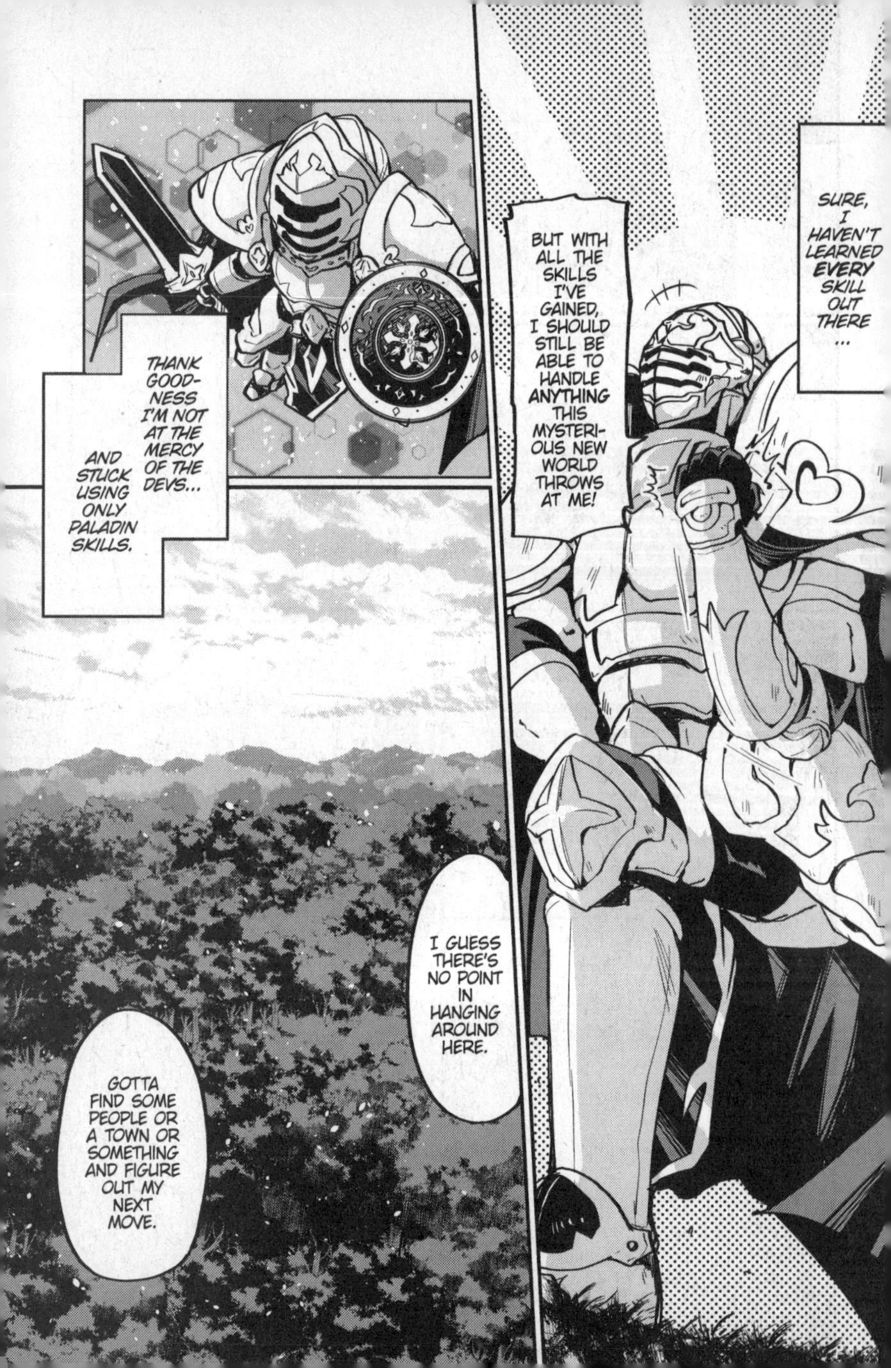
SURE, I HAVEN'T LEARNED EVERY SKILL OUT THERE...
BUT WITH ALL THE SKILLS I'VE GAINED, I SHOULD STILL BE ABLE TO HANDLE ANYTHING THIS MYSTERIOUS NEW WORLD THROWS AT ME!
THANK GOODNESS I'M NOT AT THE MERCY OF THE DEVS...
AND STUCK USING ONLY PALADIN SKILLS.
I GUESS THERE'S NO POINT IN HANGING AROUND HERE.
GOTTA FIND SOME PEOPLE OR A TOWN OR SOMETHING AND FIGURE OUT MY NEXT MOVE.

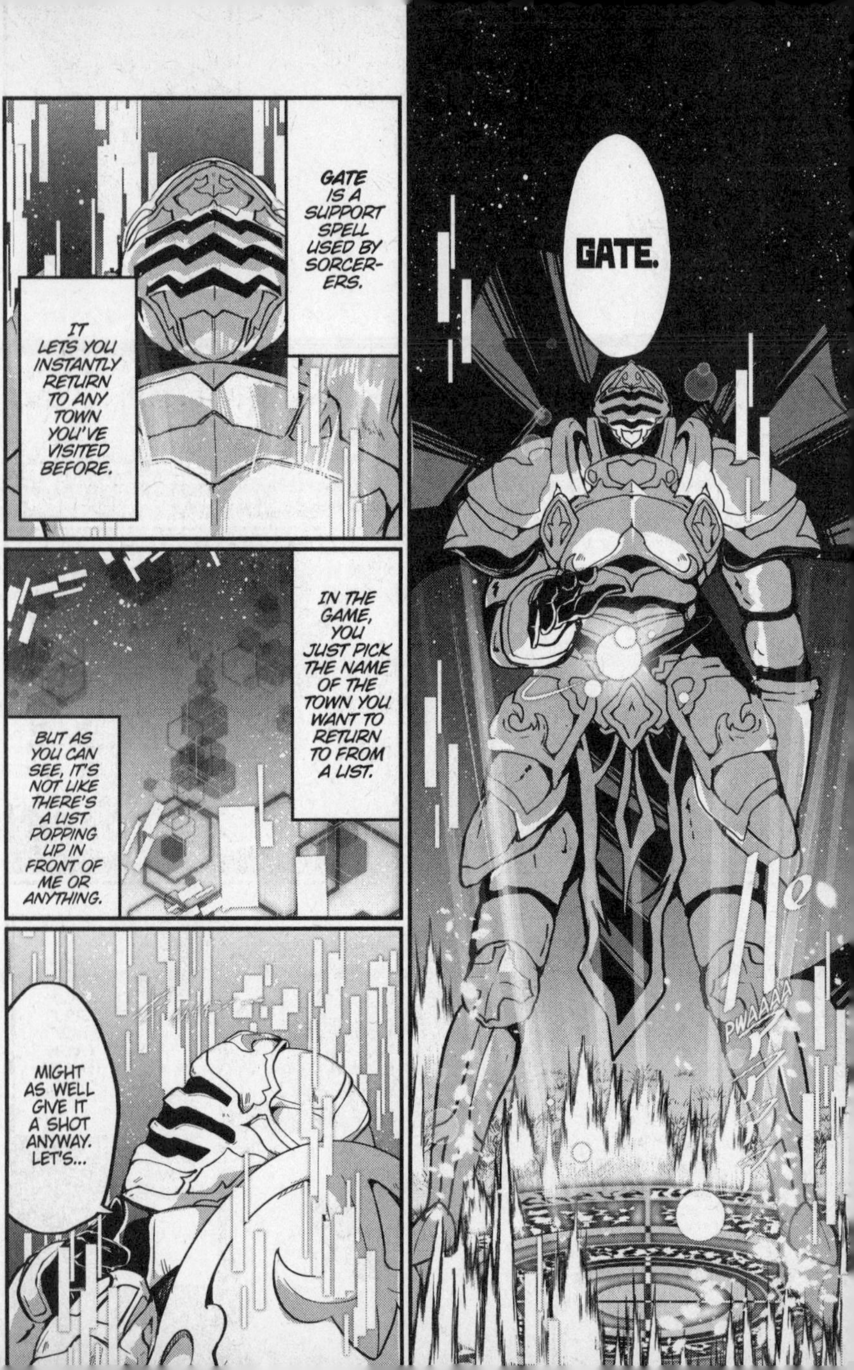
GATE IS A SUPPORT SPELL USED BY SORCERERS.
IT LETS YOU INSTANTLY RETURN TO ANY TOWN YOU'VE VISITED BEFORE.
IN THE GAME, YOU JUST PICK THE NAME OF THE TOWN YOU WANT TO RETURN TO FROM A LIST.
BUT AS YOU CAN SEE, IT'S NOT LIKE THERE'S A LIST POPPING UP IN FRONT OF ME OR ANYTHING.
MIGHT AS WELL GIVE IT A SHOT ANYWAY. LET'S...
GATE.
PWAAAA

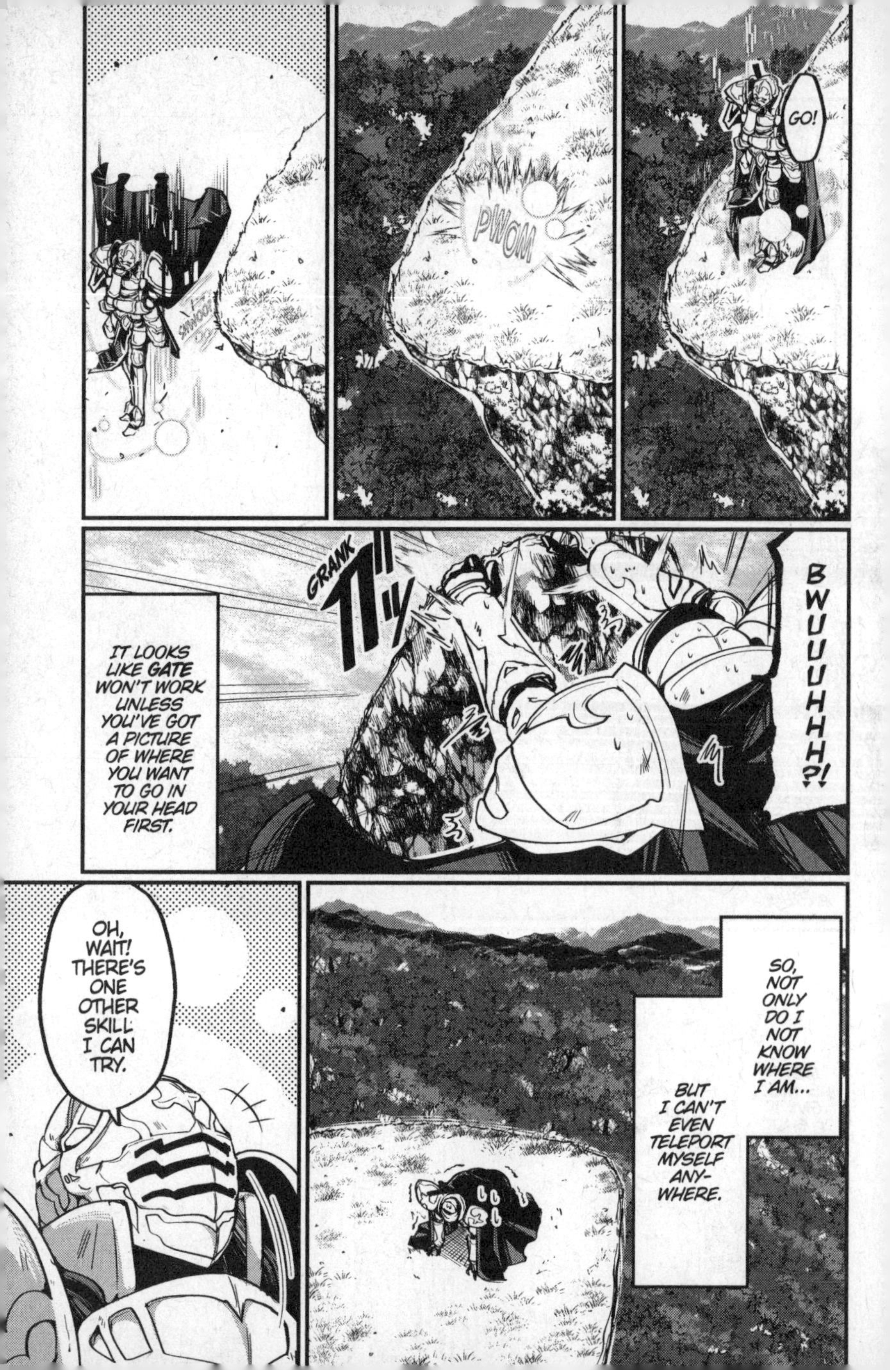
GO!
PWOM
BWUUUUHHHH?!
GRANK
IT LOOKS LIKE GATE WON'T WORK UNLESS YOU'VE GOT A PICTURE OF WHERE YOU WANT TO GO IN YOUR HEAD FIRST.
SO, NOT ONLY DO I NOT KNOW WHERE I AM...
BUT I CAN'T EVEN TELEPORT MYSELF ANY-WHERE.
OH, WAIT! THERE'S ONE OTHER SKILL I CAN TRY.

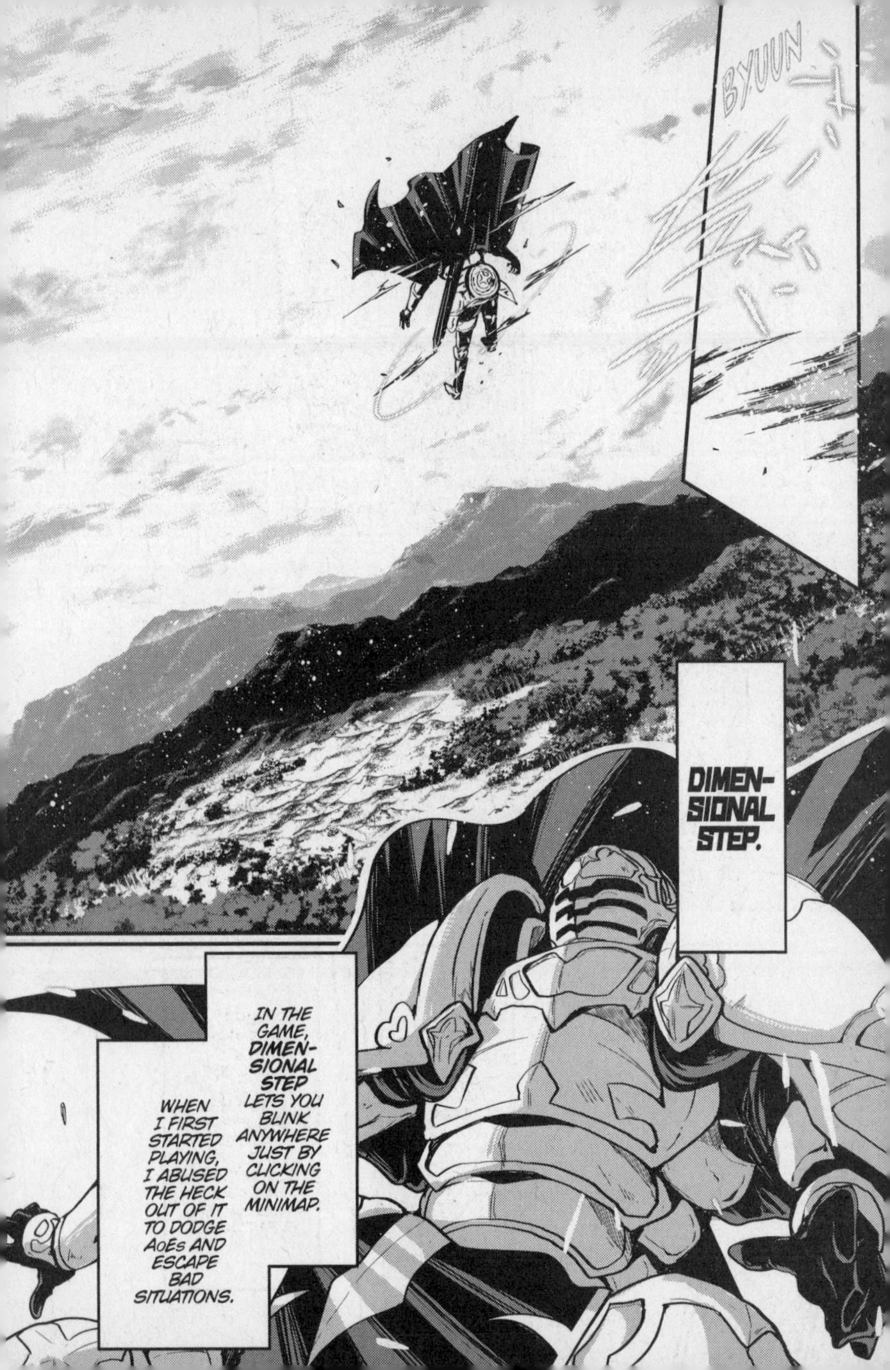
BYUUN
DIMEN-SIONAL STEP.
IN THE GAME, DIMEN-SIONAL STEP LETS YOU BLINK ANYWHERE JUST BY CLICKING ON THE MINIMAP.
WHEN I FIRST STARTED PLAYING, I ABUSED THE HECK OUT OF IT TO DODGE AoEs AND ESCAPE BAD SITUATIONS.

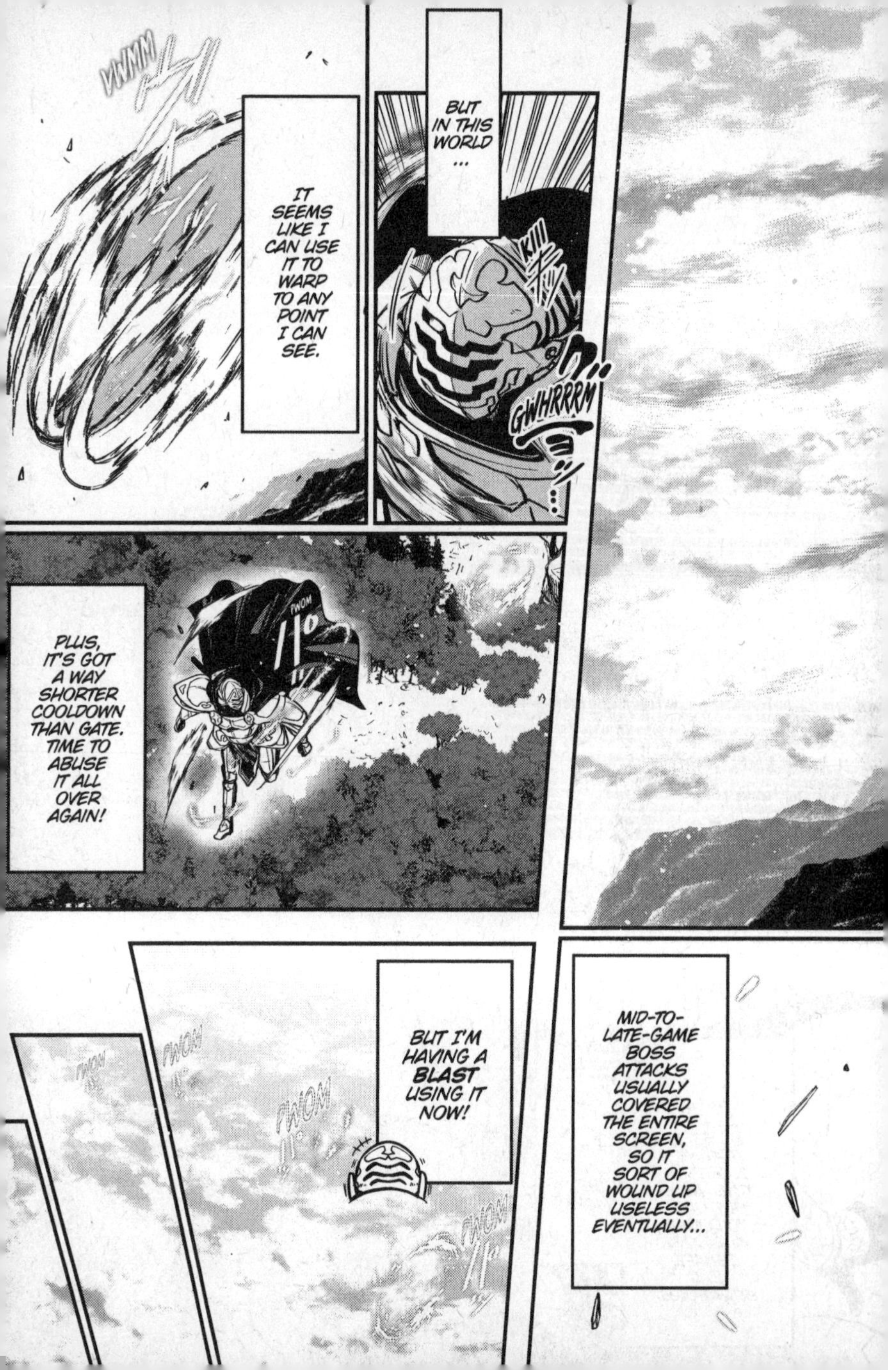
BUT IN THIS WORLD...
GWHRRRM
IT SEEMS LIKE I CAN USE IT TO WARP TO ANY POINT I CAN SEE.
VWMM
PLUS, IT'S GOT A WAY SHORTER COOLDOWN THAN GATE. TIME TO ABUSE IT ALL OVER AGAIN!
PWOM
MID-TO-LATE-GAME BOSS ATTACKS USUALLY COVERED THE ENTIRE SCREEN, SO IT SORT OF WOUND UP USELESS EVENTUALLY...
BUT I'M HAVING A **BLAST** USING IT NOW!
PWOM
PWOM
PWOM
PWOM

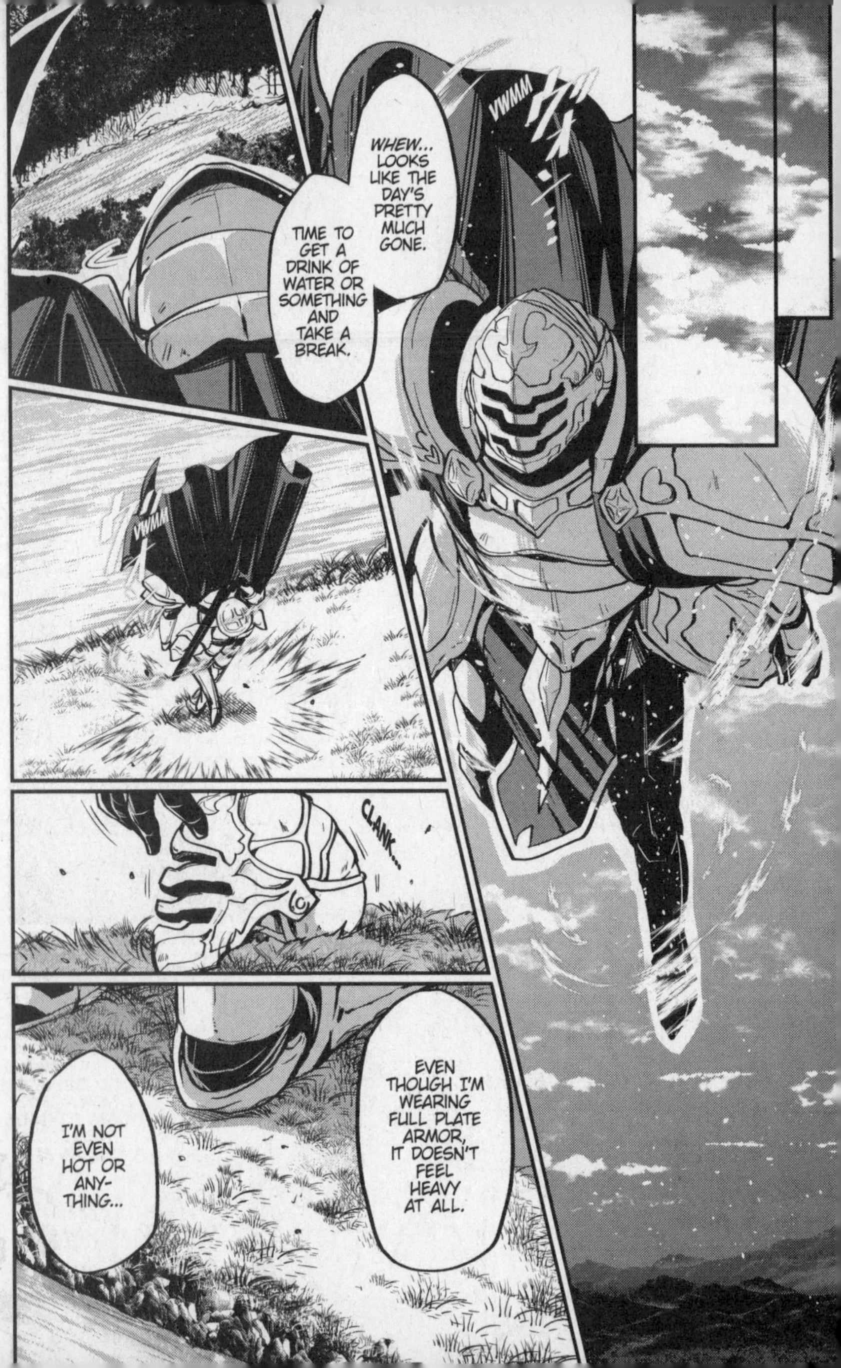
VWMM
WHEW... LOOKS LIKE THE DAY'S PRETTY MUCH GONE.
TIME TO GET A DRINK OF WATER OR SOMETHING AND TAKE A BREAK.
VWMM
CLANK...
EVEN THOUGH I'M WEARING FULL PLATE ARMOR, IT DOESN'T FEEL HEAVY AT ALL.
I'M NOT EVEN HOT OR ANY-THING...

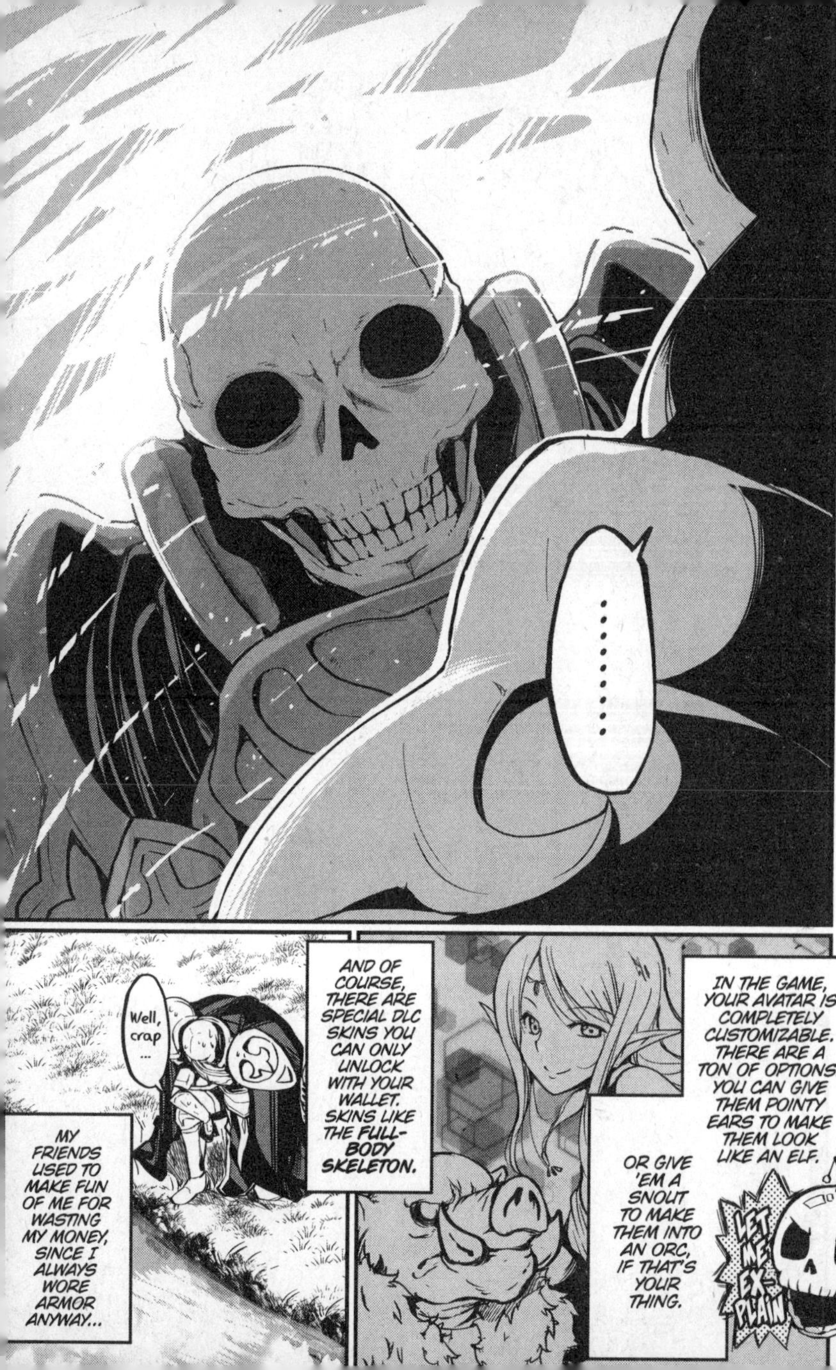
......
IN THE GAME, YOUR AVATAR IS COMPLETELY CUSTOMIZABLE. THERE ARE A TON OF OPTIONS. YOU CAN GIVE THEM POINTY EARS TO MAKE THEM LOOK LIKE AN ELF.
OR GIVE 'EM A SNOUT TO MAKE THEM INTO AN ORC, IF THAT'S YOUR THING.
LET ME EX-PLAIN
AND OF COURSE, THERE ARE SPECIAL DLC SKINS YOU CAN ONLY UNLOCK WITH YOUR WALLET. SKINS LIKE THE FULL-BODY SKELETON.
Well, crap ...
MY FRIENDS USED TO MAKE FUN OF ME FOR WASTING MY MONEY, SINCE I ALWAYS WORE ARMOR ANYWAY...

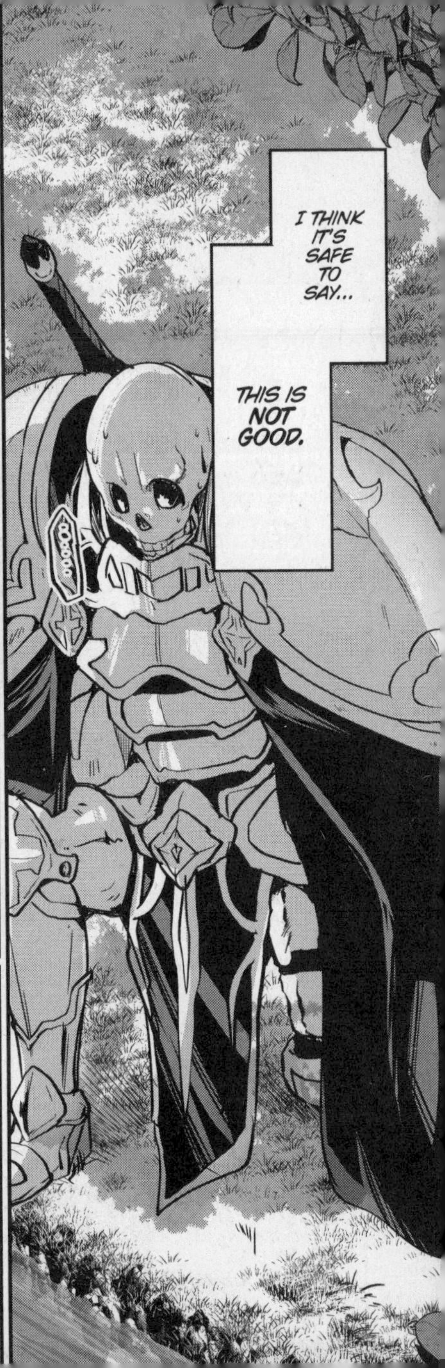
I THINK IT'S SAFE TO SAY...
THIS IS NOT GOOD.
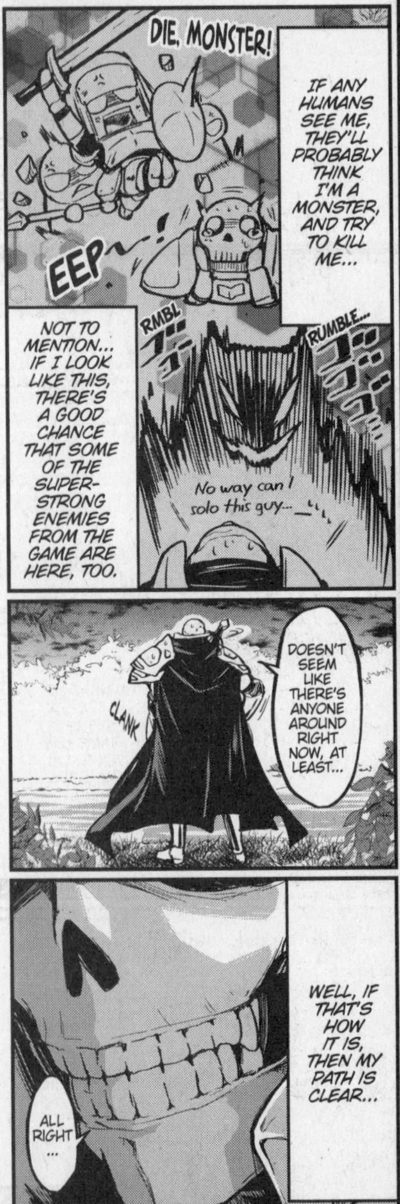
IF ANY HUMANS SEE ME, THEY'LL PROBABLY THINK I'M A MONSTER, AND TRY TO KILL ME...
DIE, MONSTER!
EEP~~!
NOT TO MENTION... IF I LOOK LIKE THIS, THERE'S A GOOD CHANCE THAT SOME OF THE SUPER-STRONG ENEMIES FROM THE GAME ARE HERE, TOO.
RUMBLE...
RMBL
No way can I solo this guy...
DOESN'T SEEM LIKE THERE'S ANYONE AROUND RIGHT NOW, AT LEAST...
CLANK
WELL, IF THAT'S HOW IT IS, THEN MY PATH IS CLEAR...
ALL RIGHT...

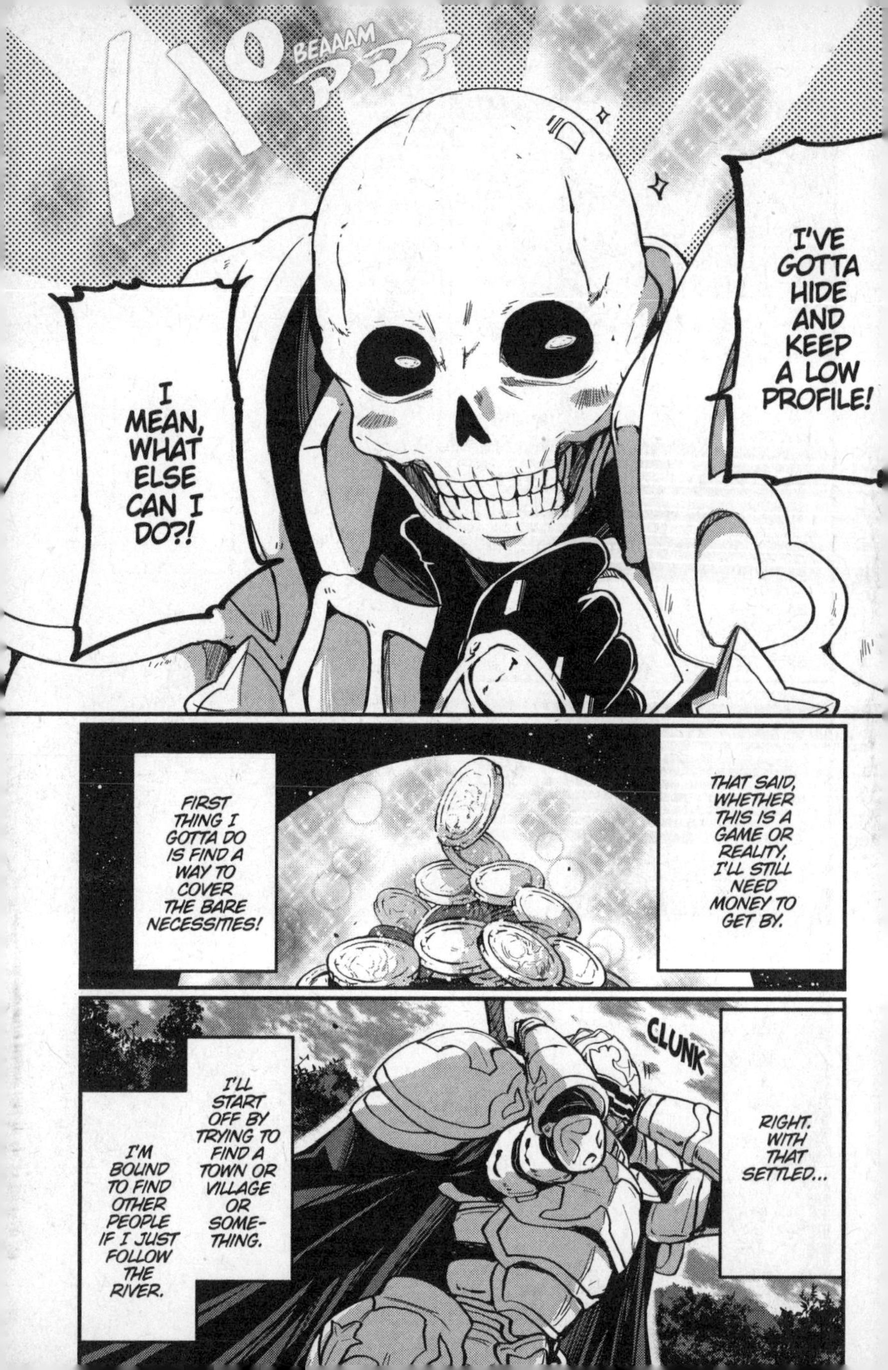
I'VE GOTTA HIDE AND KEEP A LOW PROFILE!
BEAAAM
I MEAN, WHAT ELSE CAN I DO?!
THAT SAID, WHETHER THIS IS A GAME OR REALITY, I'LL STILL NEED MONEY TO GET BY.
FIRST THING I GOTTA DO IS FIND A WAY TO COVER THE BARE NECESSITIES!
RIGHT. WITH THAT SETTLED...
CLUNK
I'LL START OFF BY TRYING TO FIND A TOWN OR VILLAGE OR SOME-THING.
I'M BOUND TO FIND OTHER PEOPLE IF I JUST FOLLOW THE RIVER.

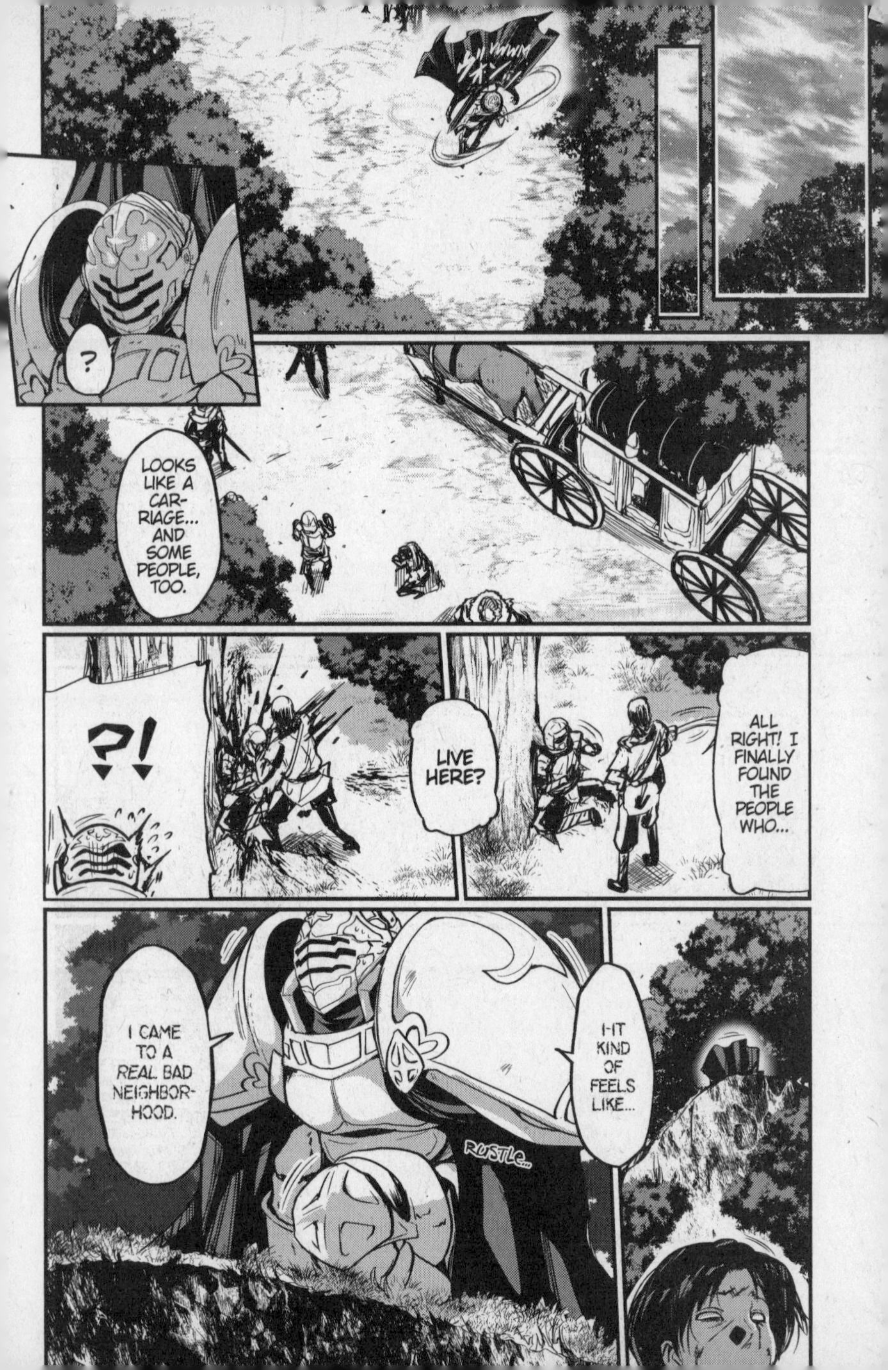
?
LOOKS LIKE A CAR-RIAGE... AND SOME PEOPLE, TOO.
ALL RIGHT! I FINALLY FOUND THE PEOPLE WHO...
LIVE HERE?
?!
I-IT KIND OF FEELS LIKE...
I CAME TO A *REAL* BAD NEIGHBOR-HOOD.
RUSTLE...

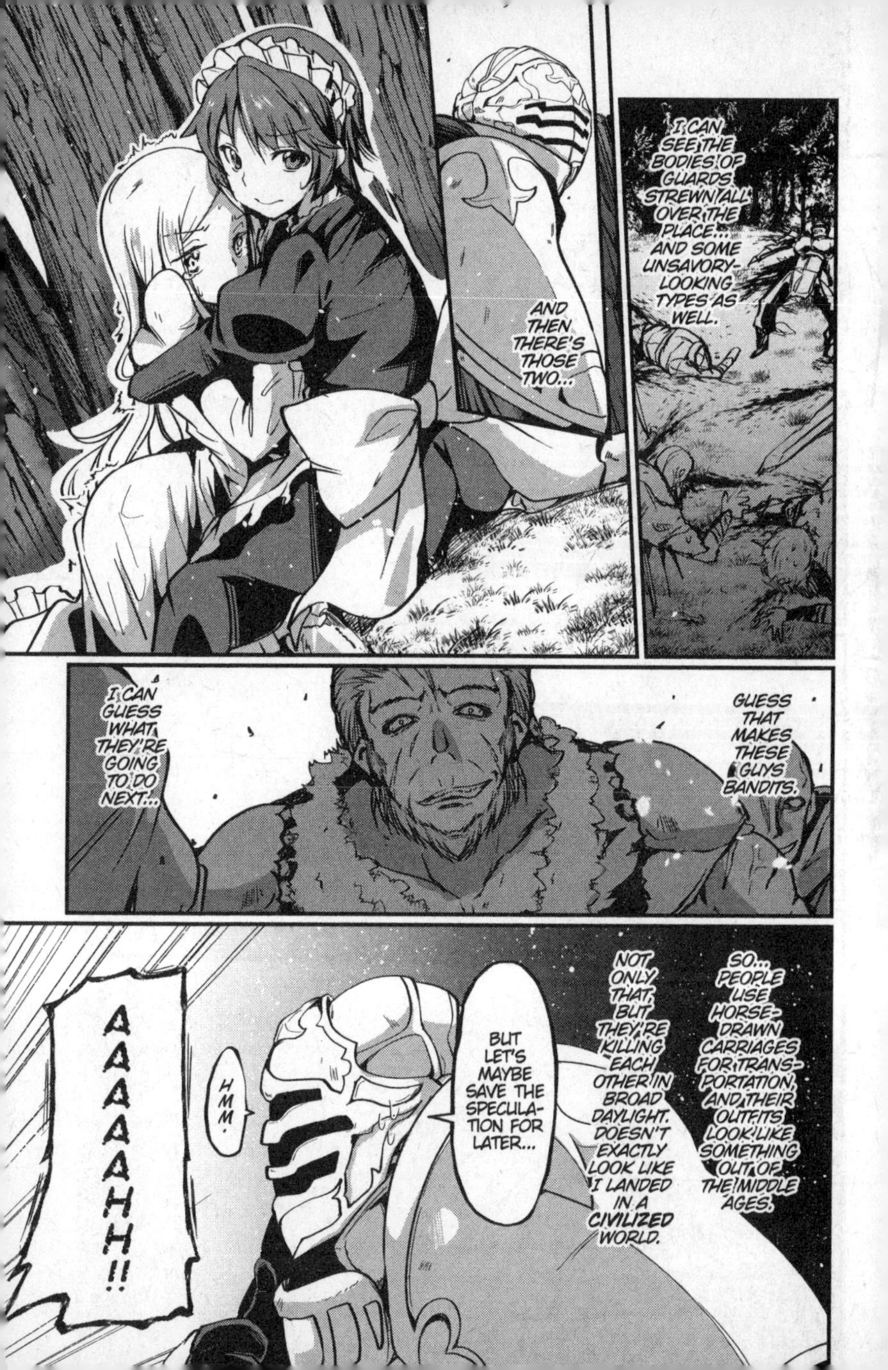
I CAN SEE THE BODIES OF GUARDS STREWN ALL OVER THE PLACE... AND SOME UNSAVORY-LOOKING TYPES AS WELL.
AND THEN THERE'S THOSE TWO...
GUESS THAT MAKES THESE GUYS BANDITS.
I CAN GUESS WHAT THEY'RE GOING TO DO NEXT...
SO... PEOPLE USE HORSE-DRAWN CARRIAGES FOR TRANS-PORTATION, AND THEIR OUTFITS LOOK LIKE SOMETHING OUT OF THE MIDDLE AGES.
NOT ONLY THAT, BUT THEY'RE KILLING EACH OTHER IN BROAD DAYLIGHT. DOESN'T EXACTLY LOOK LIKE I LANDED IN A CIVILIZED WORLD.
BUT LET'S MAYBE SAVE THE SPECULA-TION FOR LATER...
HMM.
AAAAAAAHH!!

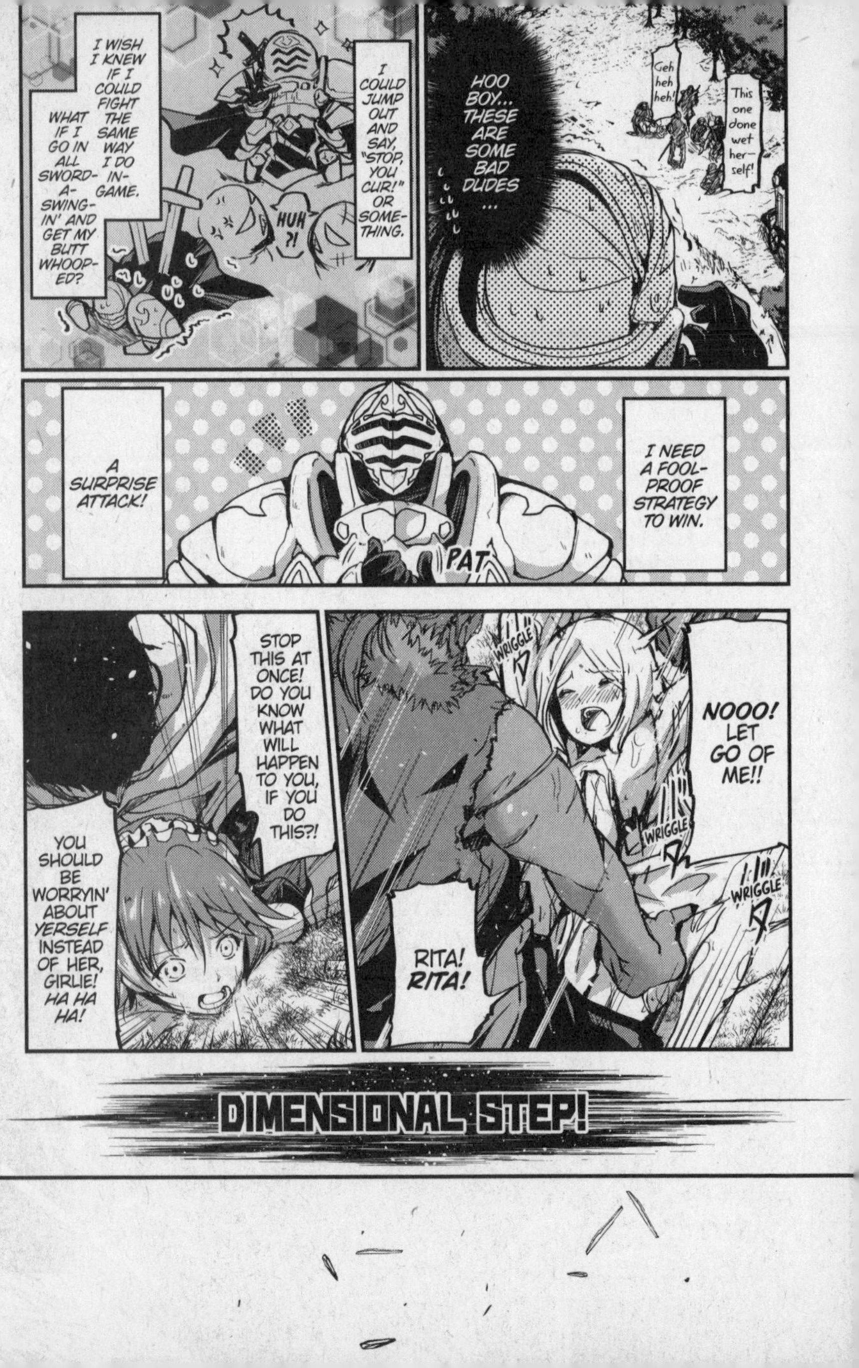
This one done wet her-self!
Geh heh heh!
HOO BOY... THESE ARE SOME BAD DUDES...
I COULD JUMP OUT AND SAY, "STOP, YOU CUR!" OR SOME-THING.
I WISH I KNEW IF I COULD FIGHT THE SAME WAY I DO IN-GAME.
WHAT IF I GO IN ALL SWORD-A-SWINGIN' AND GET MY BUTT WHOOP-ED?
HUH?!
I NEED A FOOL-PROOF STRATEGY TO WIN.
PAT
A SURPRISE ATTACK!
NOOO! LET GO OF ME!!
WRIGGLE
WRIGGLE
WRIGGLE
RITA! RITA!
STOP THIS AT ONCE! DO YOU KNOW WHAT WILL HAPPEN TO YOU, IF YOU DO THIS?!
YOU SHOULD BE WORRYIN' ABOUT YERSELF INSTEAD OF HER, GIRLIE! HA HA HA!
DIMENSIONAL STEP!

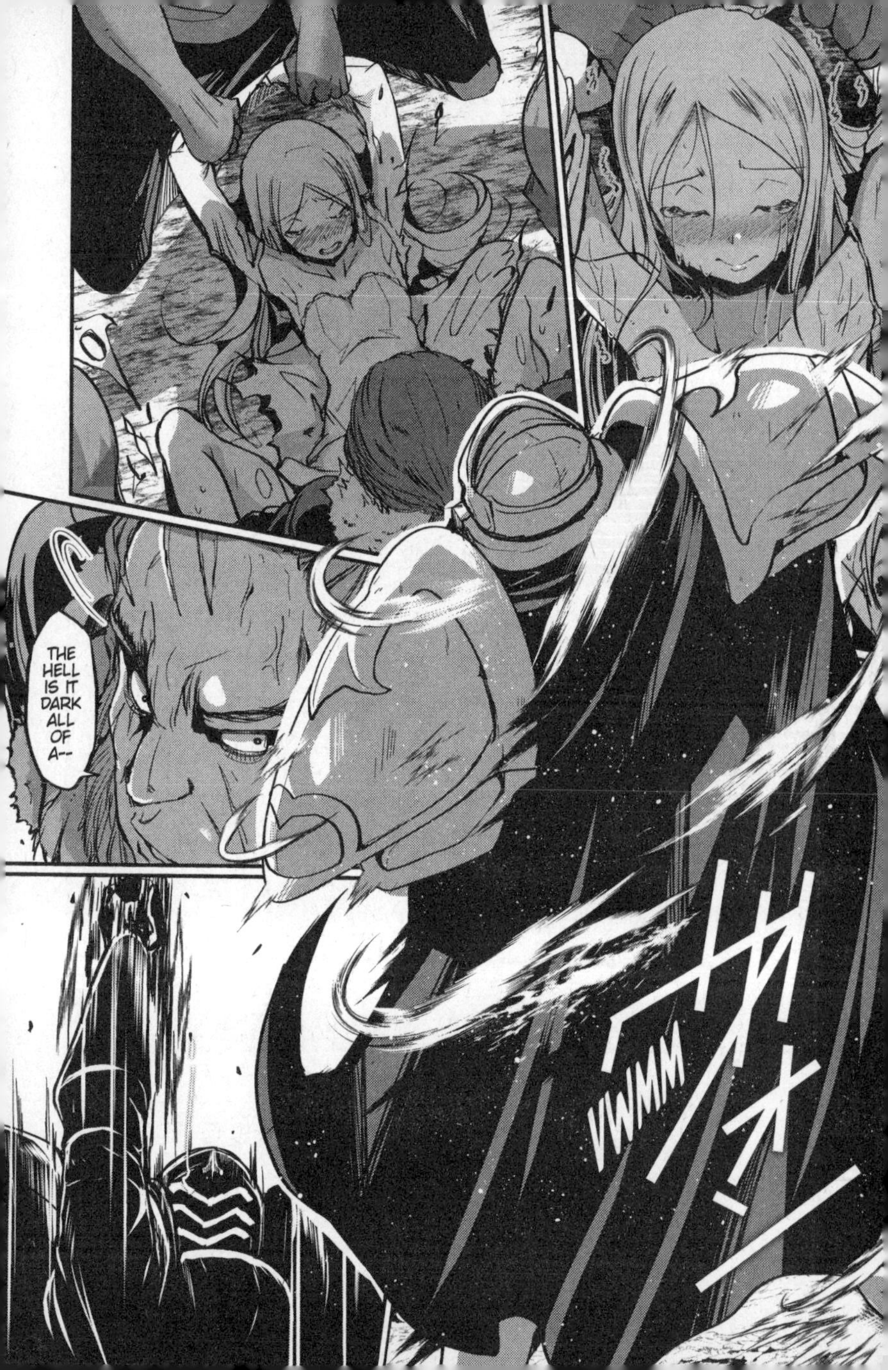
THE HELL IS IT DARK ALL OF A--
VWMM

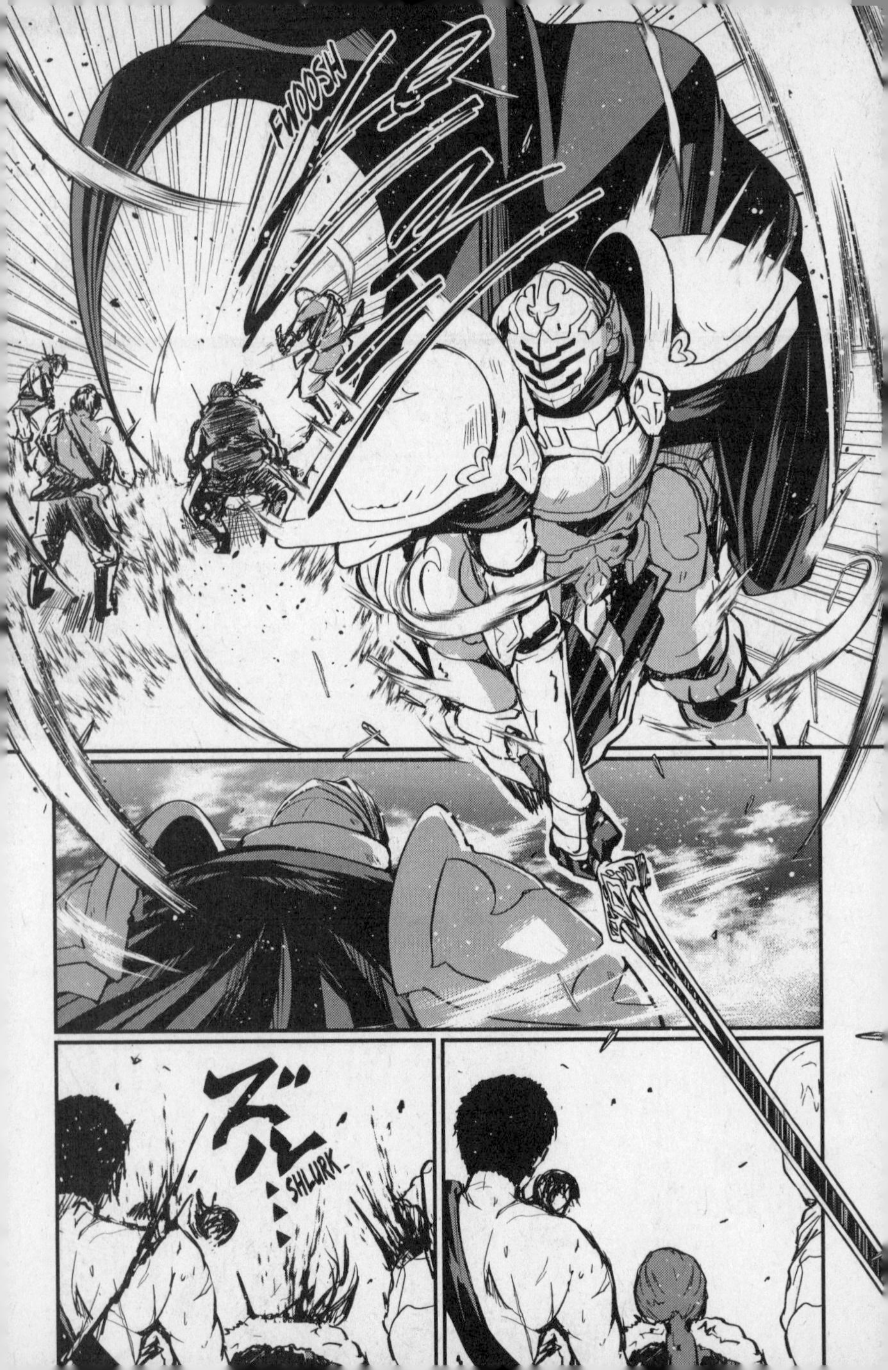
FWOOSH
SHLURK

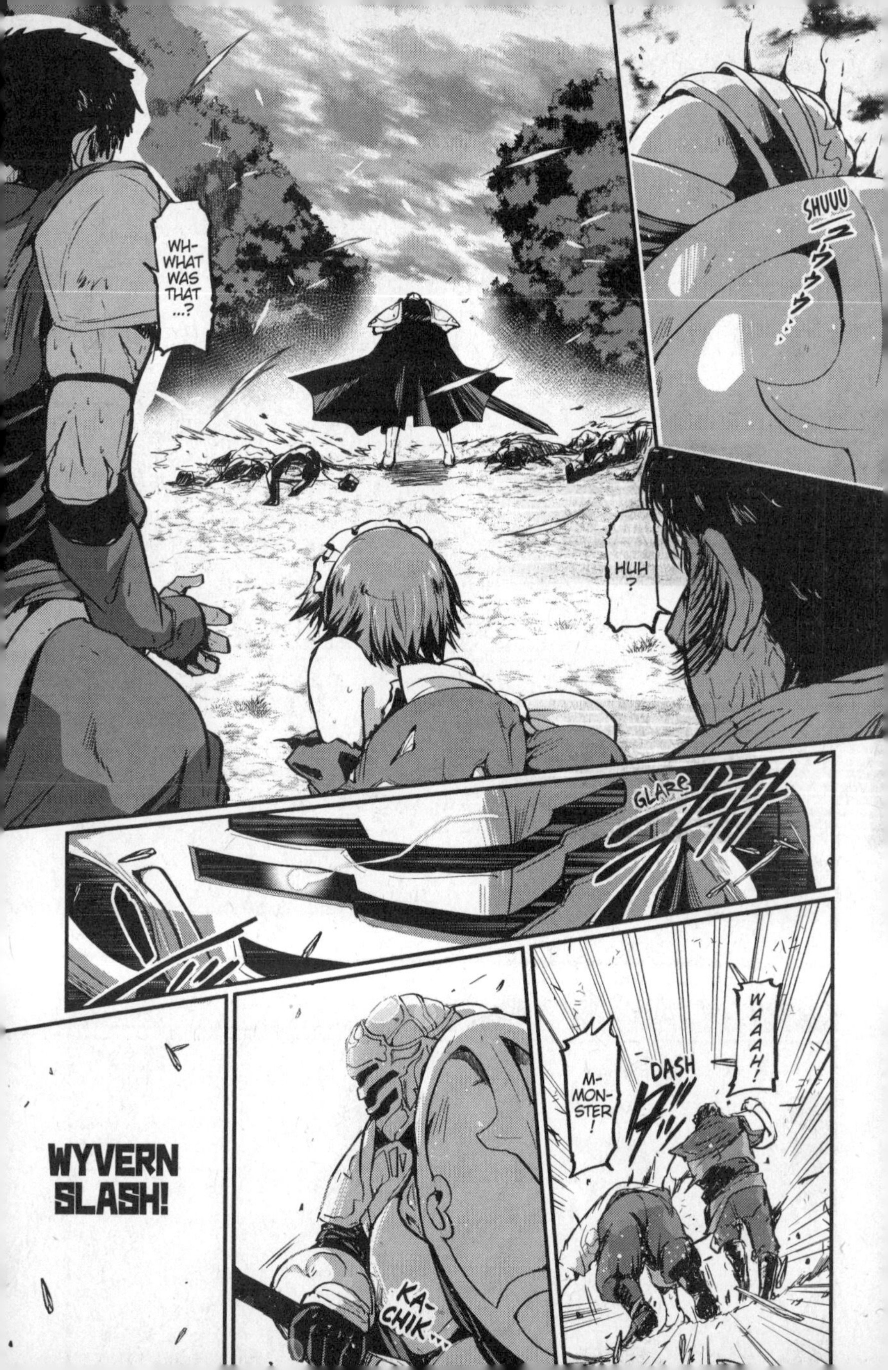

SHUUU
WH-WHAT WAS THAT ...?
HUH?
GLARE
WAAAH!
M-MONSTER!
DASH
KA-CHIK...
WYVERN SLASH!

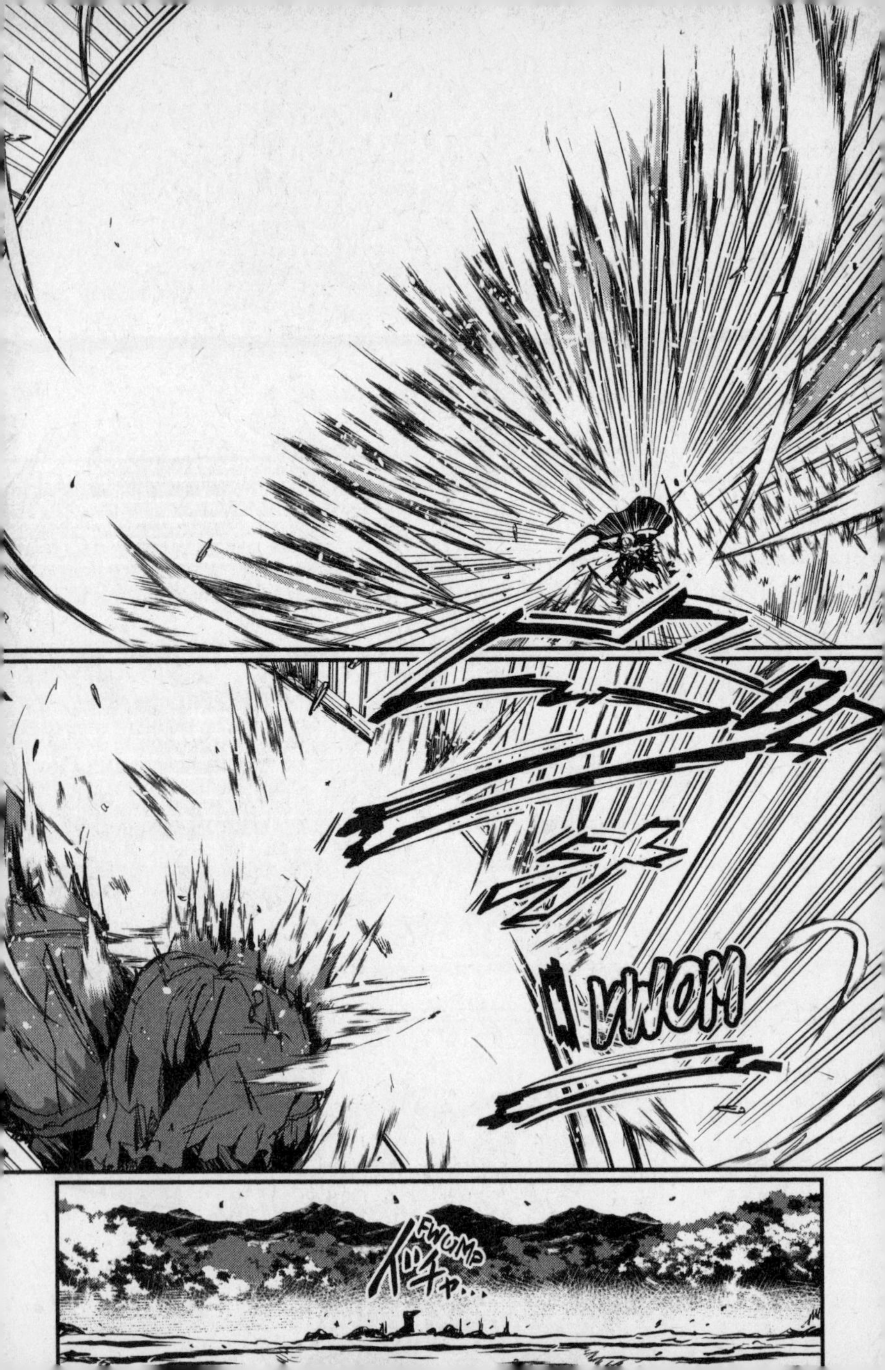
VWOM
FWOMP

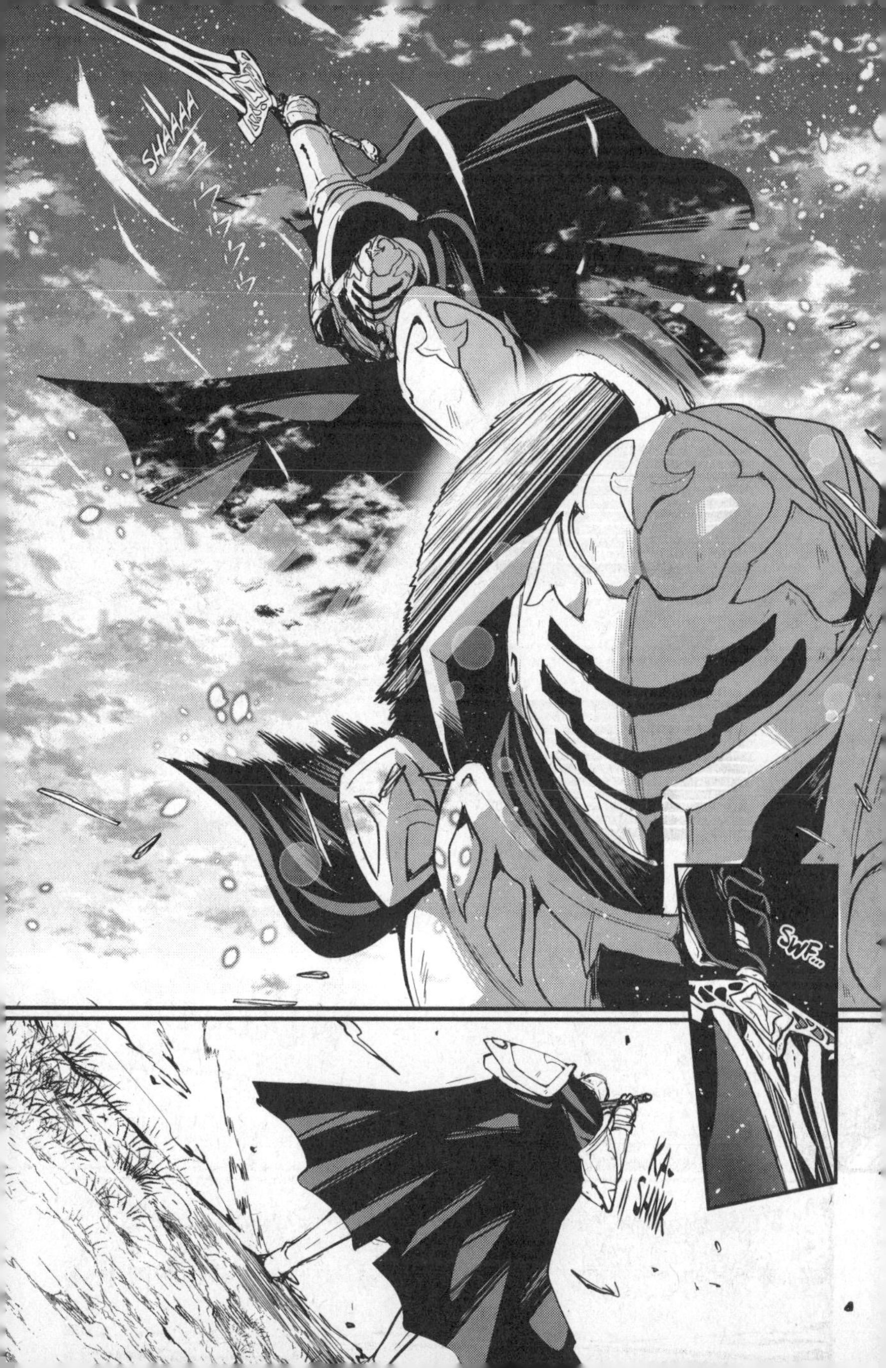
SHAAAA
SWF...
KA-SHNK

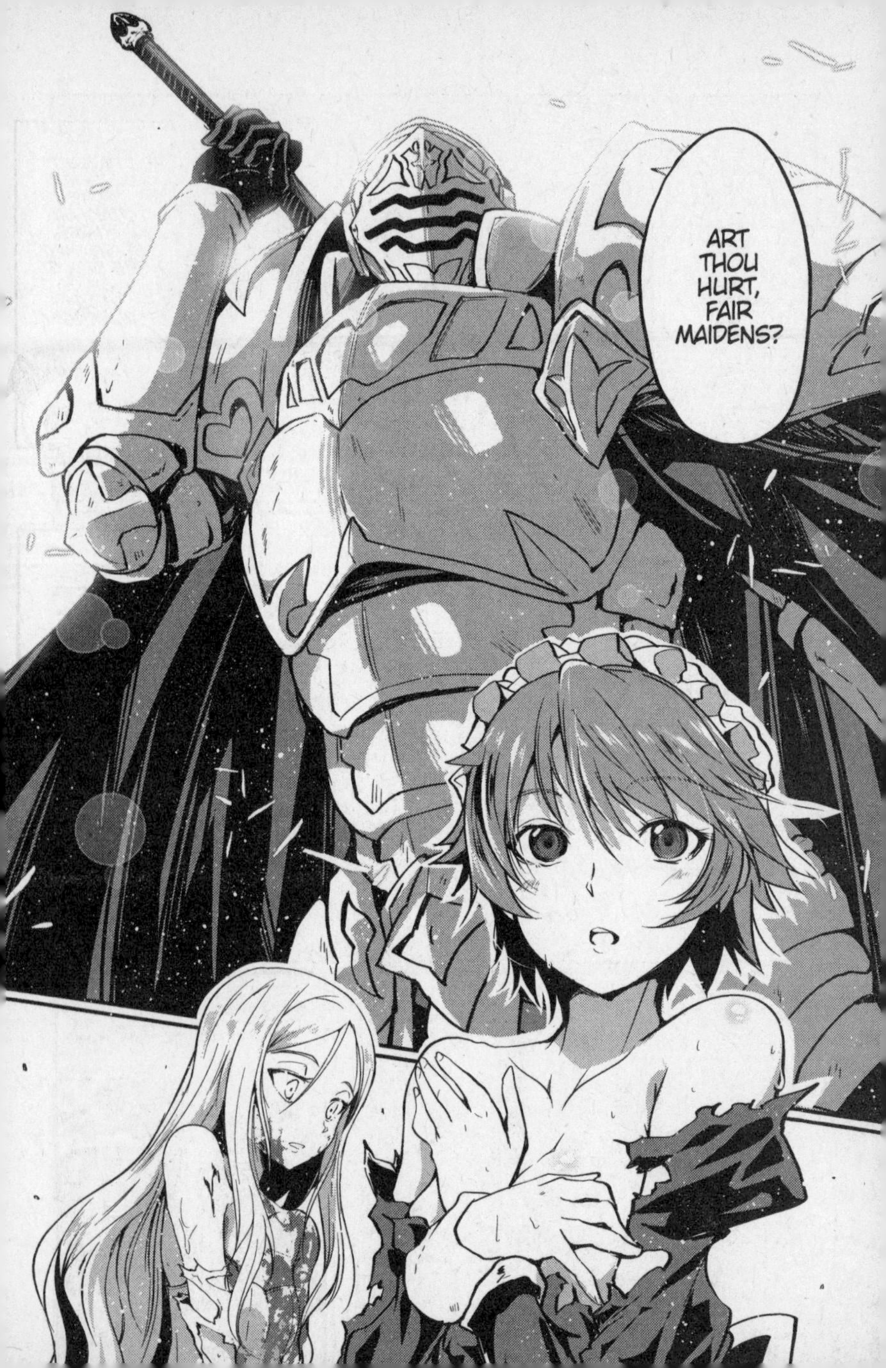
ART THOU HURT, FAIR MAIDENS?

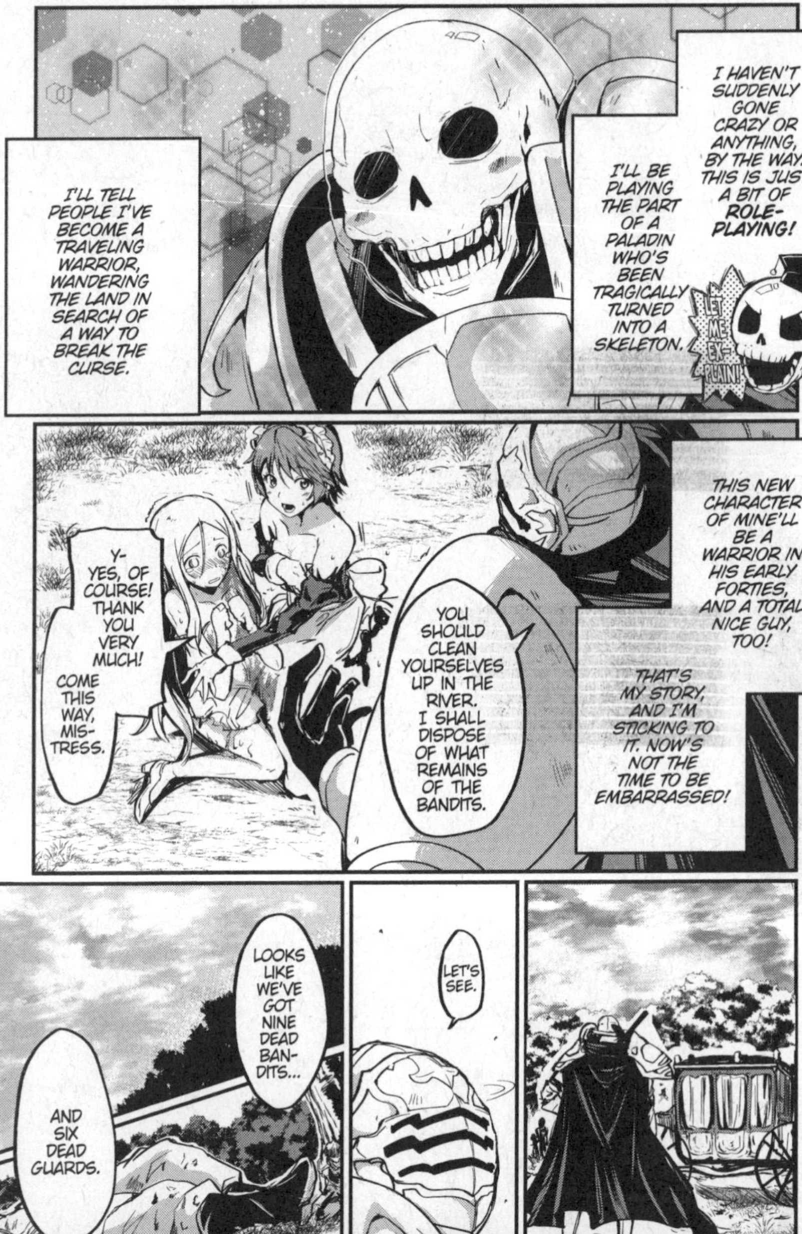
I HAVEN'T SUDDENLY GONE CRAZY OR ANYTHING, BY THE WAY. THIS IS JUST A BIT OF ROLE-PLAYING!
I'LL BE PLAYING THE PART OF A PALADIN WHO'S BEEN TRAGICALLY TURNED INTO A SKELETON.
LET ME EX-PLAIN!
I'LL TELL PEOPLE I'VE BECOME A TRAVELING WARRIOR, WANDERING THE LAND IN SEARCH OF A WAY TO BREAK THE CURSE.
THIS NEW CHARACTER OF MINE'LL BE A WARRIOR IN HIS EARLY FORTIES, AND A TOTAL NICE GUY, TOO!
THAT'S MY STORY, AND I'M STICKING TO IT. NOW'S NOT THE TIME TO BE EMBARRASSED!
YOU SHOULD CLEAN YOURSELVES UP IN THE RIVER. I SHALL DISPOSE OF WHAT REMAINS OF THE BANDITS.
Y-YES, OF COURSE! THANK YOU VERY MUCH!
COME THIS WAY, MIS-TRESS.
LET'S SEE.
LOOKS LIKE WE'VE GOT NINE DEAD BAN-DITS...
AND SIX DEAD GUARDS.

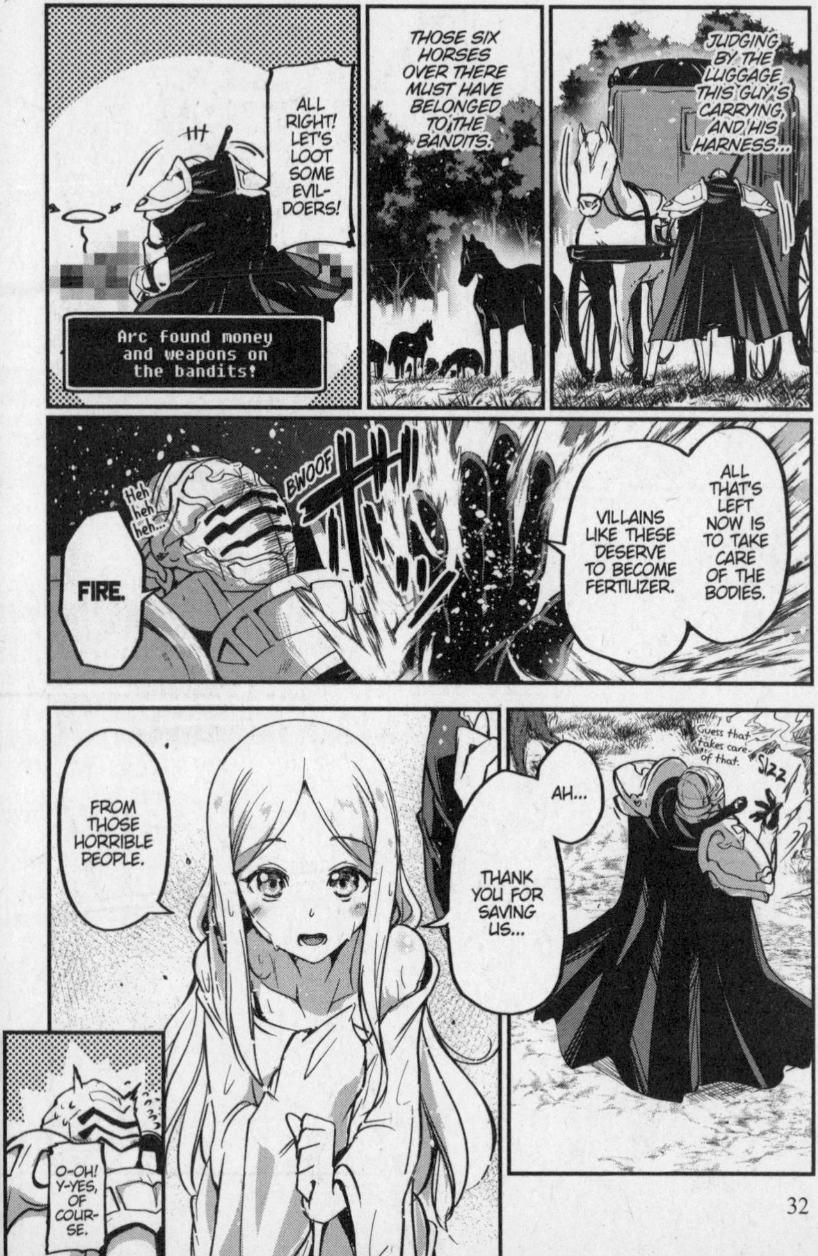
JUDGING BY THE LUGGAGE THIS GUY'S CARRYING, AND HIS HARNESS...
THOSE SIX HORSES OVER THERE MUST HAVE BELONGED TO THE BANDITS.
ALL RIGHT! LET'S LOOT SOME EVIL-DOERS!
Arc found money and weapons on the bandits!
ALL THAT'S LEFT NOW IS TO TAKE CARE OF THE BODIES.
VILLAINS LIKE THESE DESERVE TO BECOME FERTILIZER.
BWOOF
Heh heh heh...
FIRE.
Guess that takes care of that.
SIZZ
AH...
THANK YOU FOR SAVING US...
FROM THOSE HORRIBLE PEOPLE.
O-OH! Y-YES, OF COURSE.

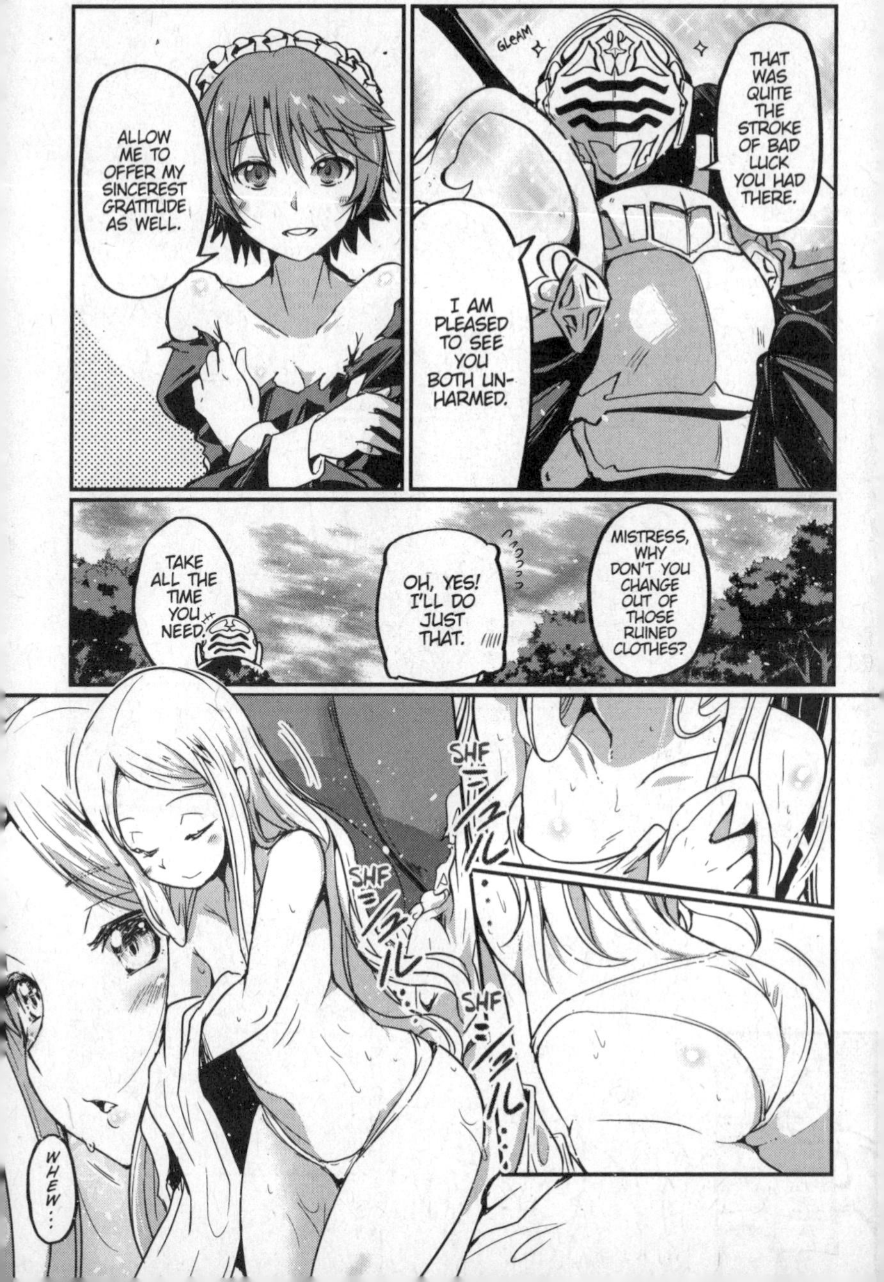
GLEAM
THAT WAS QUITE THE STROKE OF BAD LUCK YOU HAD THERE.
I AM PLEASED TO SEE YOU BOTH UN-HARMED.
ALLOW ME TO OFFER MY SINCEREST GRATITUDE AS WELL.
MISTRESS, WHY DON'T YOU CHANGE OUT OF THOSE RUINED CLOTHES?
OH, YES! I'LL DO JUST THAT.
TAKE ALL THE TIME YOU NEED.
SHF
SHF
SHF
WHEW...

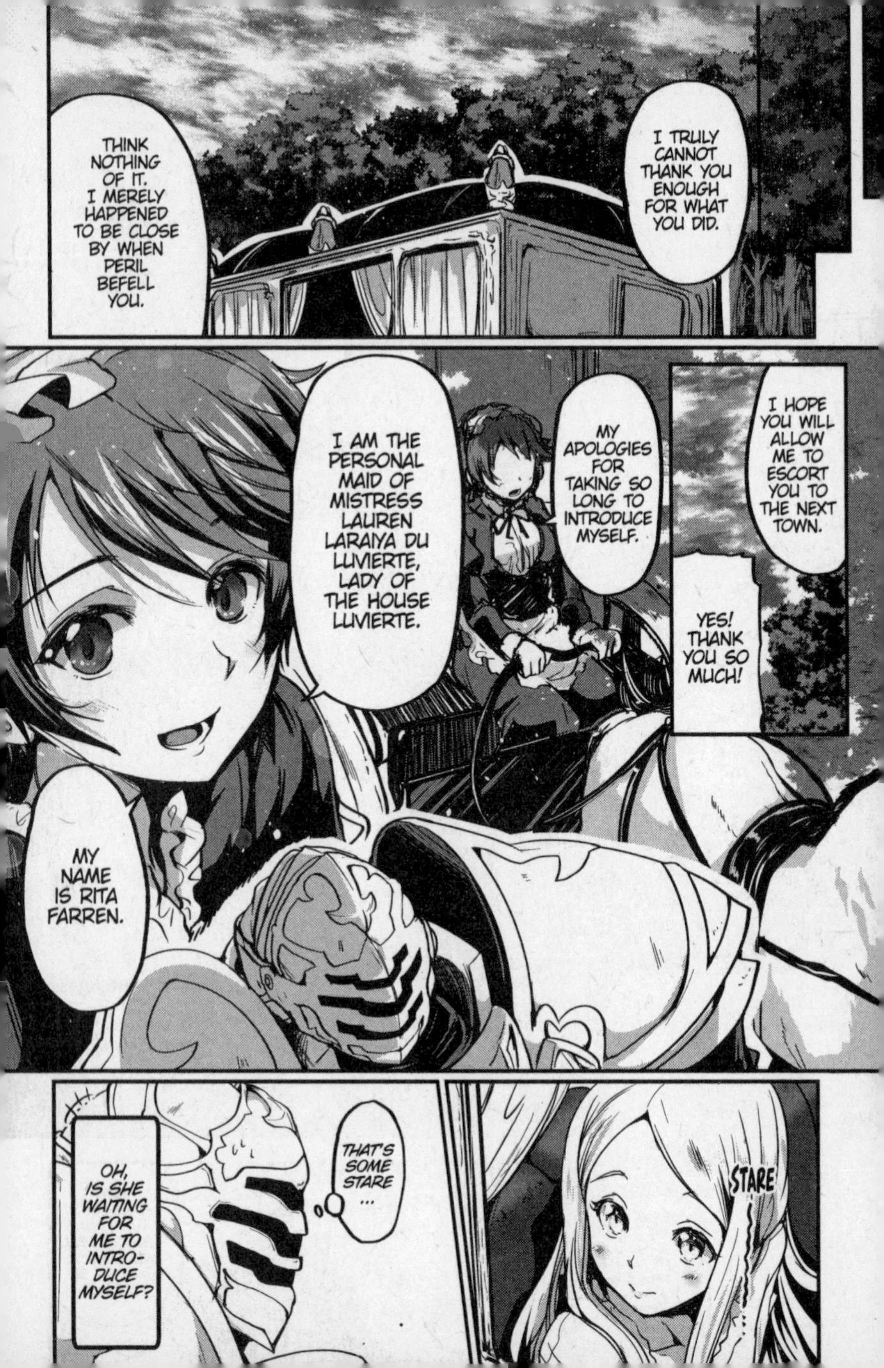
I TRULY CANNOT THANK YOU ENOUGH FOR WHAT YOU DID.
THINK NOTHING OF IT. I MERELY HAPPENED TO BE CLOSE BY WHEN PERIL BEFELL YOU.
I HOPE YOU WILL ALLOW ME TO ESCORT YOU TO THE NEXT TOWN.
YES! THANK YOU SO MUCH!
MY APOLOGIES FOR TAKING SO LONG TO INTRODUCE MYSELF.
I AM THE PERSONAL MAID OF MISTRESS LAUREN LARAIYA DU LUVIERTE, LADY OF THE HOUSE LUVIERTE.
MY NAME IS RITA FARREN.
STARE
THAT'S SOME STARE ...
OH, IS SHE WAITING FOR ME TO INTRODUCE MYSELF?

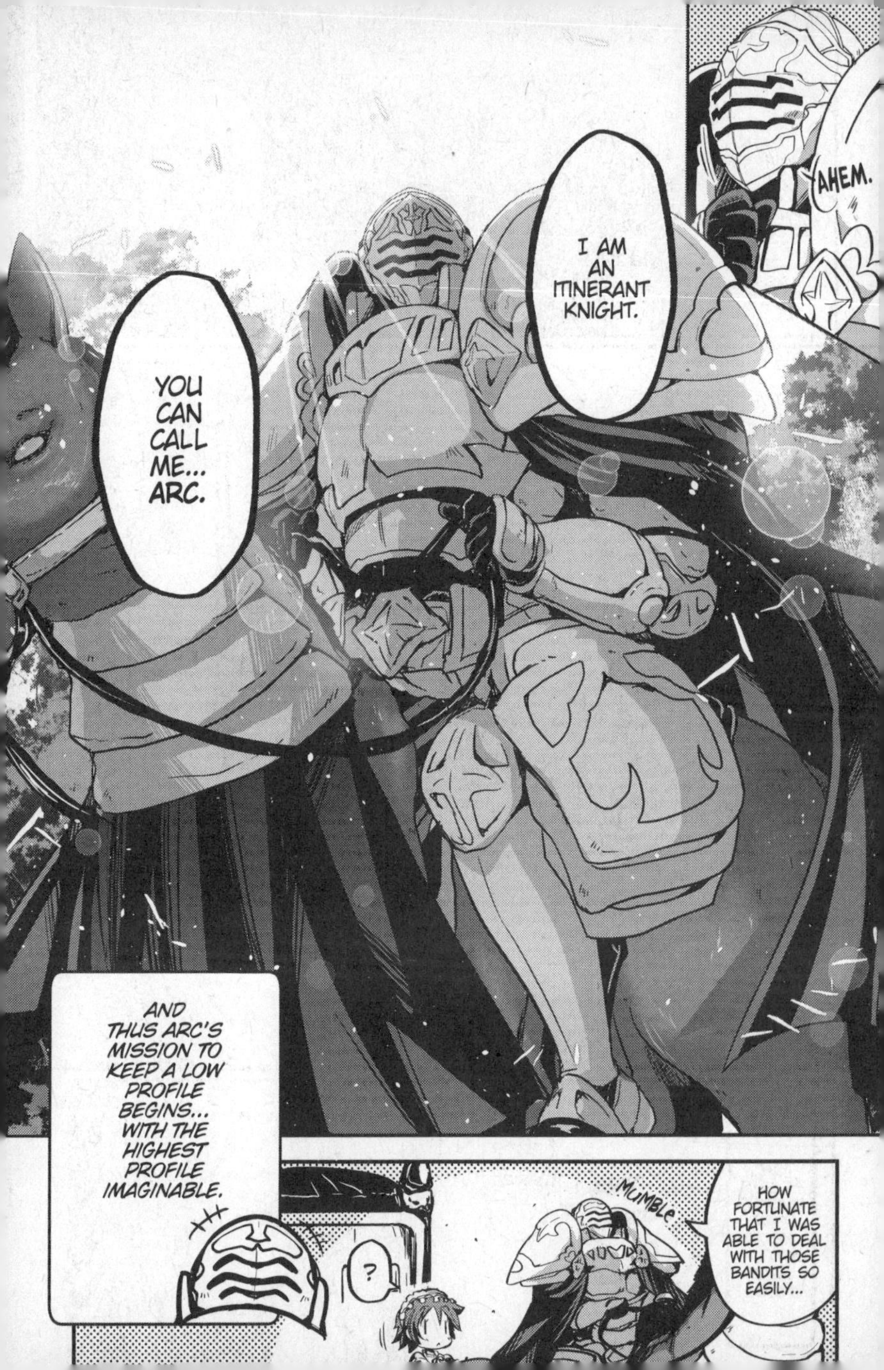
AHEM.
I AM AN ITINERANT KNIGHT.
YOU CAN CALL ME... ARC.
AND THUS ARC'S MISSION TO KEEP A LOW PROFILE BEGINS... WITH THE HIGHEST PROFILE IMAGINABLE.
HOW FORTUNATE THAT I WAS ABLE TO DEAL WITH THOSE BANDITS SO EASILY...
MUMBLE
?

SKELETON KNiGHT
IN ANOTHER WORLD

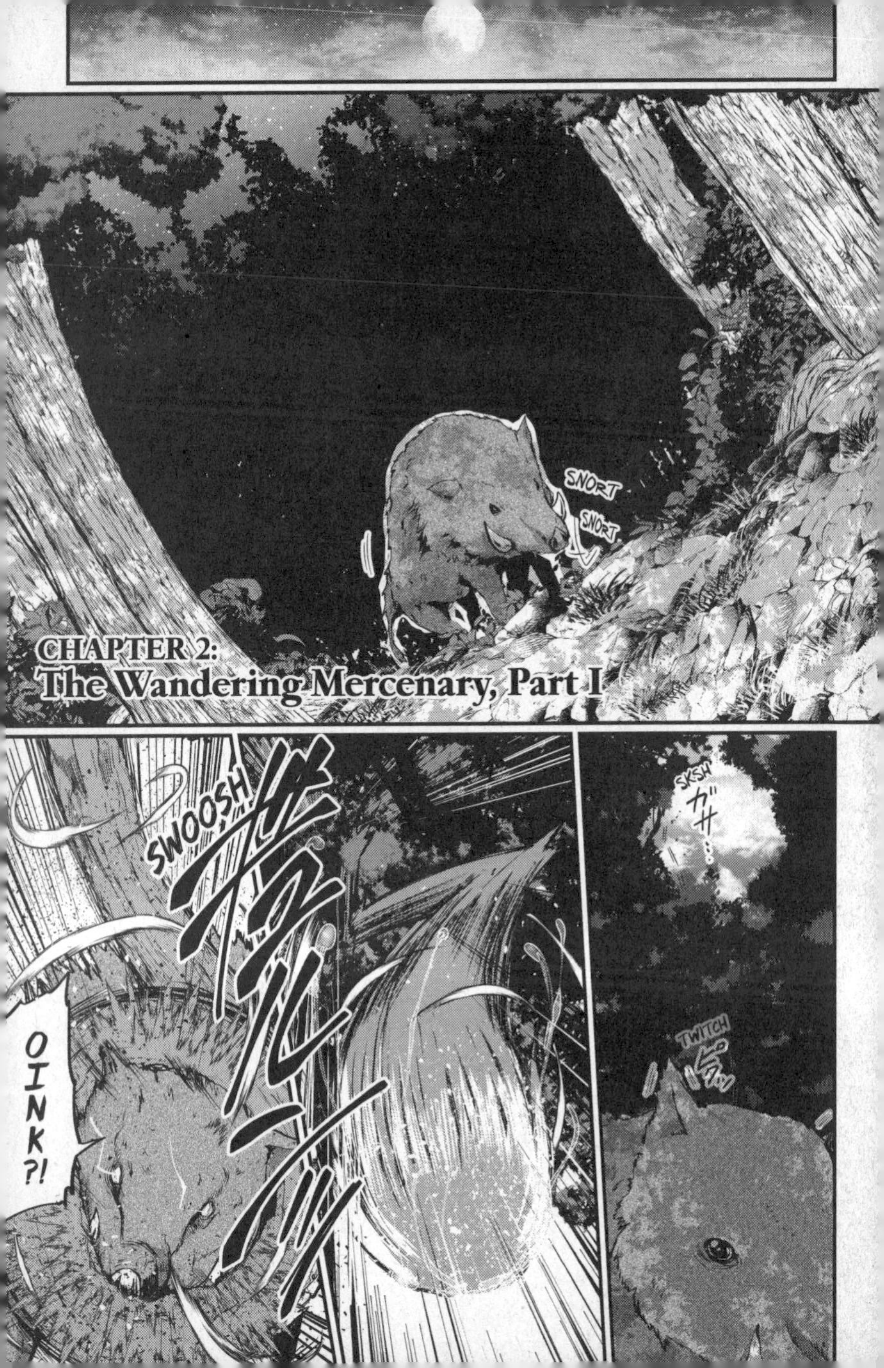
SNORT
SNORT
CHAPTER 2:
The Wandering Mercenary, Part I
SKSH
TWITCH
SWOOSH
OINK?!

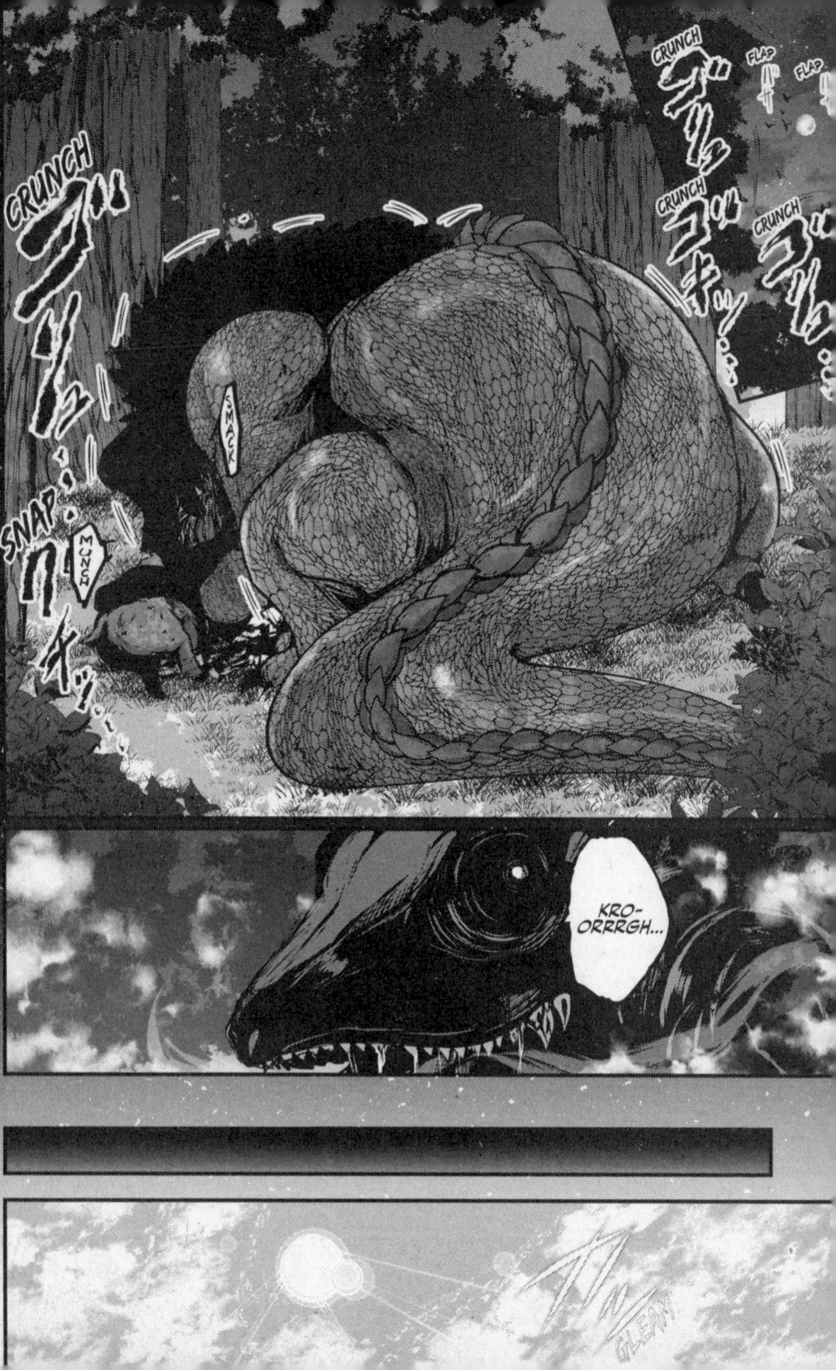
FLAP
FLAP
CRUNCH
CRUNCH
CRUNCH
SMACK
CRUNCH
MUNCH
SNAP
KRO-ORRRGH...
GLEAM

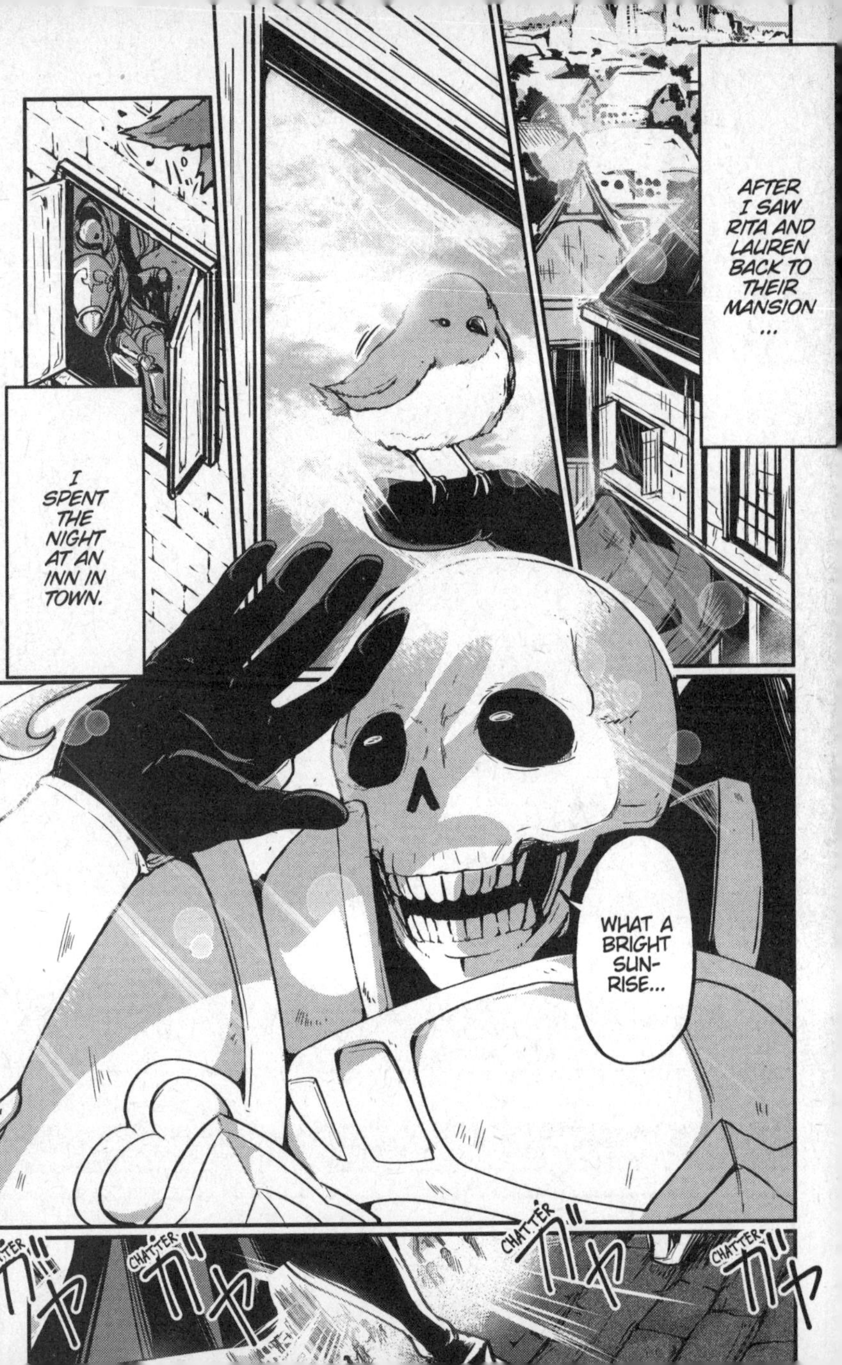
AFTER I SAW RITA AND LAUREN BACK TO THEIR MANSION ...
I SPENT THE NIGHT AT AN INN IN TOWN.
WHAT A BRIGHT SUN-RISE...
CHATTER
CHATTER
CHATTER
CHATTER

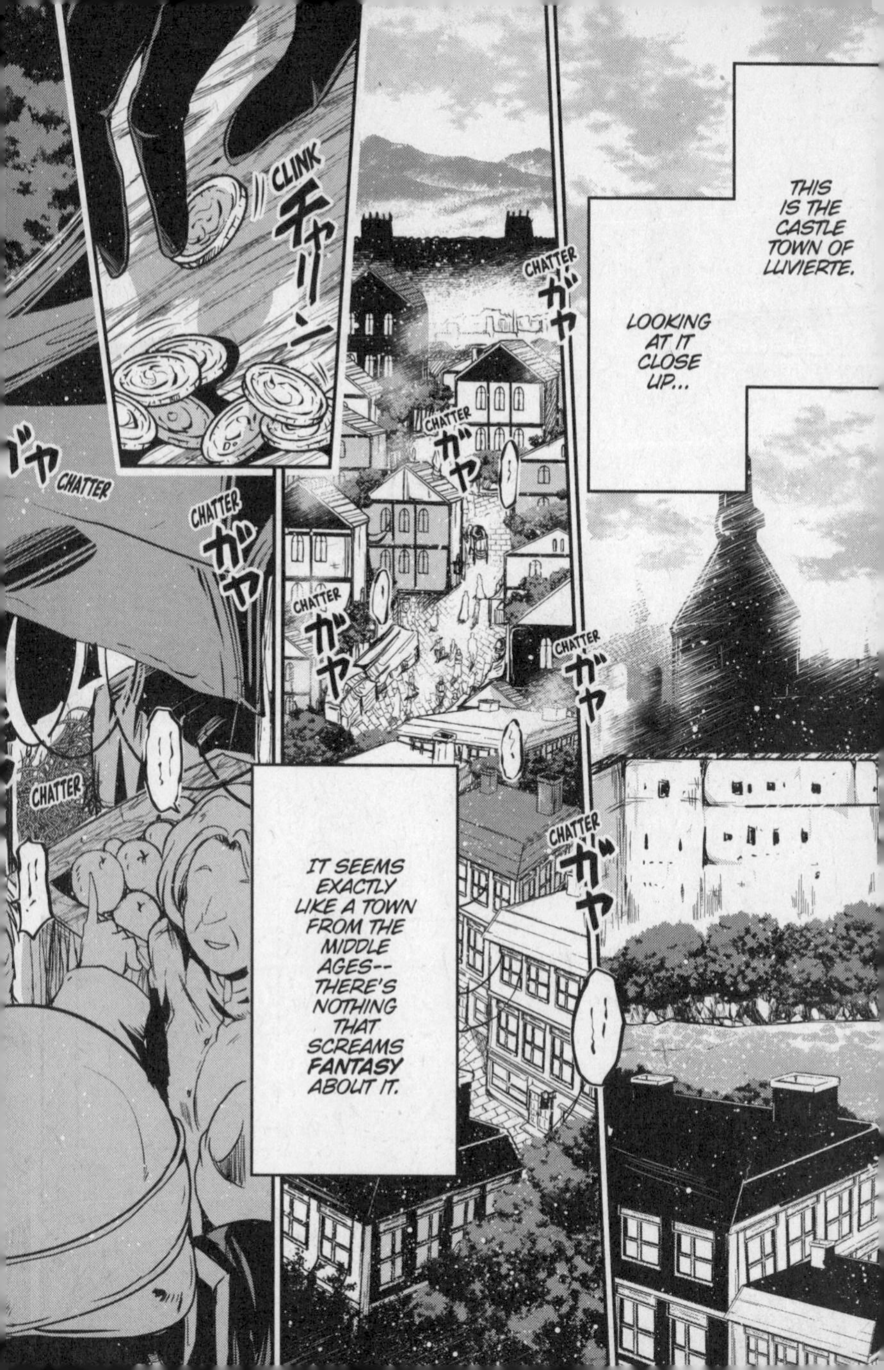
THIS IS THE CASTLE TOWN OF LUVIERTE.
LOOKING AT IT CLOSE UP...
CHATTER ガヤ
CHATTER ガヤ
CHATTER ガヤ
CHATTER ガヤ
CHATTER ガヤ
CLINK チャリーン
CHATTER ガヤ
CHATTER ガヤ
CHATTER
CHATTER ガヤ
IT SEEMS EXACTLY LIKE A TOWN FROM THE MIDDLE AGES--THERE'S NOTHING THAT SCREAMS **FANTASY** ABOUT IT.

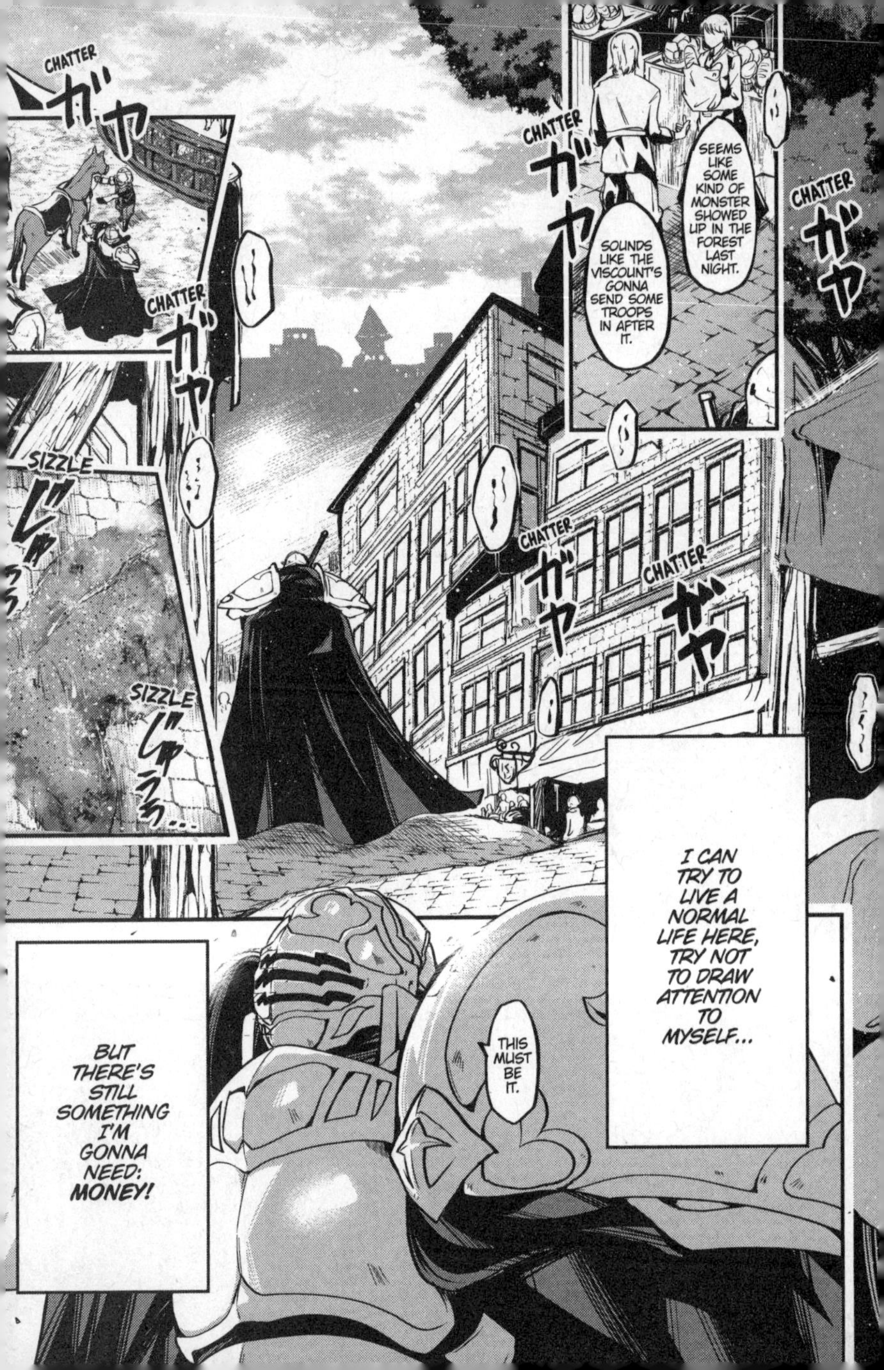
CHATTER
ガヤ
CHATTER
ガヤ
SEEMS LIKE SOME KIND OF MONSTER SHOWED UP IN THE FOREST LAST NIGHT.
SOUNDS LIKE THE VISCOUNT'S GONNA SEND SOME TROOPS IN AFTER IT.
CHATTER
ガヤ
CHATTER
ガヤ
CHATTER
ガヤ
CHATTER
ガヤ
SIZZLE
SIZZLE
I CAN TRY TO LIVE A NORMAL LIFE HERE, TRY NOT TO DRAW ATTENTION TO MYSELF...
THIS MUST BE IT.
BUT THERE'S STILL SOMETHING I'M GONNA NEED: MONEY!

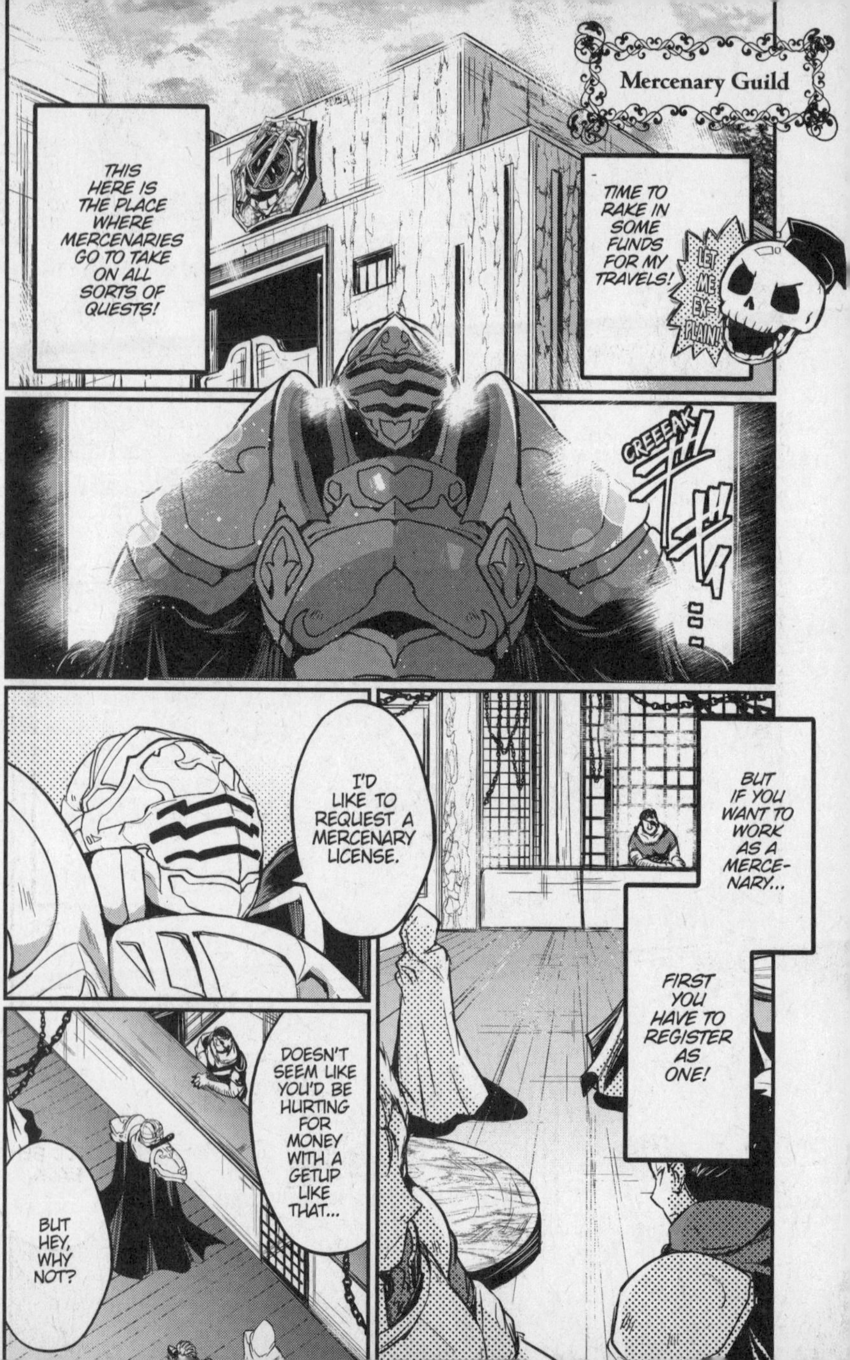
Mercenary Guild
TIME TO RAKE IN SOME FUNDS FOR MY TRAVELS!
LET ME EX-PLAIN!
THIS HERE IS THE PLACE WHERE MERCENARIES GO TO TAKE ON ALL SORTS OF QUESTS!
CREEEAK
BUT IF YOU WANT TO WORK AS A MERCE-NARY...
FIRST YOU HAVE TO REGISTER AS ONE!
I'D LIKE TO REQUEST A MERCENARY LICENSE.
DOESN'T SEEM LIKE YOU'D BE HURTING FOR MONEY WITH A GETUP LIKE THAT...
BUT HEY, WHY NOT?

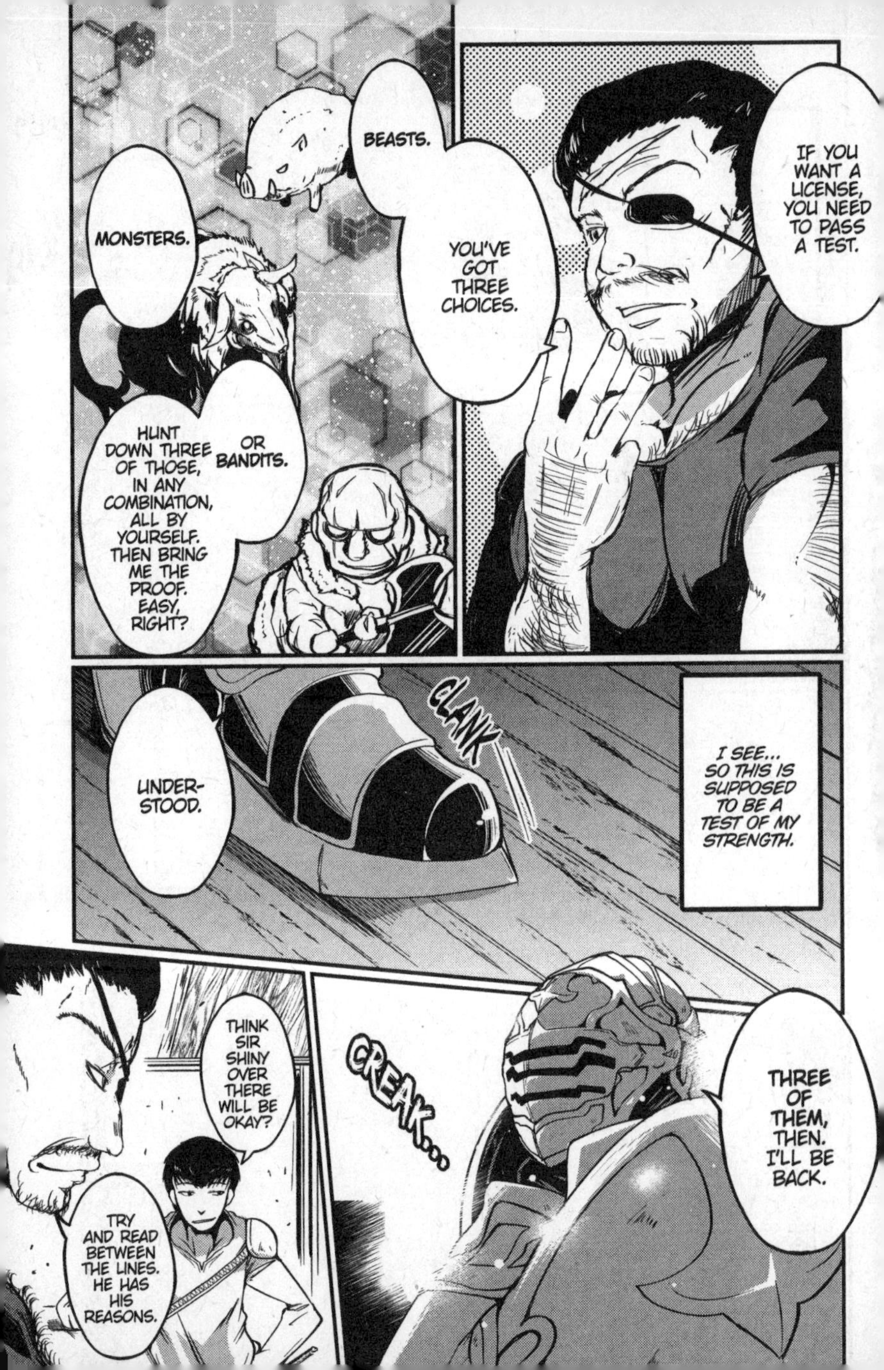
IF YOU WANT A LICENSE, YOU NEED TO PASS A TEST.
YOU'VE GOT THREE CHOICES.
BEASTS.
MONSTERS.
OR BANDITS.
HUNT DOWN THREE OF THOSE, IN ANY COMBINATION, ALL BY YOURSELF. THEN BRING ME THE PROOF. EASY, RIGHT?
I SEE... SO THIS IS SUPPOSED TO BE A TEST OF MY STRENGTH.
CLANK
UNDER-STOOD.
THREE OF THEM, THEN. I'LL BE BACK.
CREAK...
THINK SIR SHINY OVER THERE WILL BE OKAY?
TRY AND READ BETWEEN THE LINES. HE HAS HIS REASONS.

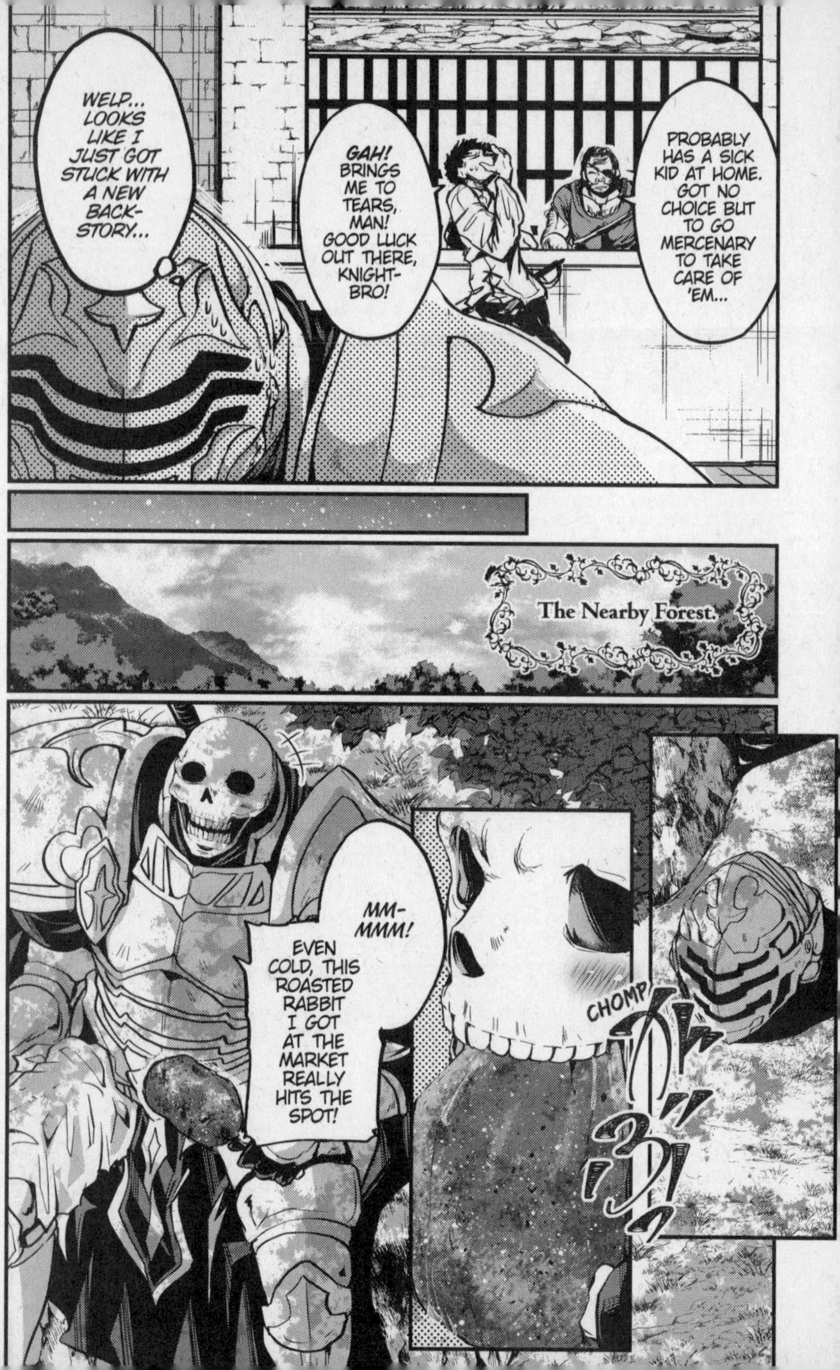
PROBABLY HAS A SICK KID AT HOME. GOT NO CHOICE BUT TO GO MERCENARY TO TAKE CARE OF 'EM...
GAH! BRINGS ME TO TEARS, MAN! GOOD LUCK OUT THERE, KNIGHT-BRO!
WELP... LOOKS LIKE I JUST GOT STUCK WITH A NEW BACK-STORY...
The Nearby Forest.
CHOMP
MM-MMM!
EVEN COLD, THIS ROASTED RABBIT I GOT AT THE MARKET REALLY HITS THE SPOT!

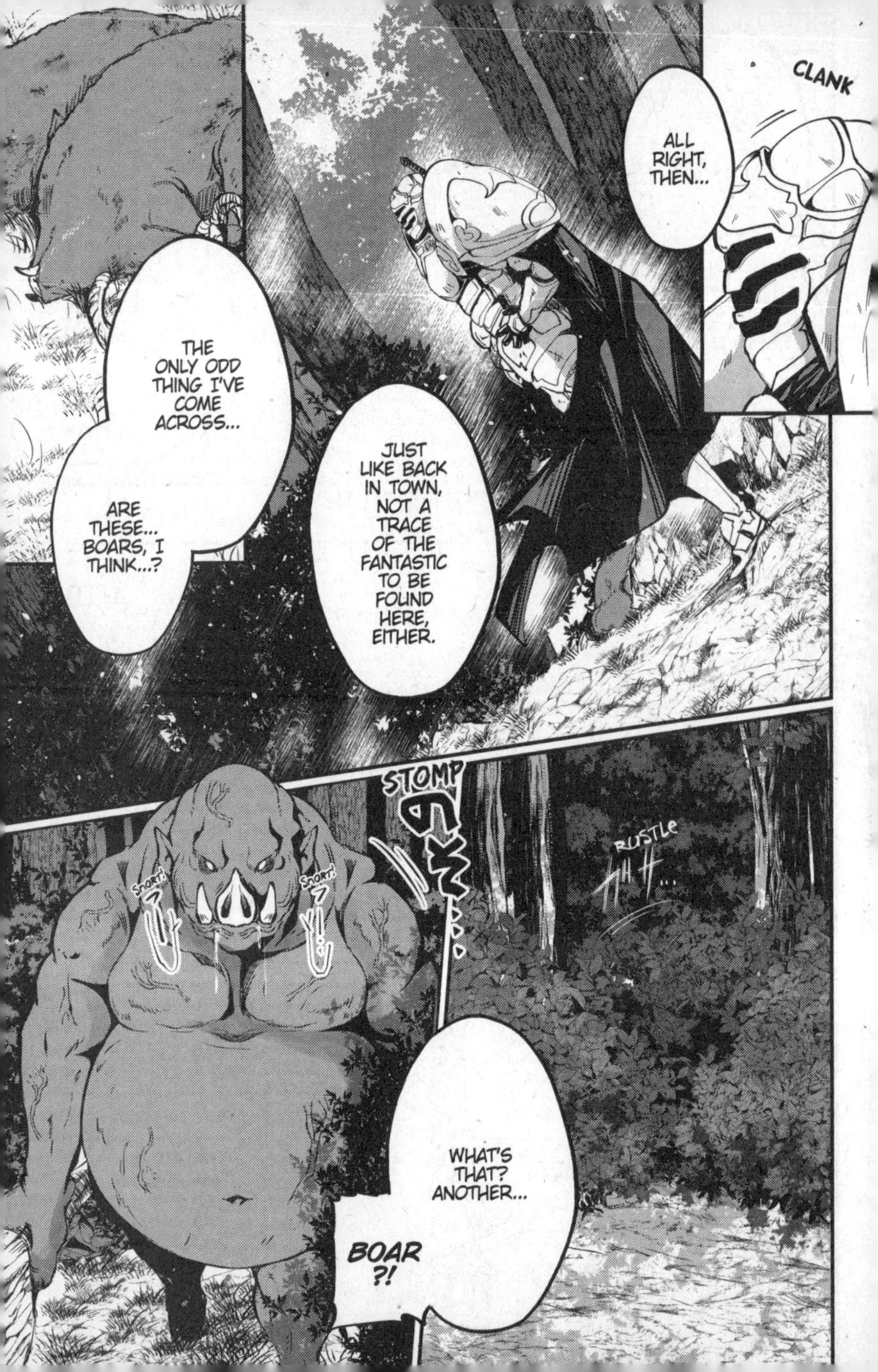
CLANK
ALL RIGHT, THEN...
JUST LIKE BACK IN TOWN, NOT A TRACE OF THE FANTASTIC TO BE FOUND HERE, EITHER.
THE ONLY ODD THING I'VE COME ACROSS...
ARE THESE... BOARS, I THINK...?
RUSTLE
STOMP
Snort
Snort
WHAT'S THAT? ANOTHER...
BOAR ?!

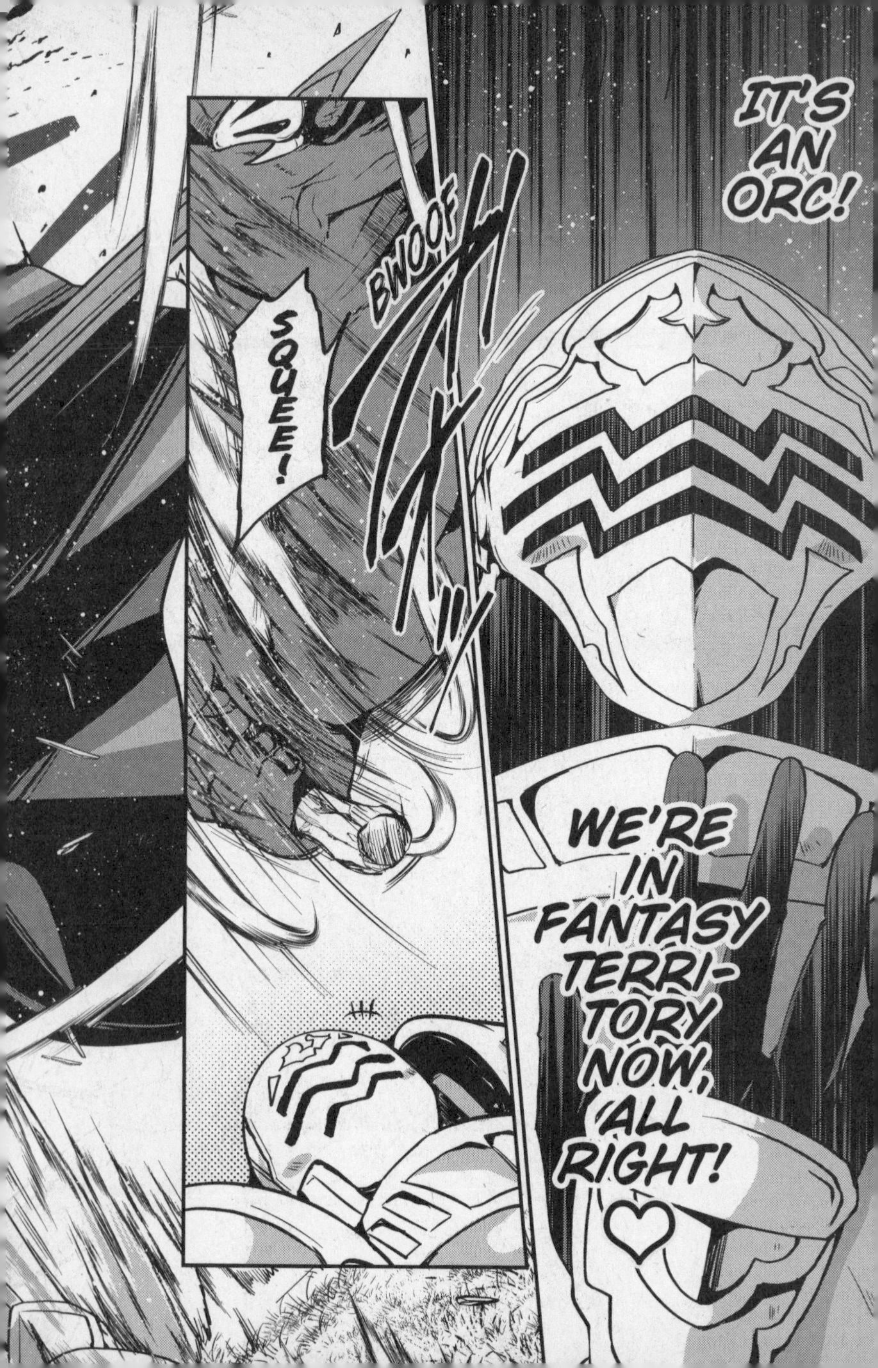
IT'S AN ORC!
BWOOF
SQUEEE!
WE'RE IN FANTASY TERRI-TORY NOW, ALL RIGHT! ♥

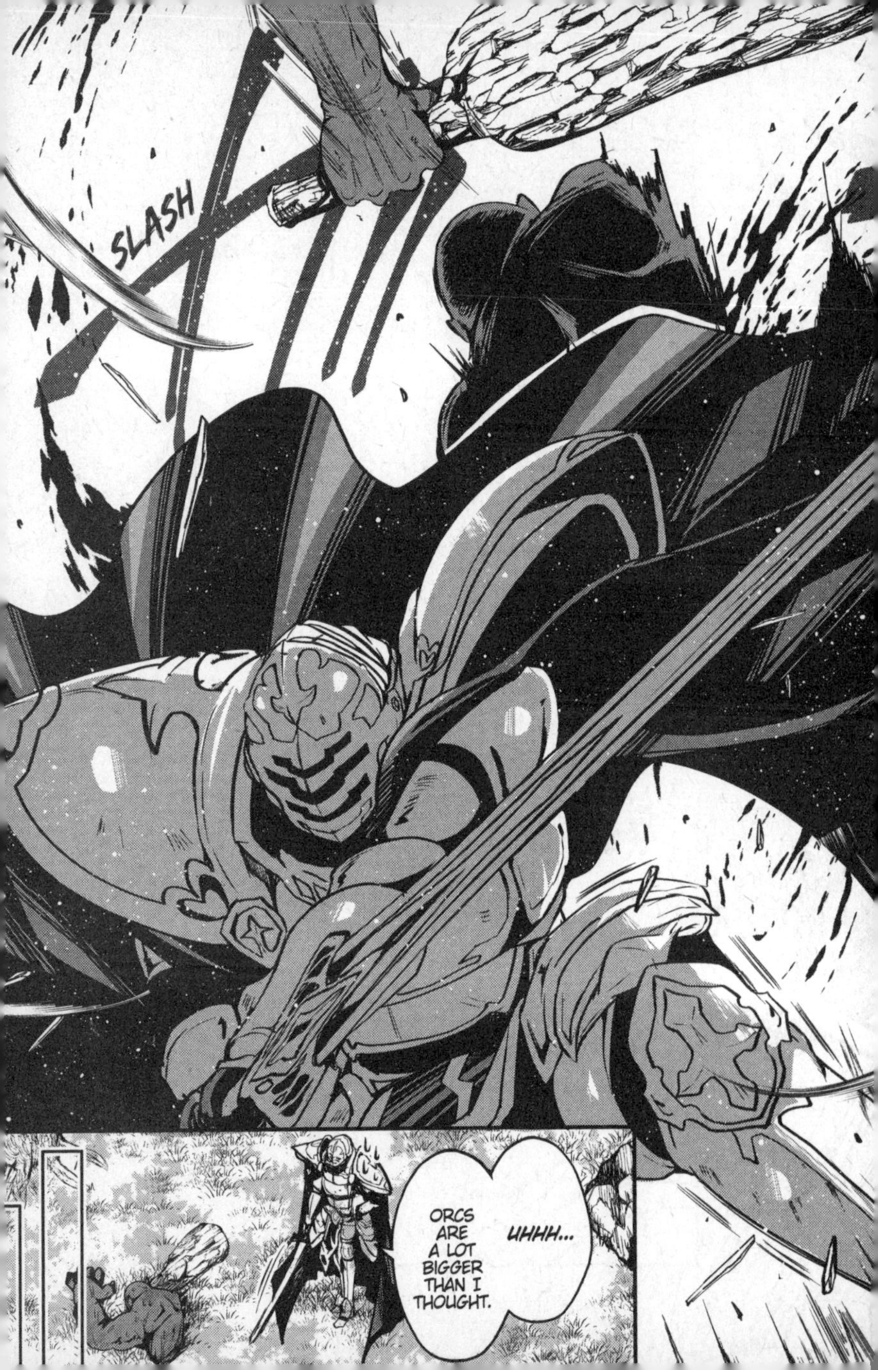
SLASH
UHHH...
ORCS ARE A LOT BIGGER THAN I THOUGHT.

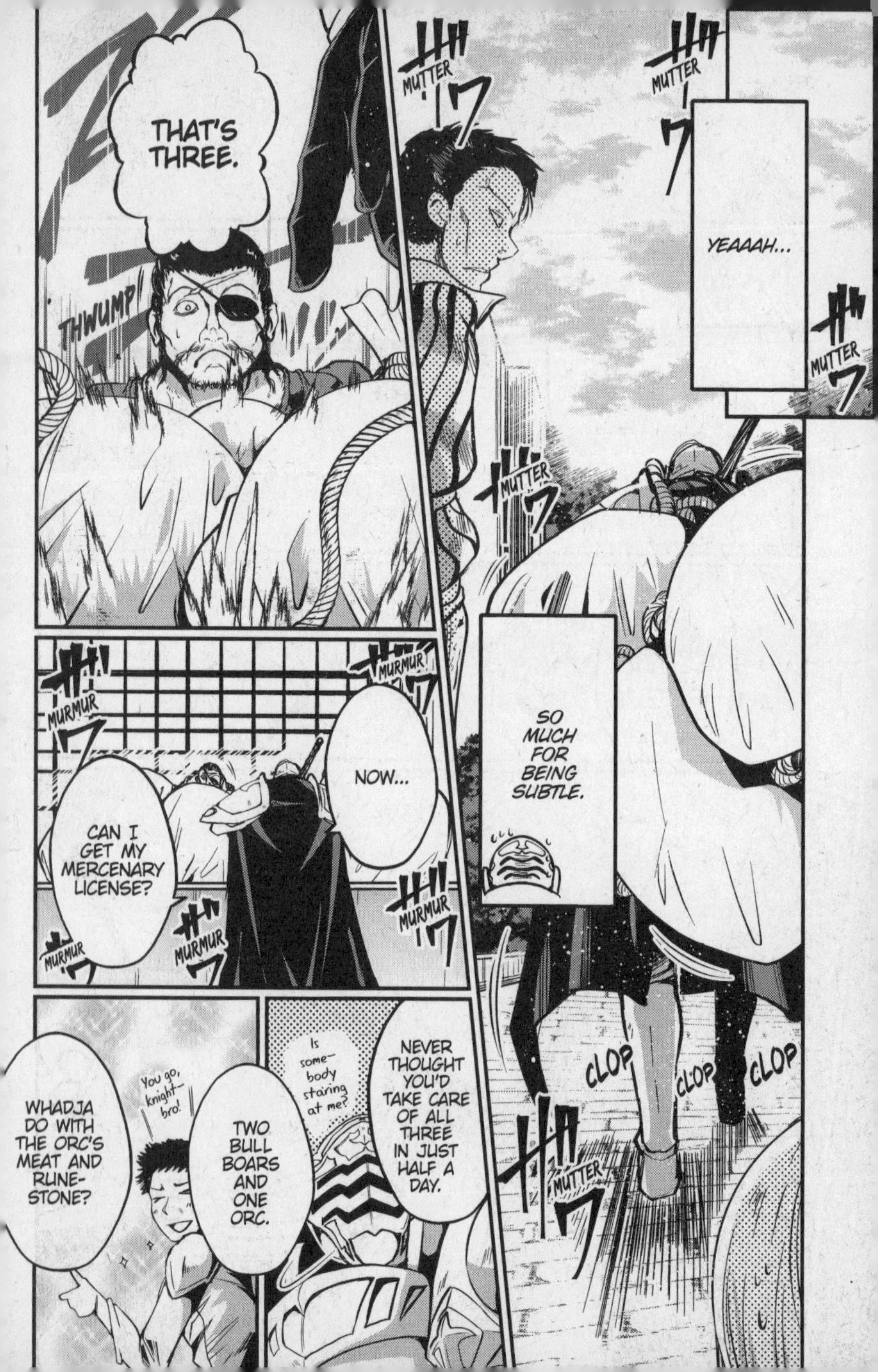
MUTTER
MUTTER
YEAAAH...
MUTTER
MUTTER
SO MUCH FOR BEING SUBTLE.
CLOP
CLOP
CLOP
MUTTER
THAT'S THREE.
THWUMP
MURMUR
NOW...
CAN I GET MY MERCENARY LICENSE?
MURMUR
MURMUR
MURMUR
MURMUR
NEVER THOUGHT YOU'D TAKE CARE OF ALL THREE IN JUST HALF A DAY.
Is somebody staring at me?
TWO BULL BOARS AND ONE ORC.
You go, knight-bro!
WHADJA DO WITH THE ORC'S MEAT AND RUNE-STONE?

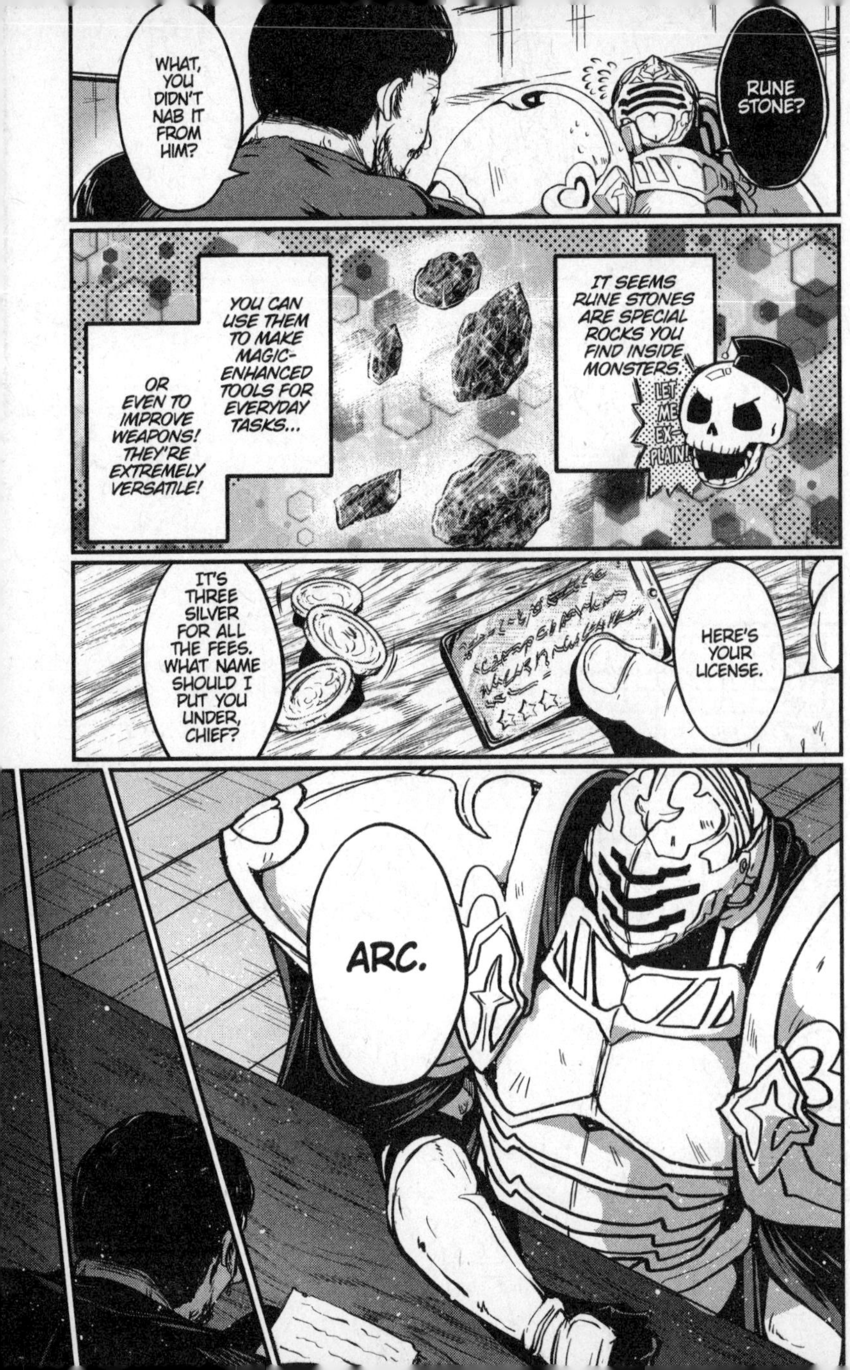
RUNE STONE?
WHAT, YOU DIDN'T NAB IT FROM HIM?
IT SEEMS RUNE STONES ARE SPECIAL ROCKS YOU FIND INSIDE MONSTERS.
LET ME EX-PLAIN!
YOU CAN USE THEM TO MAKE MAGIC-ENHANCED TOOLS FOR EVERYDAY TASKS...
OR EVEN TO IMPROVE WEAPONS! THEY'RE EXTREMELY VERSATILE!
HERE'S YOUR LICENSE.
IT'S THREE SILVER FOR ALL THE FEES. WHAT NAME SHOULD I PUT YOU UNDER, CHIEF?
ARC.

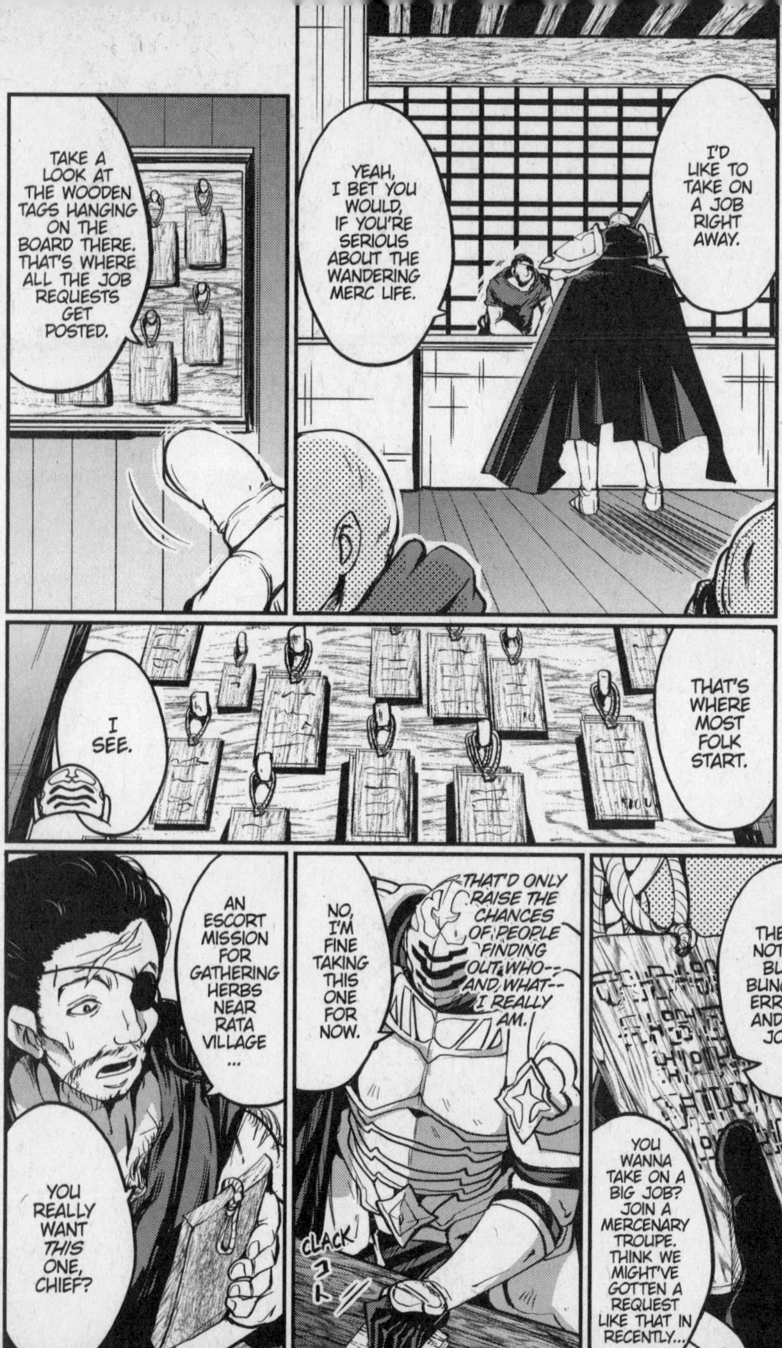
I'D LIKE TO TAKE ON A JOB RIGHT AWAY.
YEAH, I BET YOU WOULD, IF YOU'RE SERIOUS ABOUT THE WANDERING MERC LIFE.
TAKE A LOOK AT THE WOODEN TAGS HANGING ON THE BOARD THERE. THAT'S WHERE ALL THE JOB REQUESTS GET POSTED.
THAT'S WHERE MOST FOLK START.
I SEE.
THEY'RE NOTHING BUT A BUNCH OF ERRANDS AND ODD JOBS.
YOU WANNA TAKE ON A BIG JOB? JOIN A MERCENARY TROUPE. THINK WE MIGHT'VE GOTTEN A REQUEST LIKE THAT IN RECENTLY...
THAT'D ONLY RAISE THE CHANCES OF PEOPLE FINDING OUT WHO--AND WHAT--I REALLY AM.
NO, I'M FINE TAKING THIS ONE FOR NOW.
CLACK
AN ESCORT MISSION FOR GATHERING HERBS NEAR RATA VILLAGE...
YOU REALLY WANT *THIS* ONE, CHIEF?

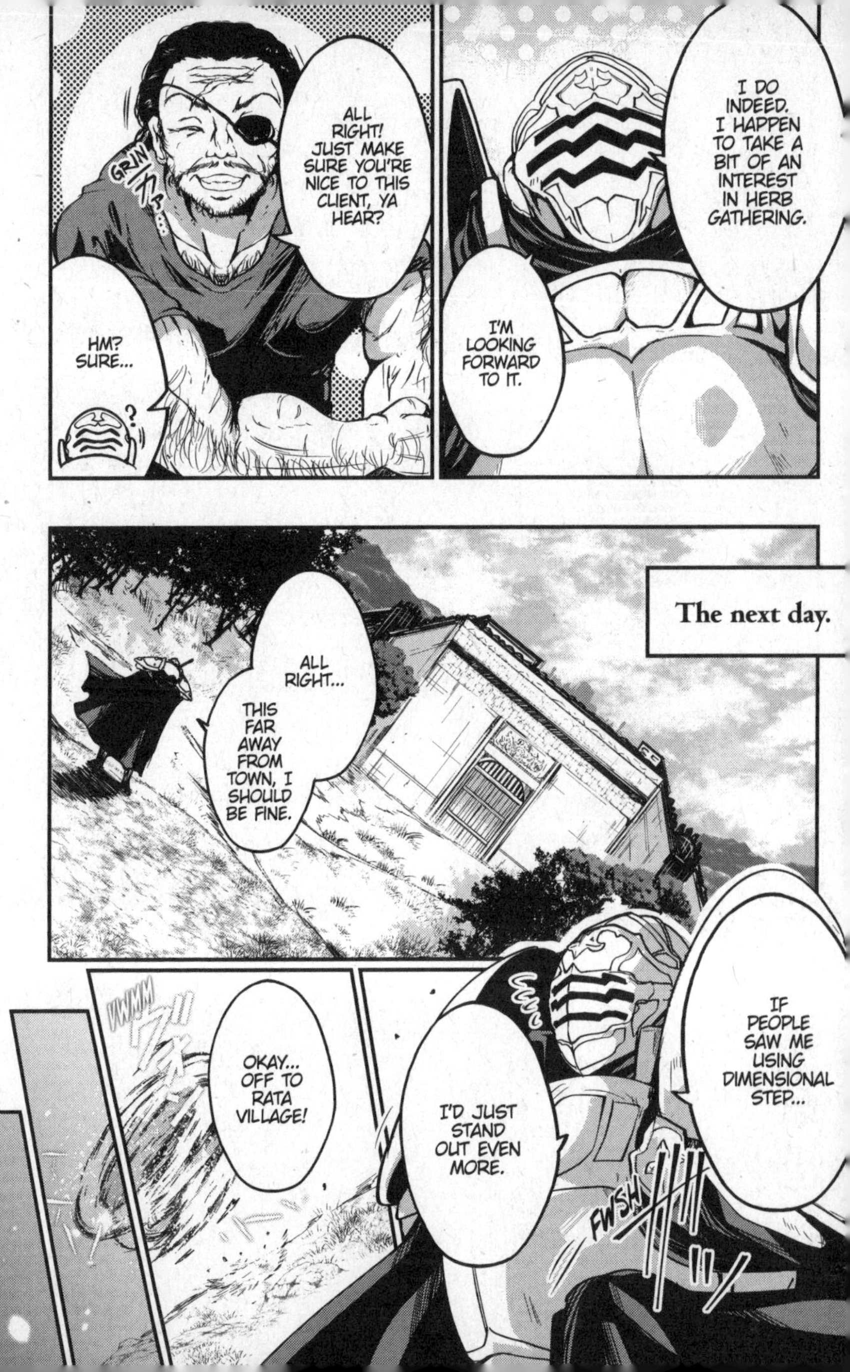
I DO INDEED. I HAPPEN TO TAKE A BIT OF AN INTEREST IN HERB GATHERING.
I'M LOOKING FORWARD TO IT.
ALL RIGHT! JUST MAKE SURE YOU'RE NICE TO THIS CLIENT, YA HEAR?
GRIN
HM? SURE...
The next day.
ALL RIGHT... THIS FAR AWAY FROM TOWN, I SHOULD BE FINE.
IF PEOPLE SAW ME USING DIMENSIONAL STEP...
I'D JUST STAND OUT EVEN MORE.
FWSH
VWMM
OKAY... OFF TO RATA VILLAGE!

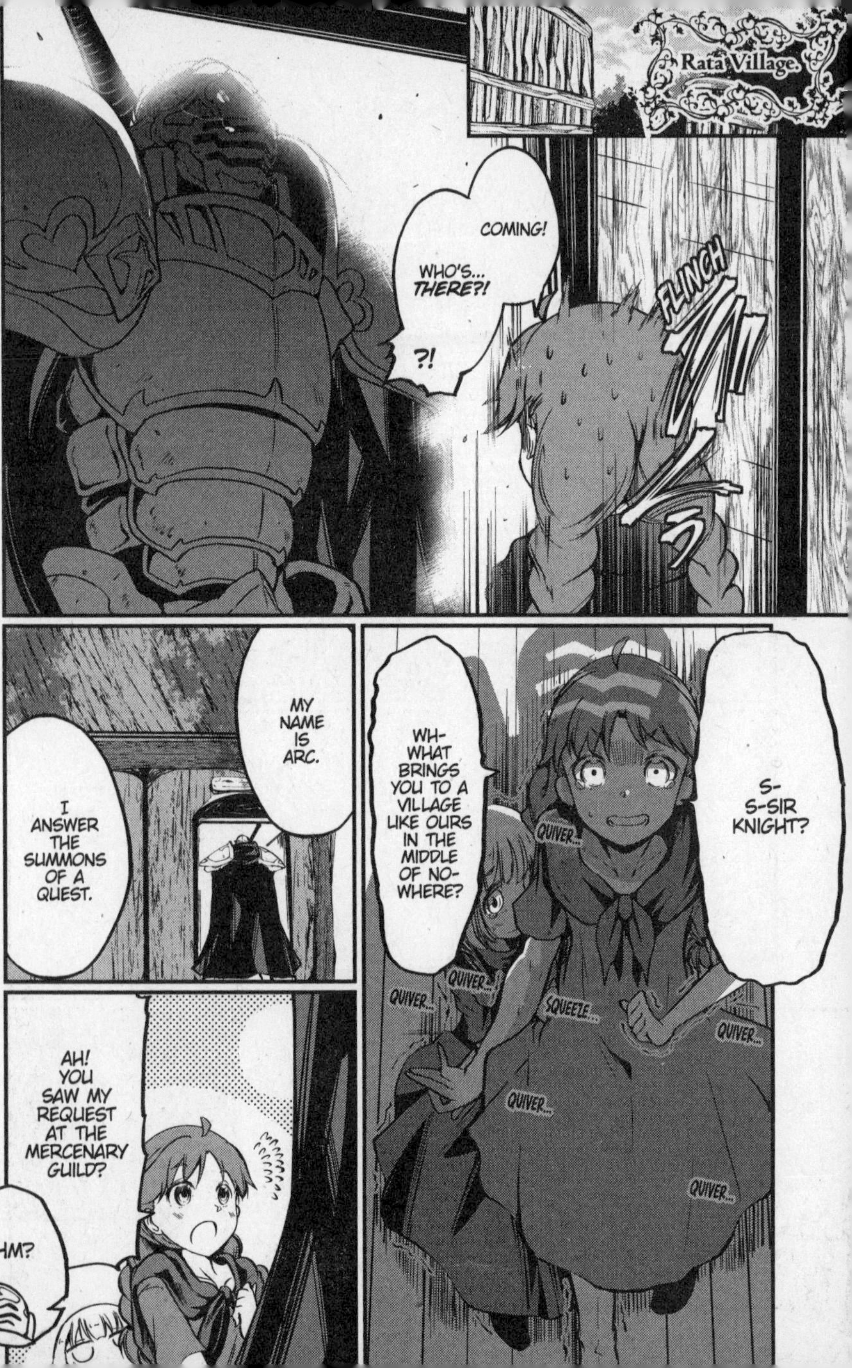
Rata Village.
COMING!
WHO'S... THERE?!
?!
FLINCH
S-S-SIR KNIGHT?
WH-WHAT BRINGS YOU TO A VILLAGE LIKE OURS IN THE MIDDLE OF NO-WHERE?
QUIVER...
QUIVER...
SQUEEZE...
QUIVER...
QUIVER...
QUIVER...
QUIVER...
MY NAME IS ARC.
I ANSWER THE SUMMONS OF A QUEST.
AH! YOU SAW MY REQUEST AT THE MERCENARY GUILD?
HM?

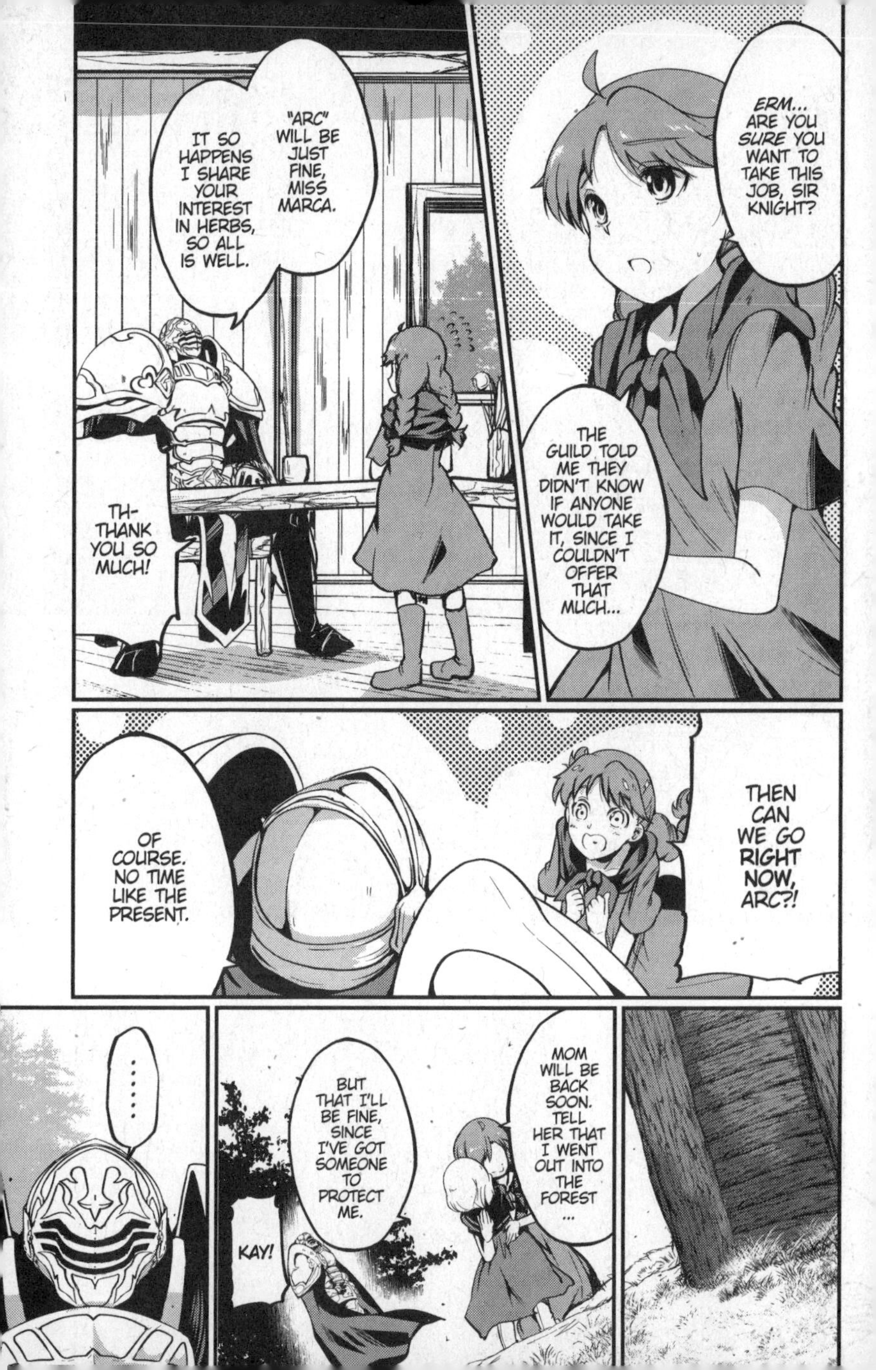
ERM... ARE YOU SURE YOU WANT TO TAKE THIS JOB, SIR KNIGHT?
THE GUILD TOLD ME THEY DIDN'T KNOW IF ANYONE WOULD TAKE IT, SINCE I COULDN'T OFFER THAT MUCH...
"ARC" WILL BE JUST FINE, MISS MARCA.
IT SO HAPPENS I SHARE YOUR INTEREST IN HERBS, SO ALL IS WELL.
TH-THANK YOU SO MUCH!
THEN CAN WE GO RIGHT NOW, ARC?!
OF COURSE. NO TIME LIKE THE PRESENT.
MOM WILL BE BACK SOON. TELL HER THAT I WENT OUT INTO THE FOREST ...
BUT THAT I'LL BE FINE, SINCE I'VE GOT SOMEONE TO PROTECT ME.
KAY!
......

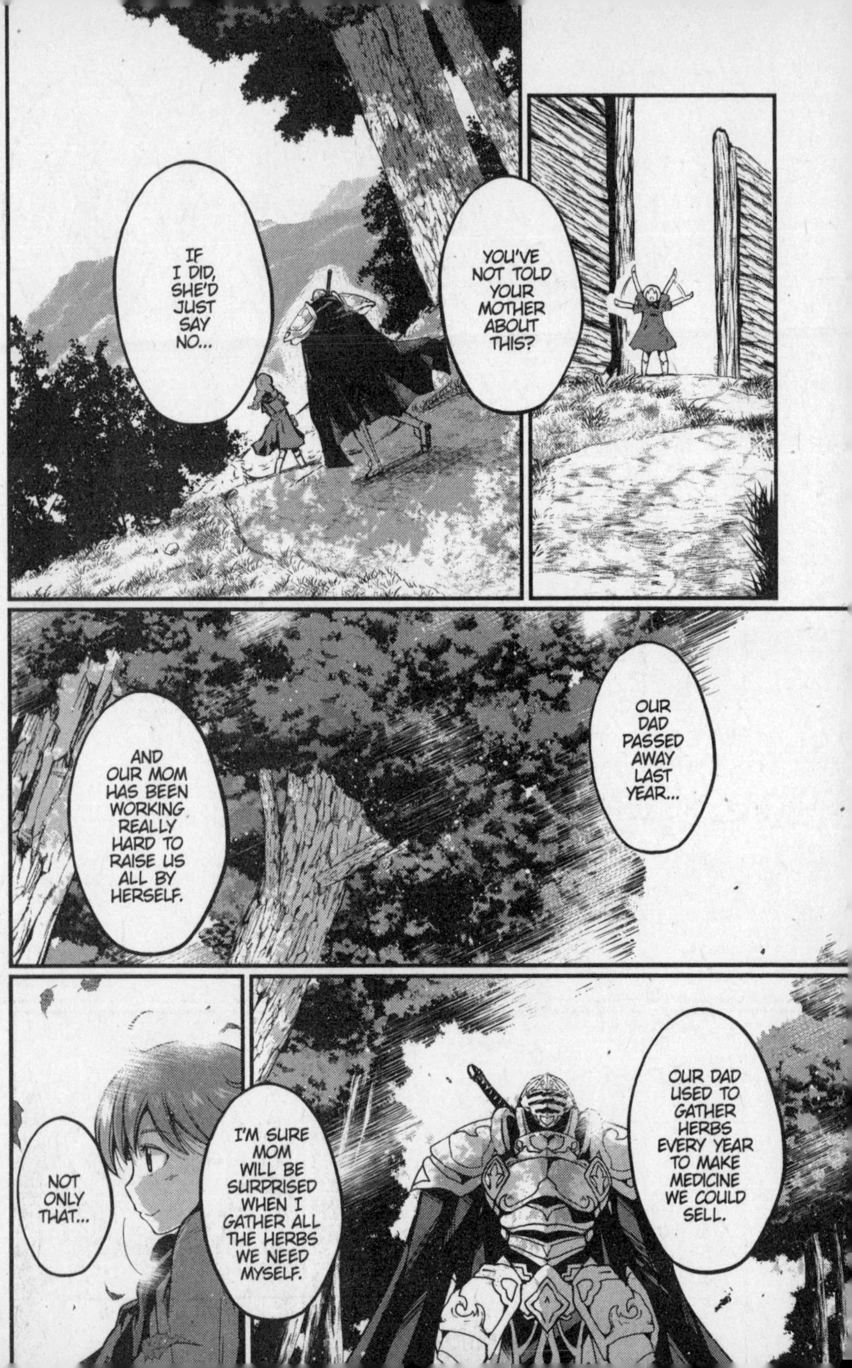
YOU'VE NOT TOLD YOUR MOTHER ABOUT THIS?
IF I DID, SHE'D JUST SAY NO...
OUR DAD PASSED AWAY LAST YEAR...
AND OUR MOM HAS BEEN WORKING REALLY HARD TO RAISE US ALL BY HERSELF.
OUR DAD USED TO GATHER HERBS EVERY YEAR TO MAKE MEDICINE WE COULD SELL.
I'M SURE MOM WILL BE SURPRISED WHEN I GATHER ALL THE HERBS WE NEED MYSELF.
NOT ONLY THAT...

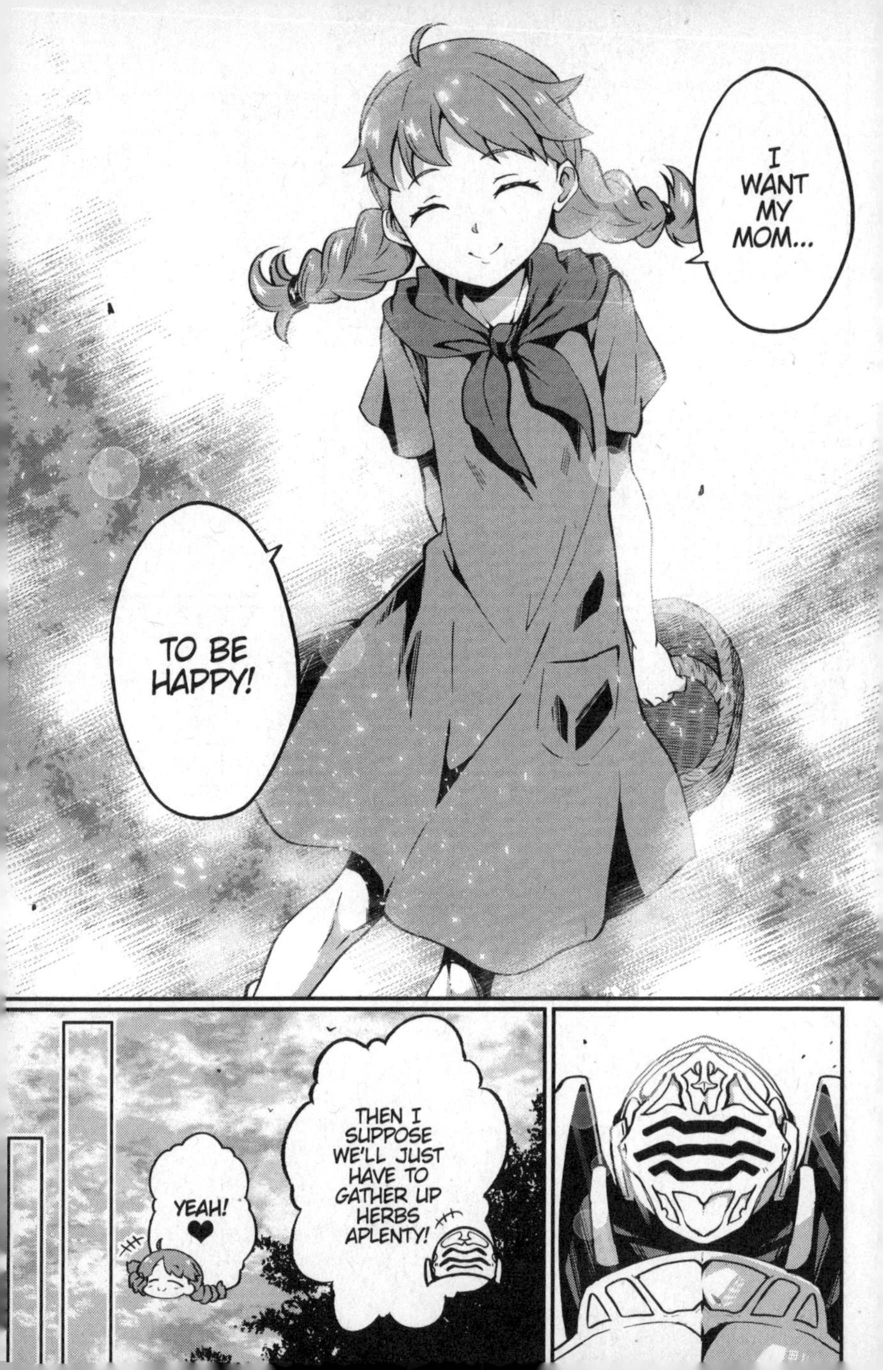
I WANT MY MOM...
TO BE HAPPY!
THEN I SUPPOSE WE'LL JUST HAVE TO GATHER UP HERBS APLENTY!
YEAH! ♥

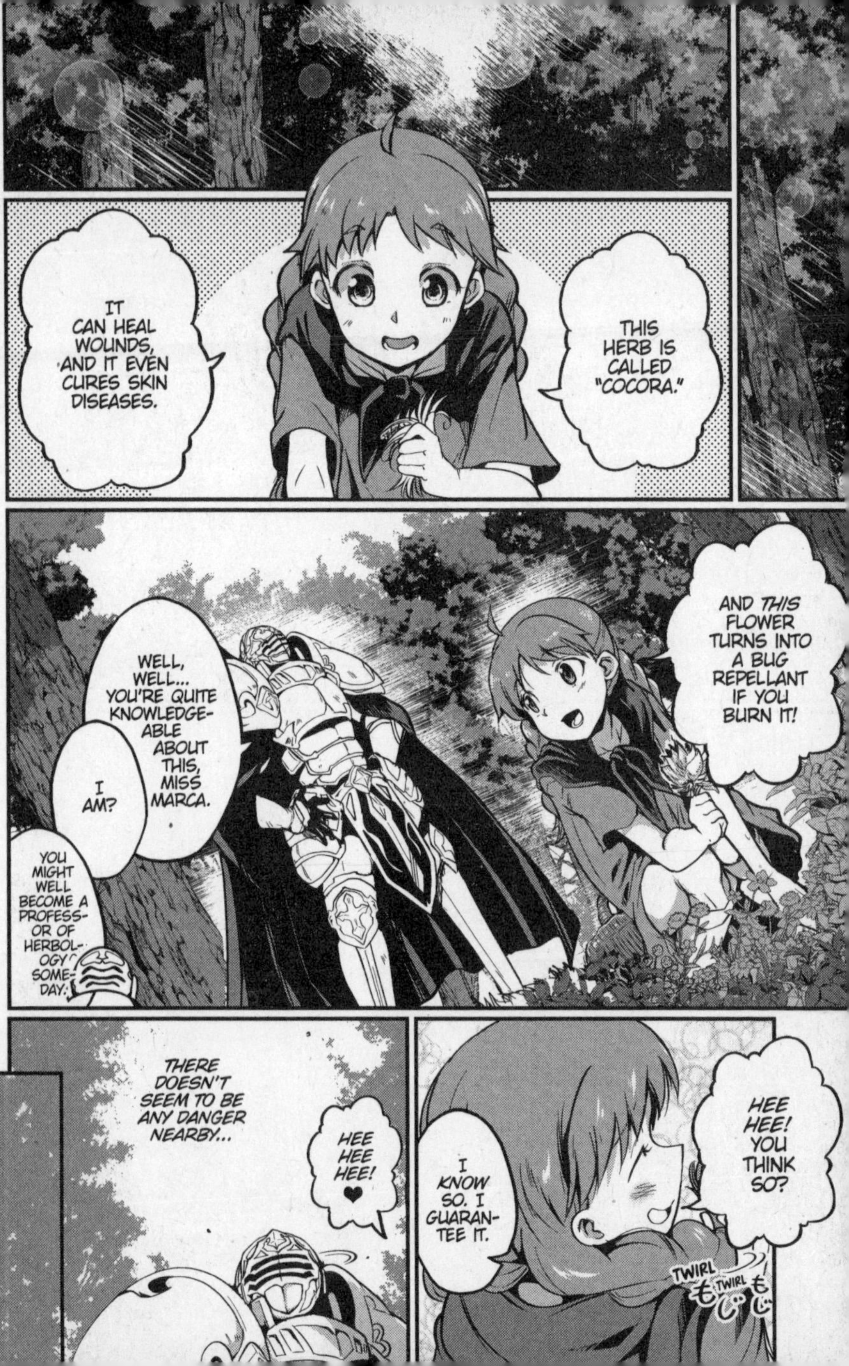
THIS HERB IS CALLED "COCORA."
IT CAN HEAL WOUNDS, AND IT EVEN CURES SKIN DISEASES.
AND *THIS* FLOWER TURNS INTO A BUG REPELLANT IF YOU BURN IT!
WELL, WELL... YOU'RE QUITE KNOWLEDGEABLE ABOUT THIS, MISS MARCA.
I AM?
YOU MIGHT WELL BECOME A PROFESSOR OF HERBOLOGY SOMEDAY.
HEE HEE! YOU THINK SO?
I KNOW SO. I GUARANTEE IT.
TWIRL TWIRL もじもじ
HEE HEE HEE! ♥
THERE DOESN'T SEEM TO BE ANY DANGER NEARBY...

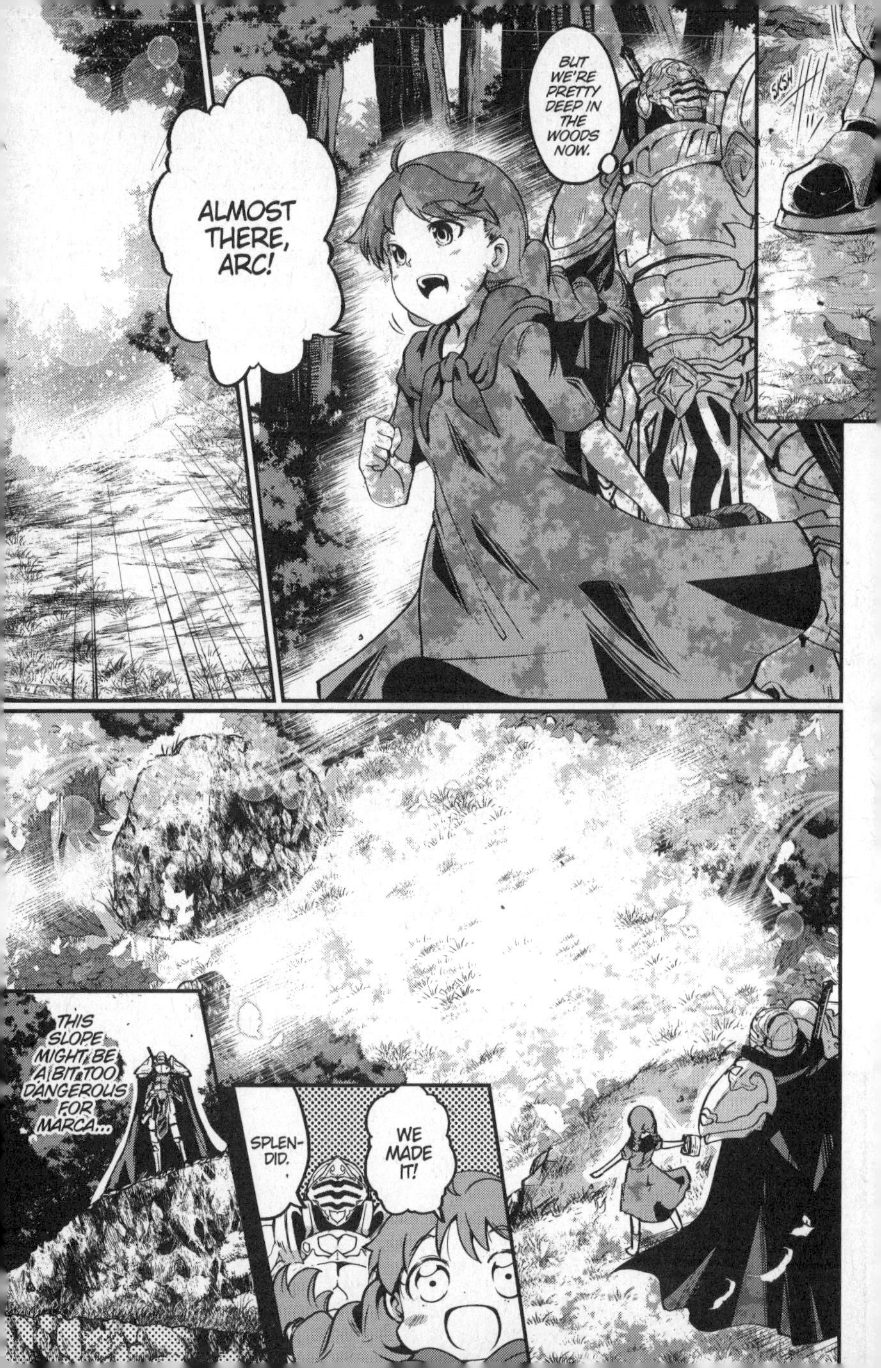
SKSH
BUT WE'RE PRETTY DEEP IN THE WOODS NOW.
ALMOST THERE, ARC!
WE MADE IT!
SPLEN-DID.
THIS SLOPE MIGHT BE A BIT TOO DANGEROUS FOR MARCA...

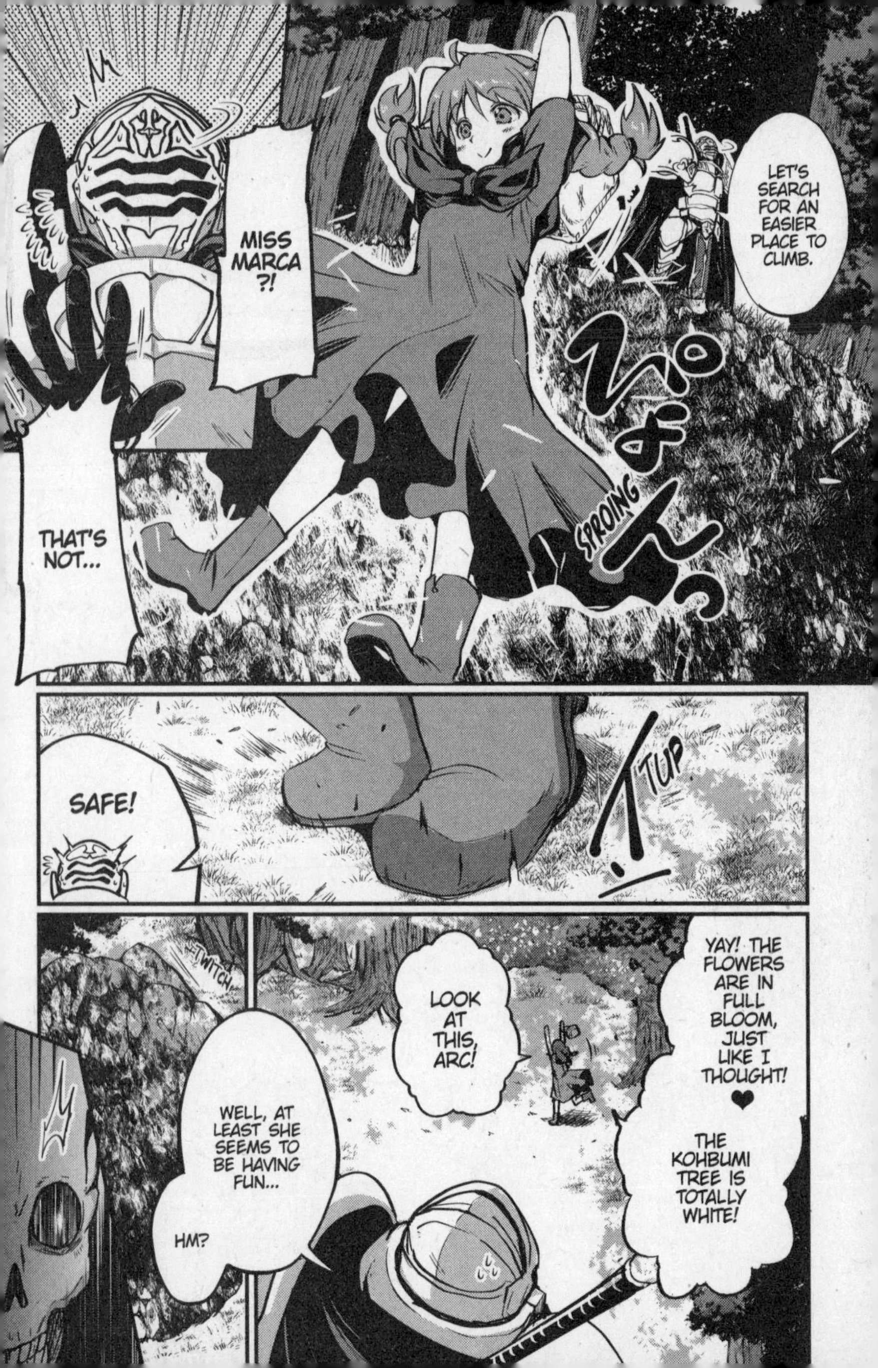
LET'S SEARCH FOR AN EASIER PLACE TO CLIMB.
SPROING
MISS MARCA?!
THAT'S NOT...
TUP
SAFE!
YAY! THE FLOWERS ARE IN FULL BLOOM, JUST LIKE I THOUGHT! ♥
THE KOHBUMI TREE IS TOTALLY WHITE!
LOOK AT THIS, ARC!
TWITCH
WELL, AT LEAST SHE SEEMS TO BE HAVING FUN...
HM?

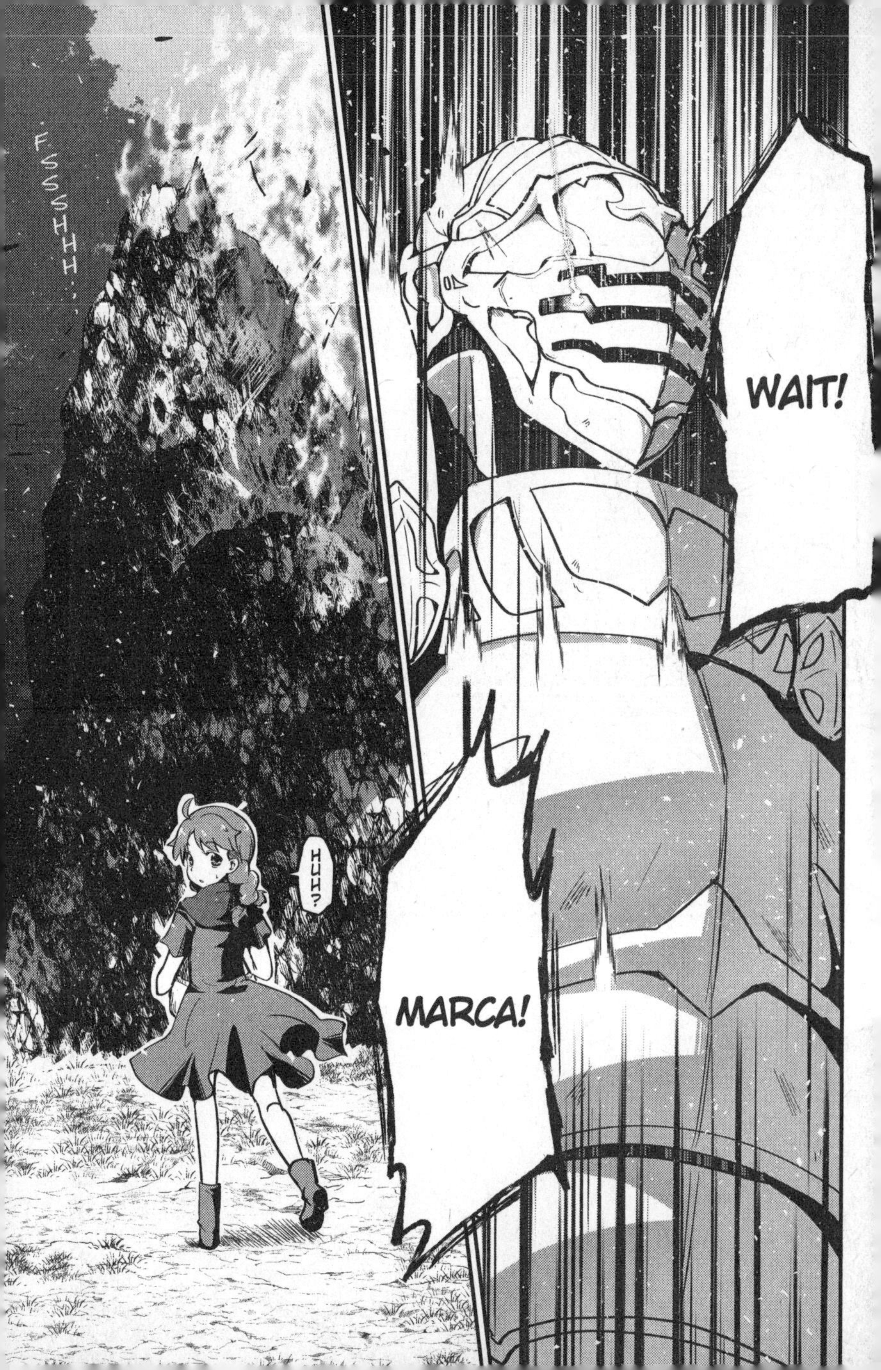
WAIT!
MARCA!
FSSSHHH...
HUH?

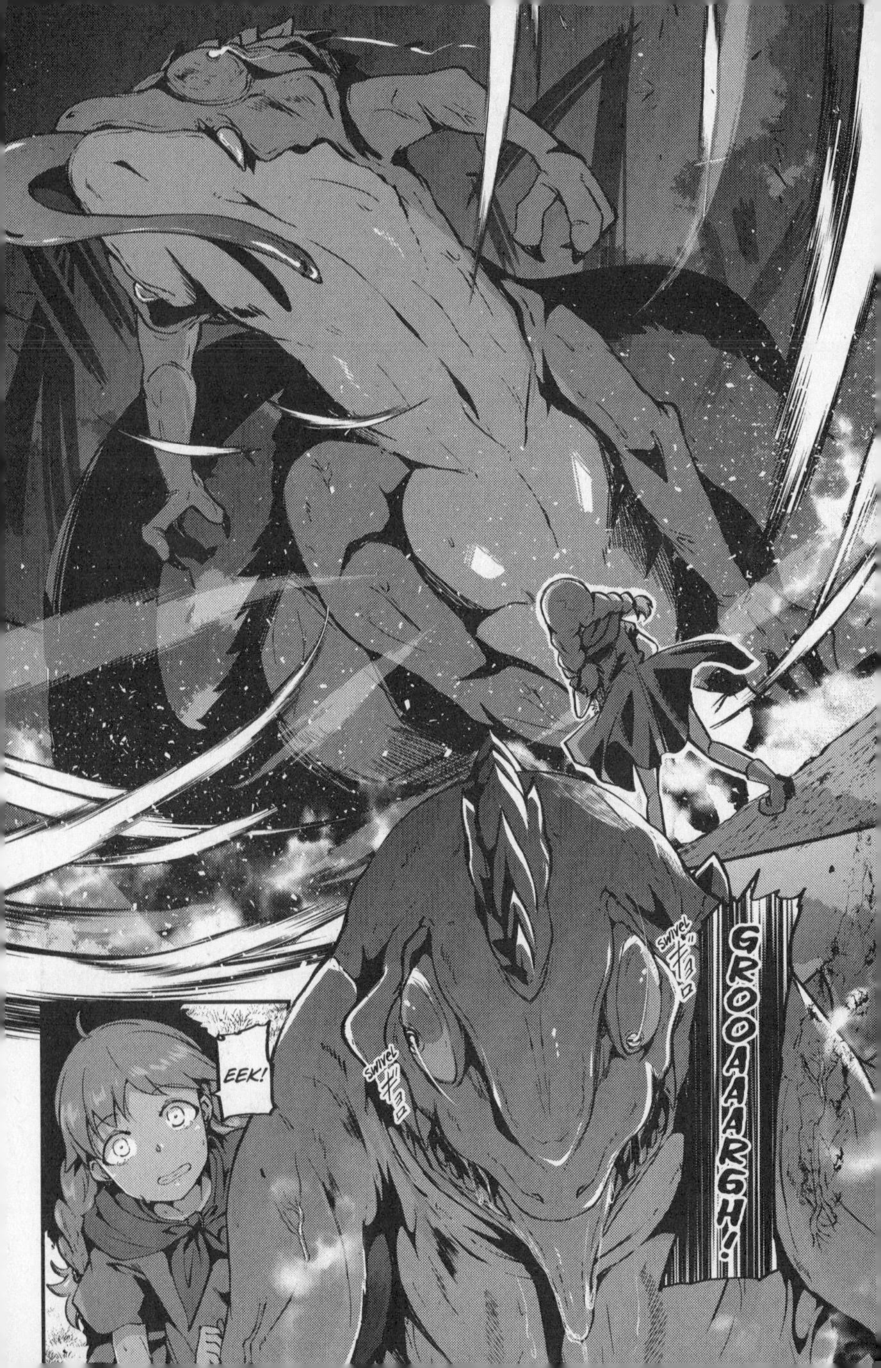
swivel
GROOOAAARGH!
swivel
EEK!

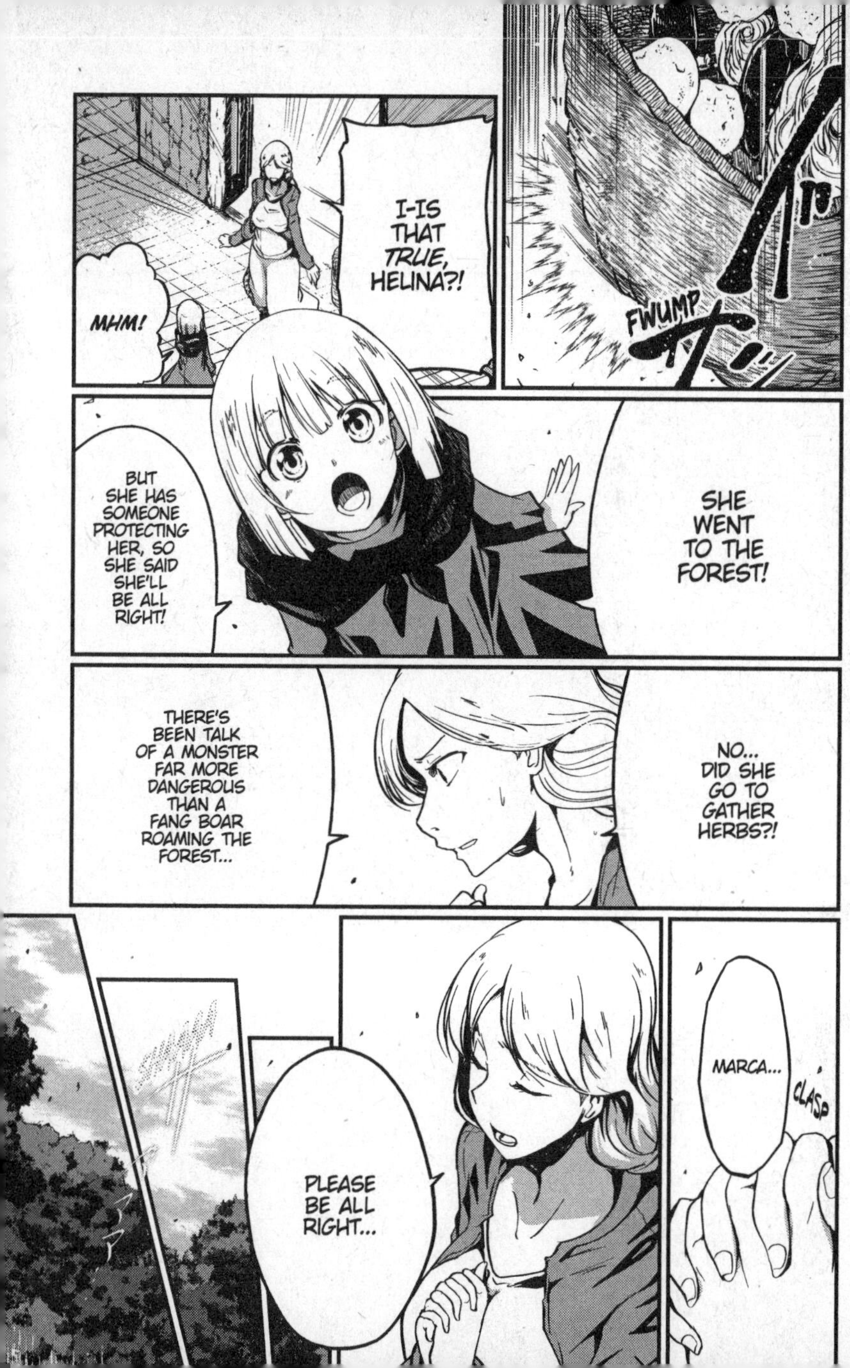
FWUMP
I-IS THAT TRUE, HELINA?!
MHM!
SHE WENT TO THE FOREST!
BUT SHE HAS SOMEONE PROTECTING HER, SO SHE SAID SHE'LL BE ALL RIGHT!
NO... DID SHE GO TO GATHER HERBS?!
THERE'S BEEN TALK OF A MONSTER FAR MORE DANGEROUS THAN A FANG BOAR ROAMING THE FOREST...
MARCA...
CLASP
PLEASE BE ALL RIGHT...

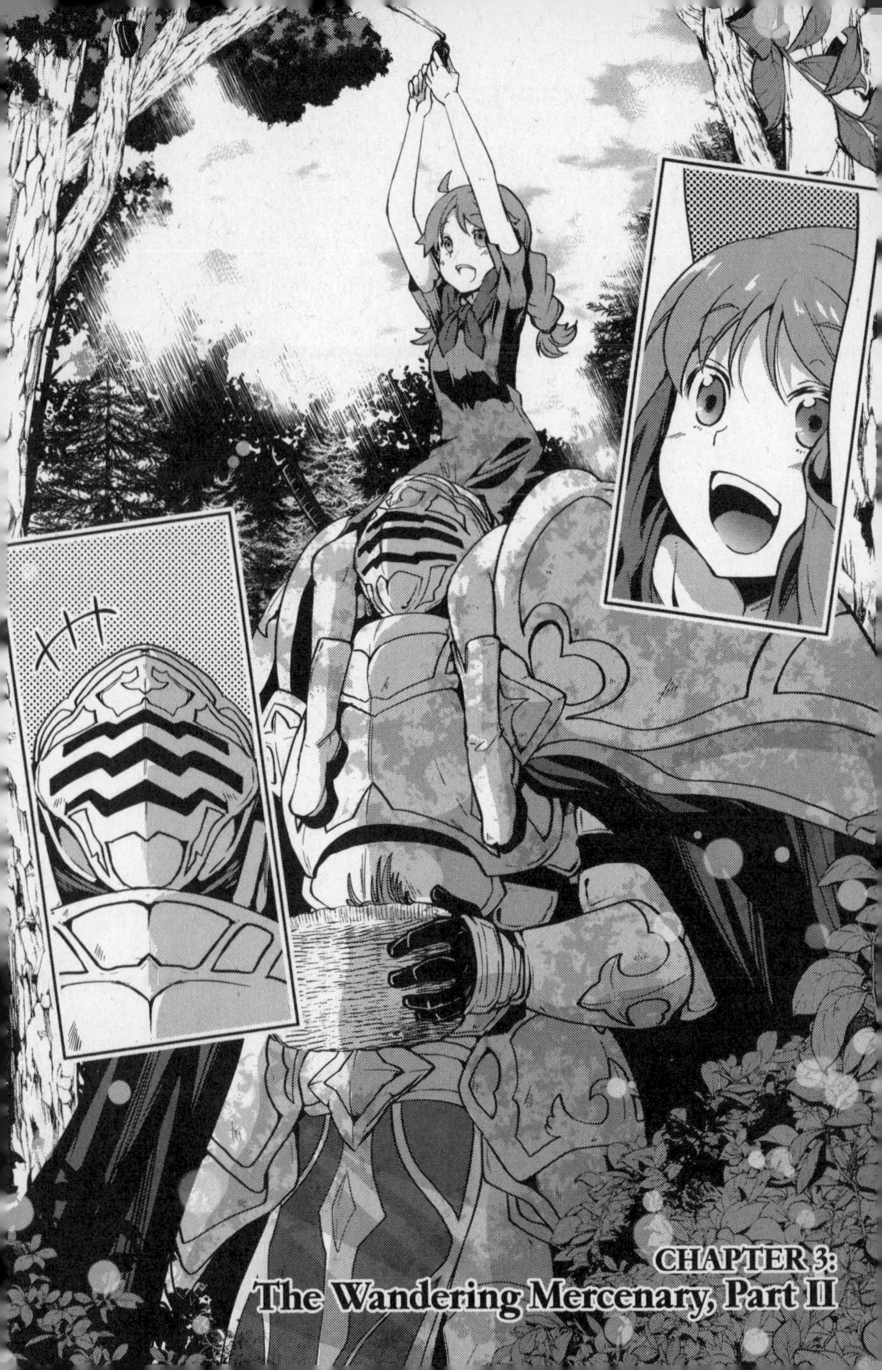
CHAPTER 3:
The Wandering Mercenary, Part II

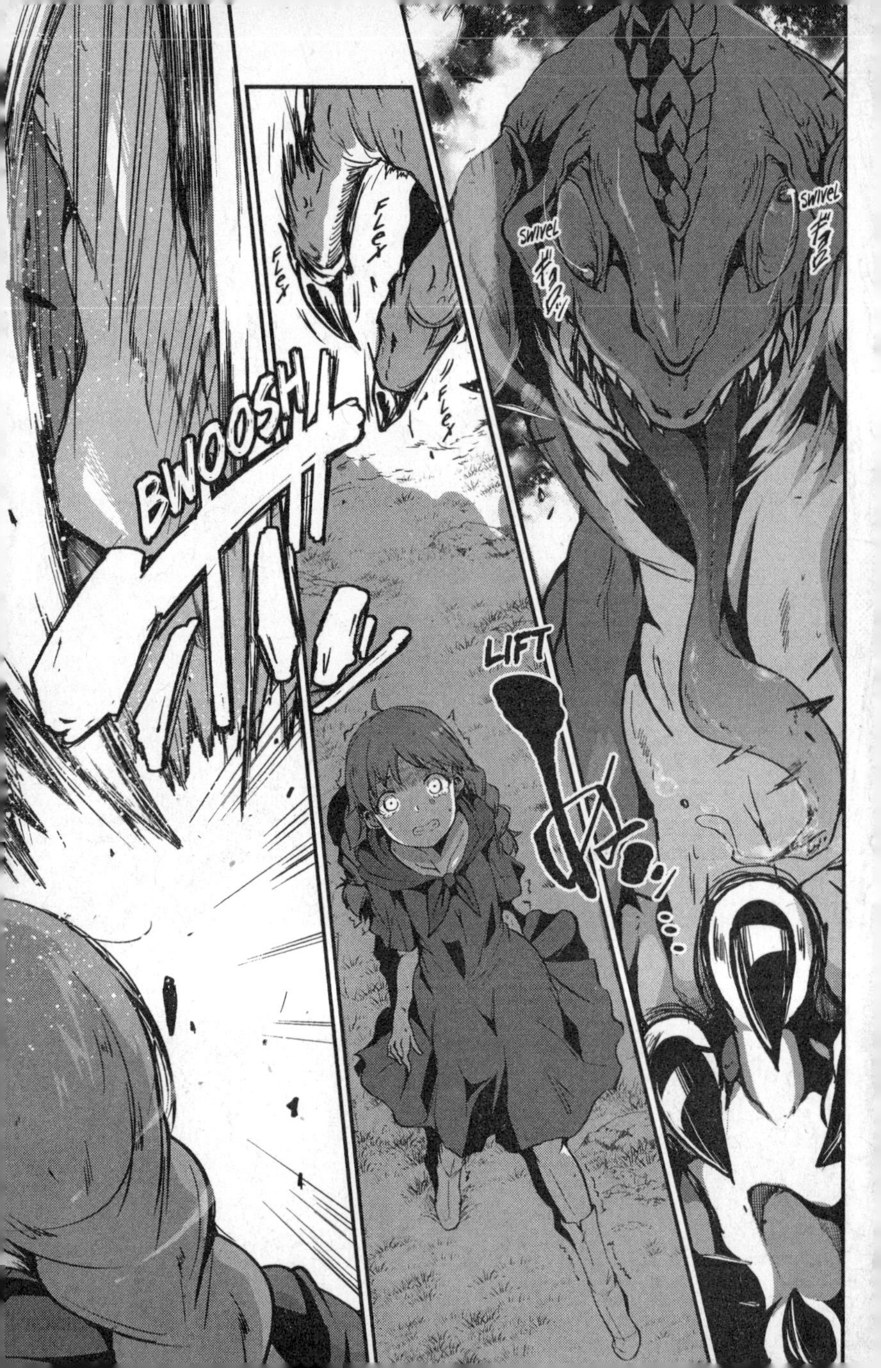
SWIVEL
SWIVEL
LIFT
FLEX
FLEX
FLEX
BWOOSH!

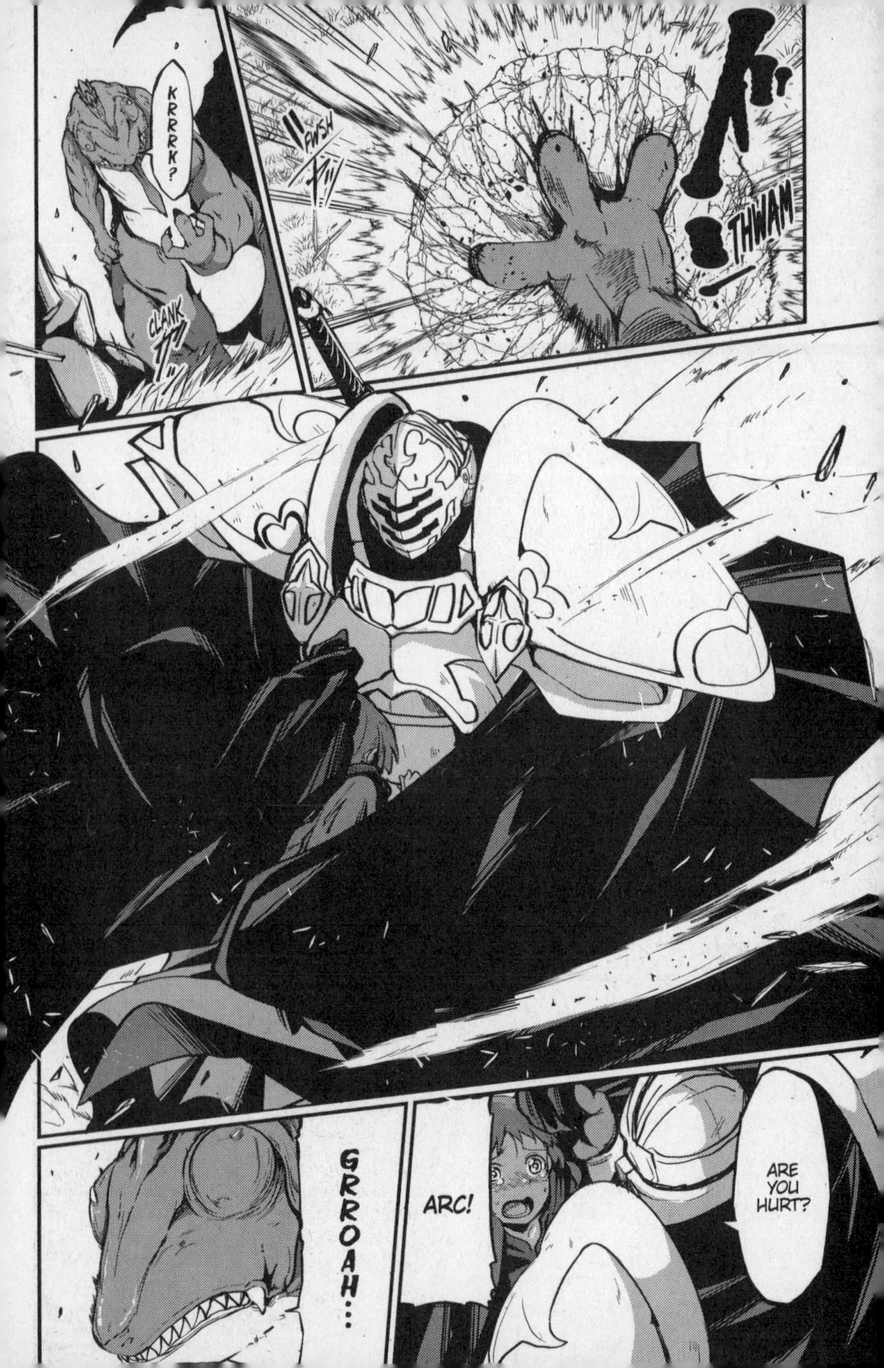
THWAM
FWSH
KRRRK?
CLANK
ARE YOU HURT?
ARC!
GRROAH...

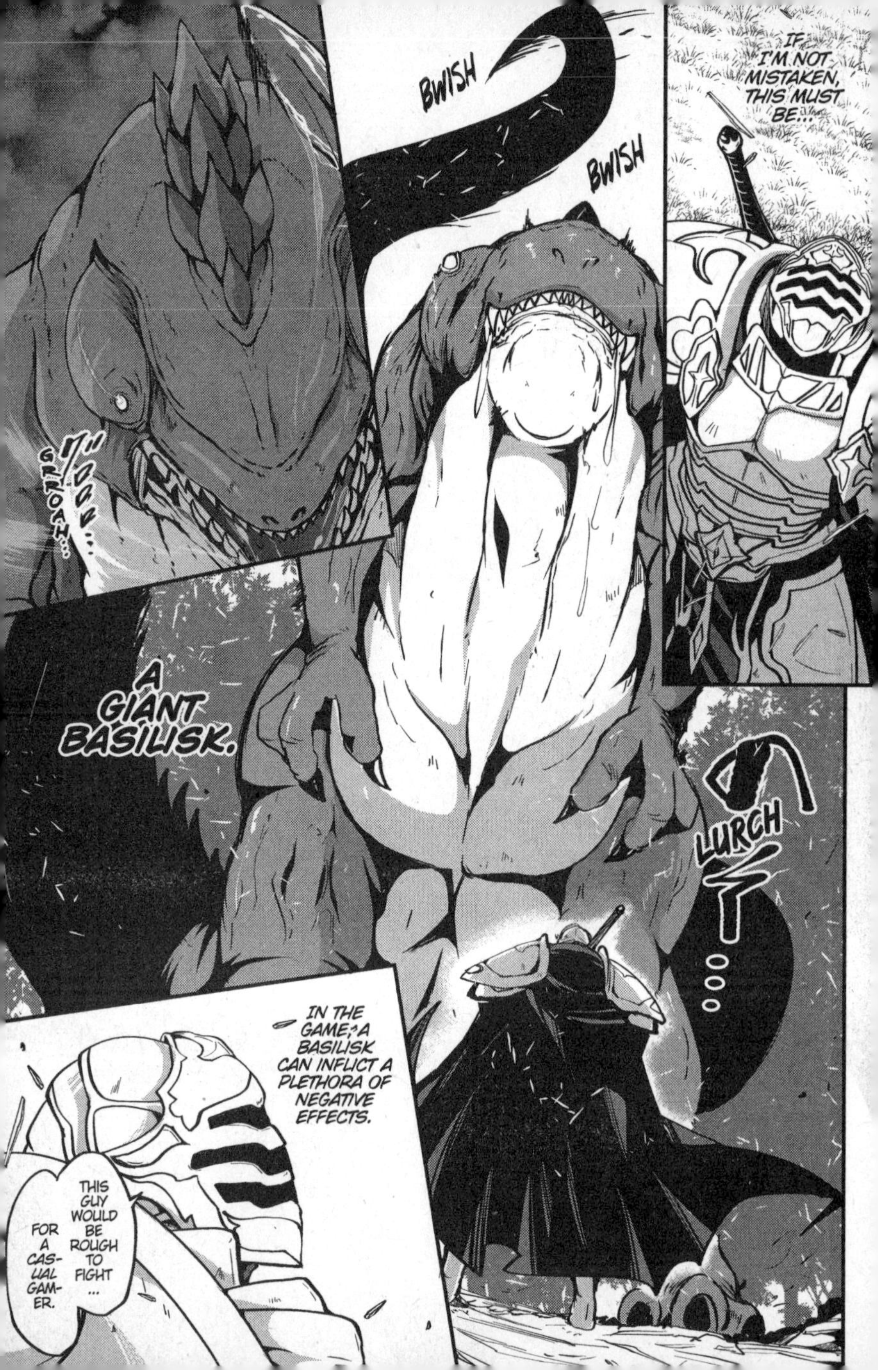
IF I'M NOT MISTAKEN, THIS MUST BE...
BWISH
BWISH
GRROAH...
A GIANT BASILISK.
LURCH
...
IN THE GAME, A BASILISK CAN INFLICT A PLETHORA OF NEGATIVE EFFECTS.
THIS GUY WOULD BE ROUGH TO FIGHT... FOR A CASUAL GAMER.

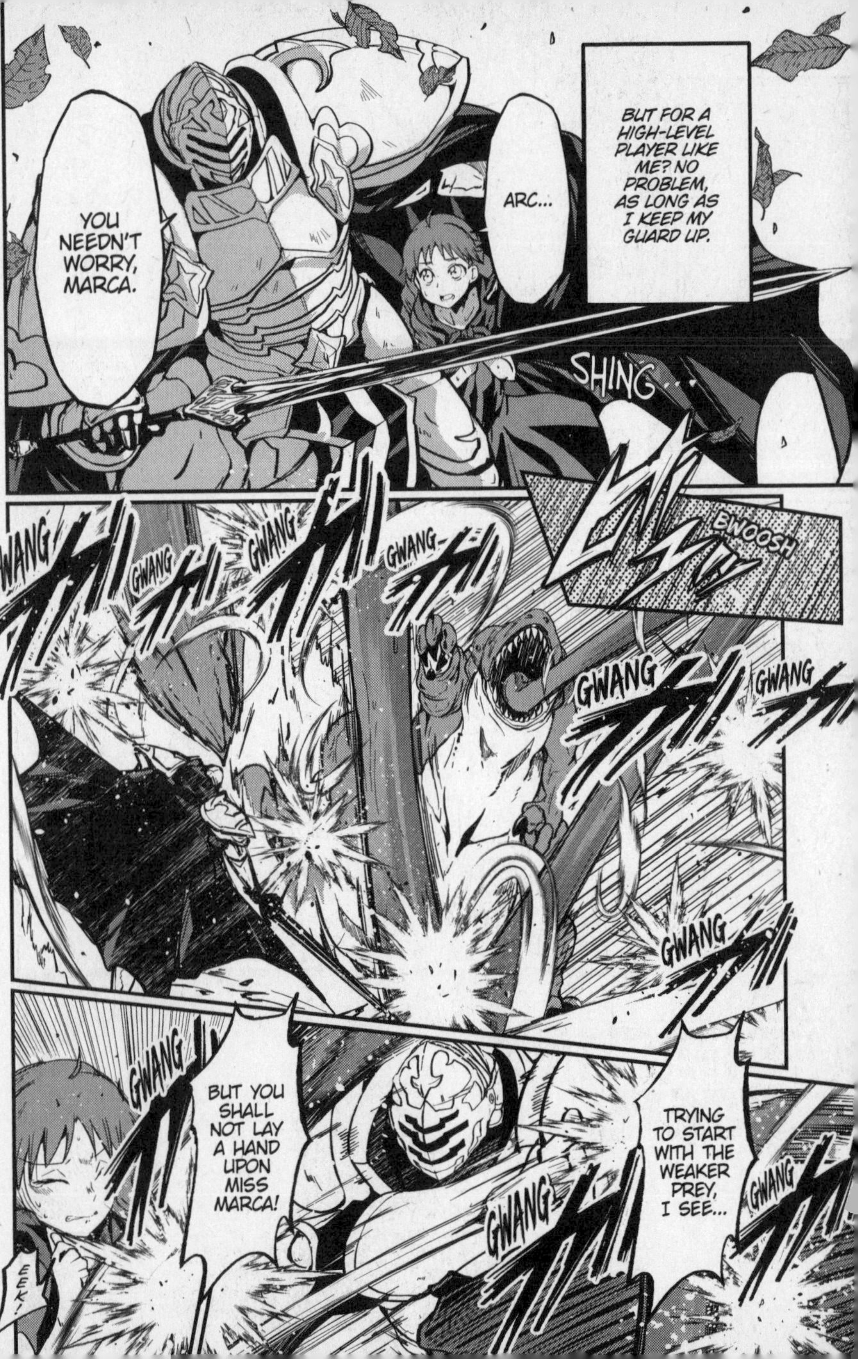
BUT FOR A HIGH-LEVEL PLAYER LIKE ME? NO PROBLEM, AS LONG AS I KEEP MY GUARD UP.
ARC...
YOU NEEDN'T WORRY, MARCA.
SHING
BWOOSH
GWANG
GWANG
GWANG
GWANG
GWANG
GWANG
GWANG
TRYING TO START WITH THE WEAKER PREY, I SEE...
GWANG
GWANG
BUT YOU SHALL NOT LAY A HAND UPON MISS MARCA!
GWANG
EEK!

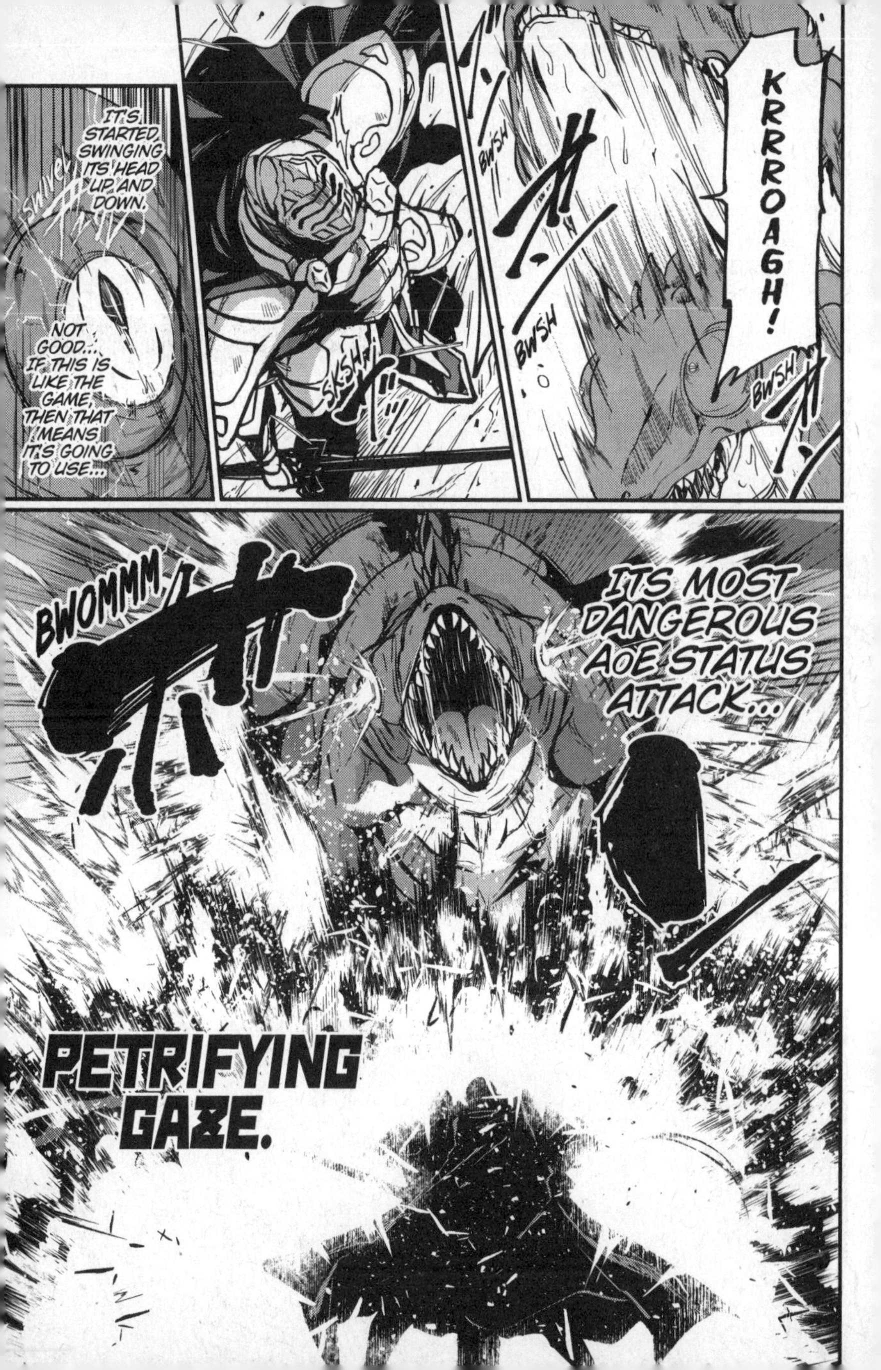
KRRROAGH!
BWSH
BWSH
BWSH
SKSH
SWIVEL
IT'S STARTED SWINGING ITS HEAD UP AND DOWN.
NOT GOOD... IF THIS IS LIKE THE GAME, THEN THAT MEANS IT'S GOING TO USE...
ITS MOST DANGEROUS AoE STATUS ATTACK...
BWOMMM
PETRIFYING GAZE.

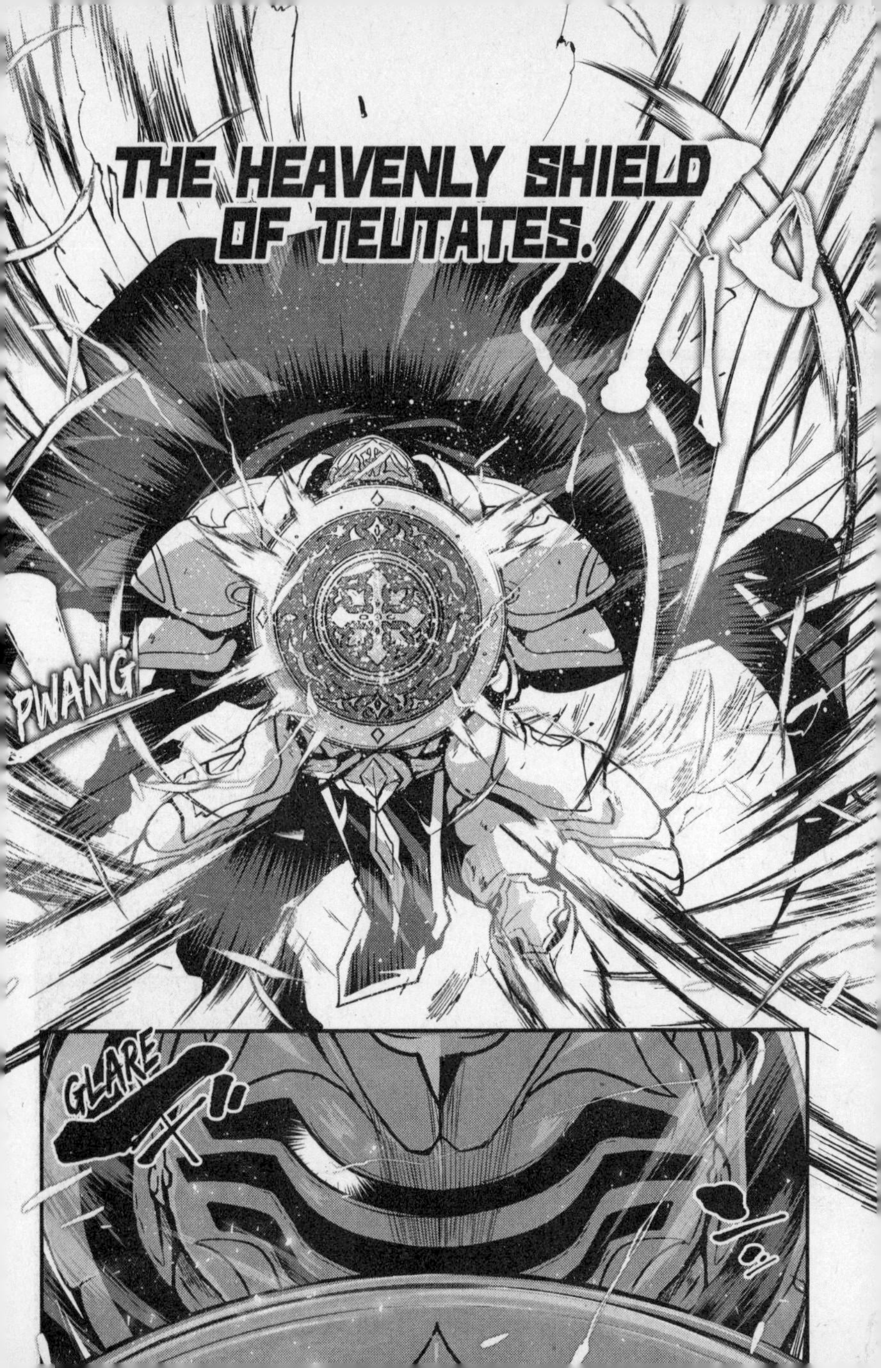
THE HEAVENLY SHIELD OF TEUTATES.
PWANG
GLARE

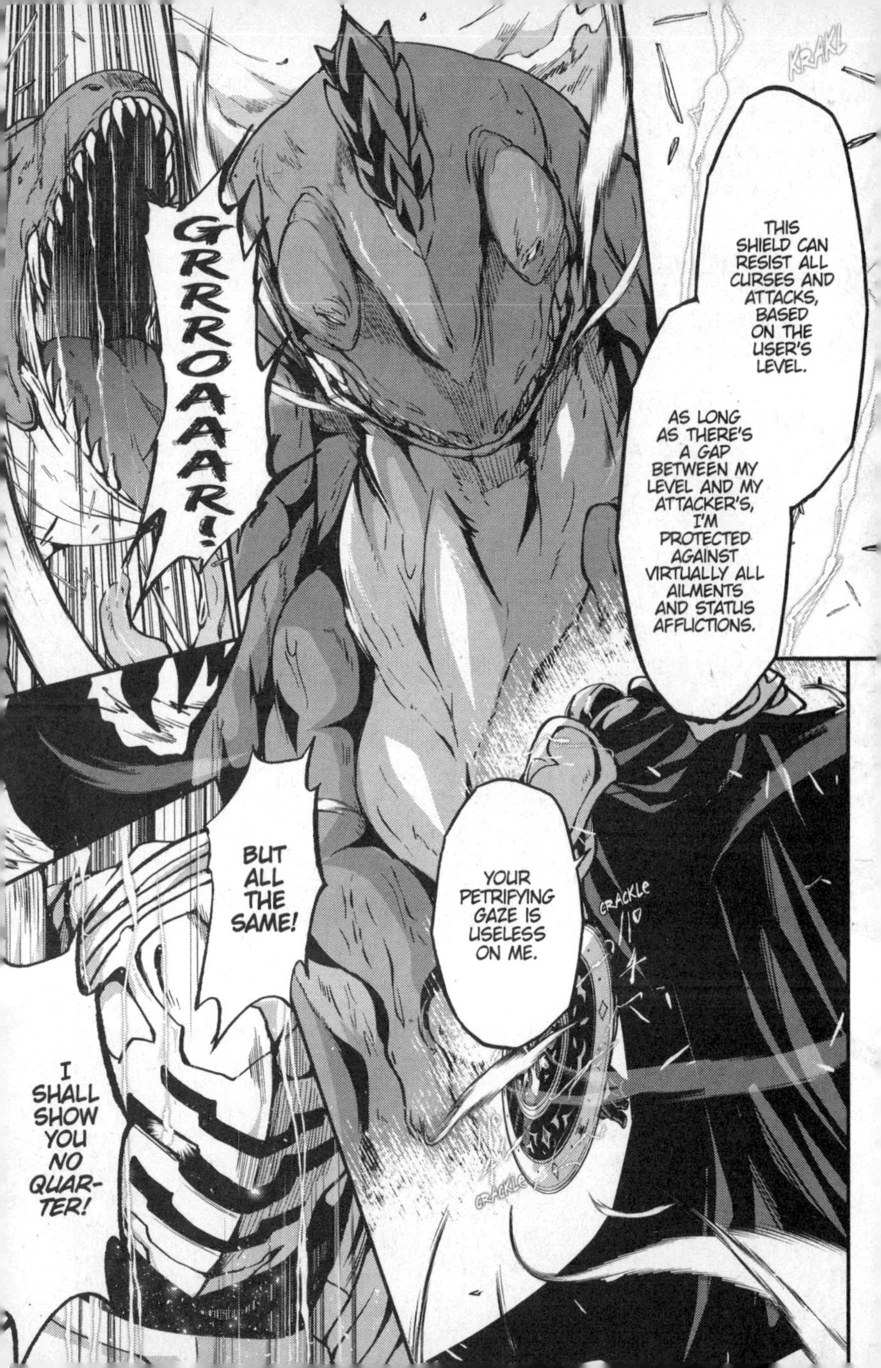
KRAKL
THIS SHIELD CAN RESIST ALL CURSES AND ATTACKS, BASED ON THE USER'S LEVEL.
AS LONG AS THERE'S A GAP BETWEEN MY LEVEL AND MY ATTACKER'S, I'M PROTECTED AGAINST VIRTUALLY ALL AILMENTS AND STATUS AFFLICTIONS.
GRRROAAAAR!
YOUR PETRIFYING GAZE IS USELESS ON ME.
CRACKLE
BUT ALL THE SAME!
I SHALL SHOW YOU NO QUARTER!
CRACKLE

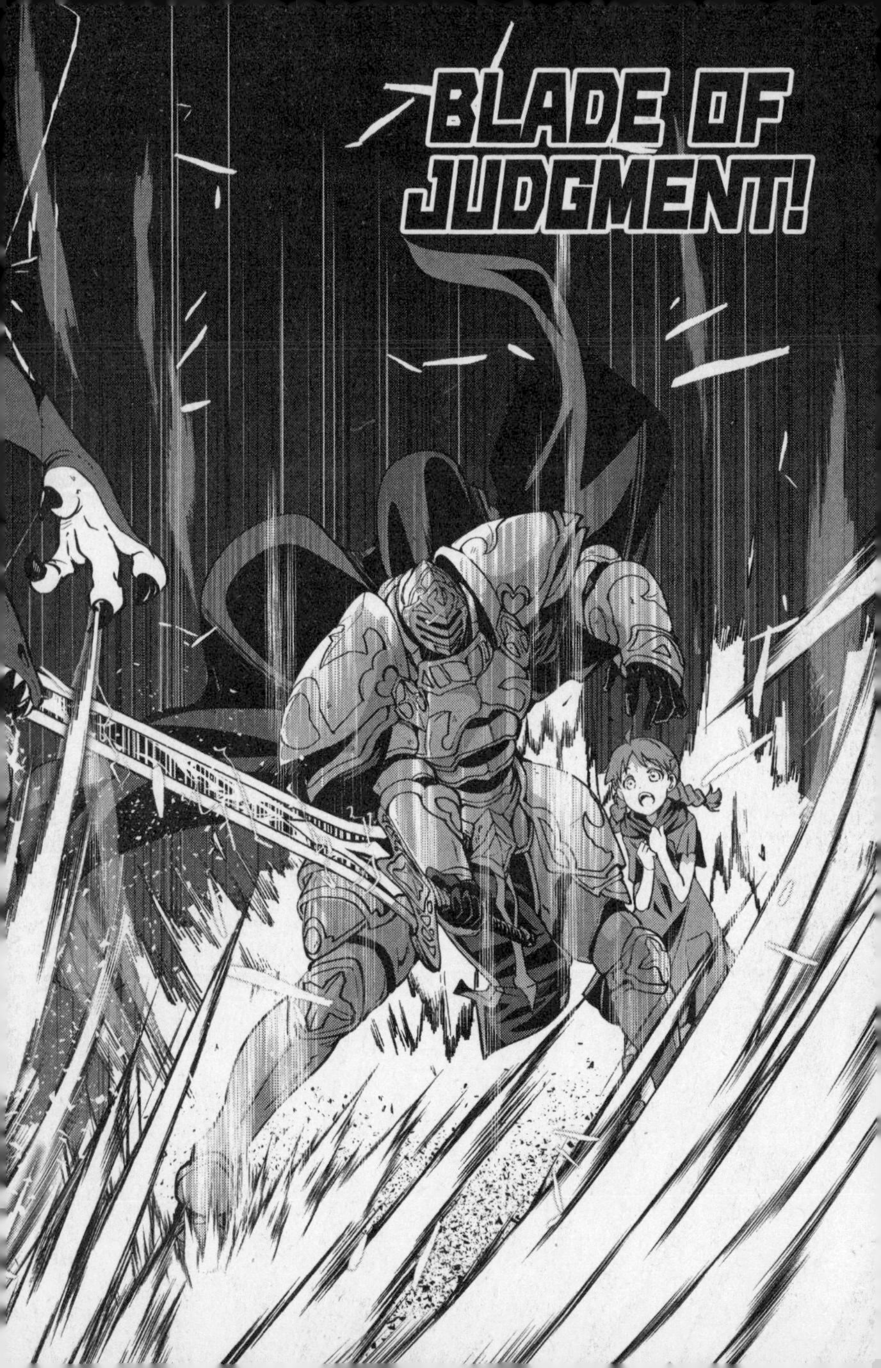
BLADE OF JUDGMENT!

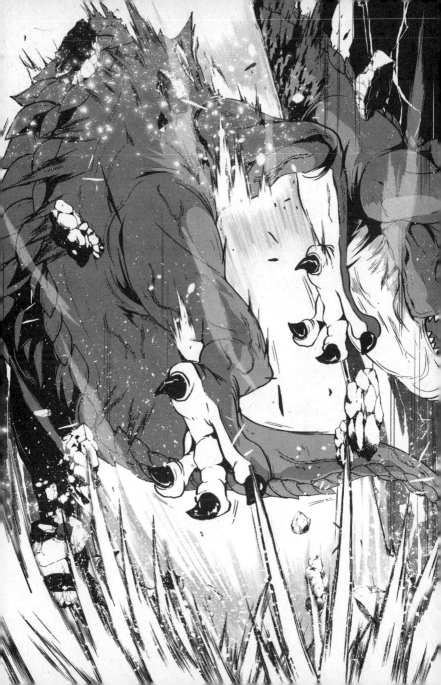

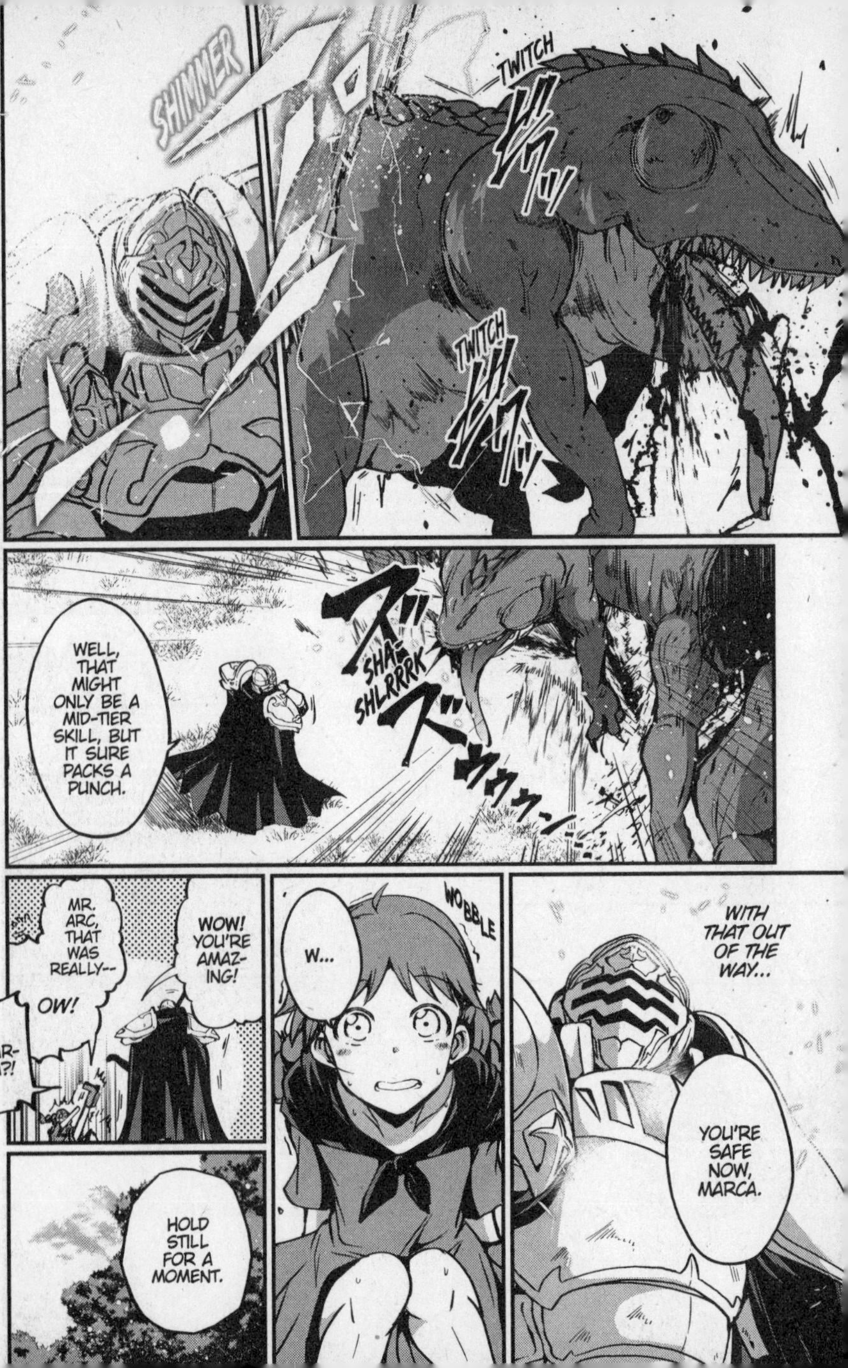
TWITCH
TWITCH
SHIMMER
SHA-
SHLRRRK
WELL, THAT MIGHT ONLY BE A MID-TIER SKILL, BUT IT SURE PACKS A PUNCH.
WITH THAT OUT OF THE WAY...
YOU'RE SAFE NOW, MARCA.
WOBBLE
W...
WOW! YOU'RE AMAZ-ING!
MR. ARC, THAT WAS REALLY--
OW!
MAR-CA?!
HOLD STILL FOR A MOMENT.

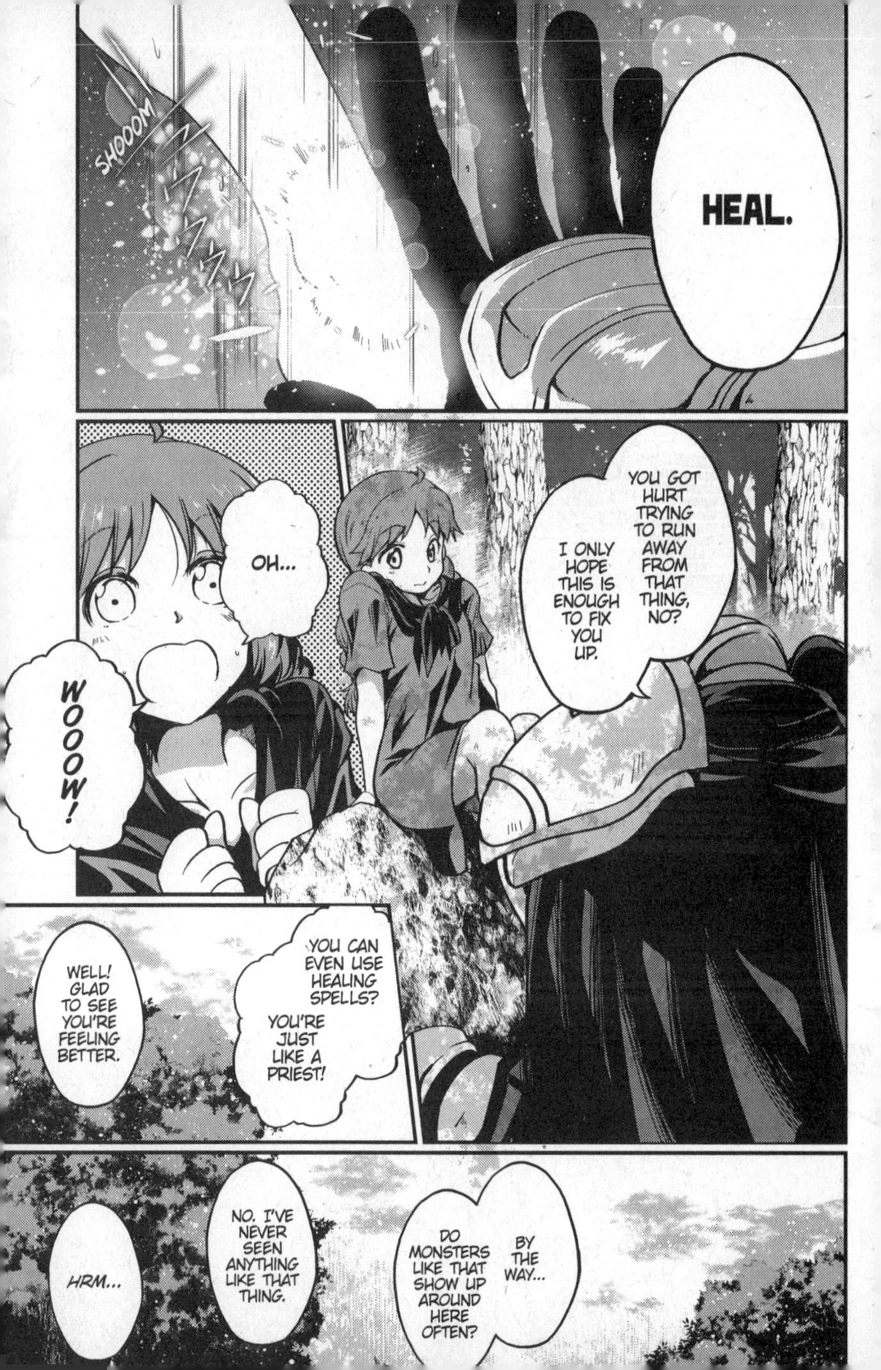
HEAL.
SHOOOM
YOU GOT HURT TRYING TO RUN AWAY FROM THAT THING, NO?
I ONLY HOPE THIS IS ENOUGH TO FIX YOU UP.
OH...
WOOOOW!
YOU CAN EVEN USE HEALING SPELLS?
YOU'RE JUST LIKE A PRIEST!
WELL! GLAD TO SEE YOU'RE FEELING BETTER.
BY THE WAY...
DO MONSTERS LIKE THAT SHOW UP AROUND HERE OFTEN?
NO. I'VE NEVER SEEN ANYTHING LIKE THAT THING.
HRM...

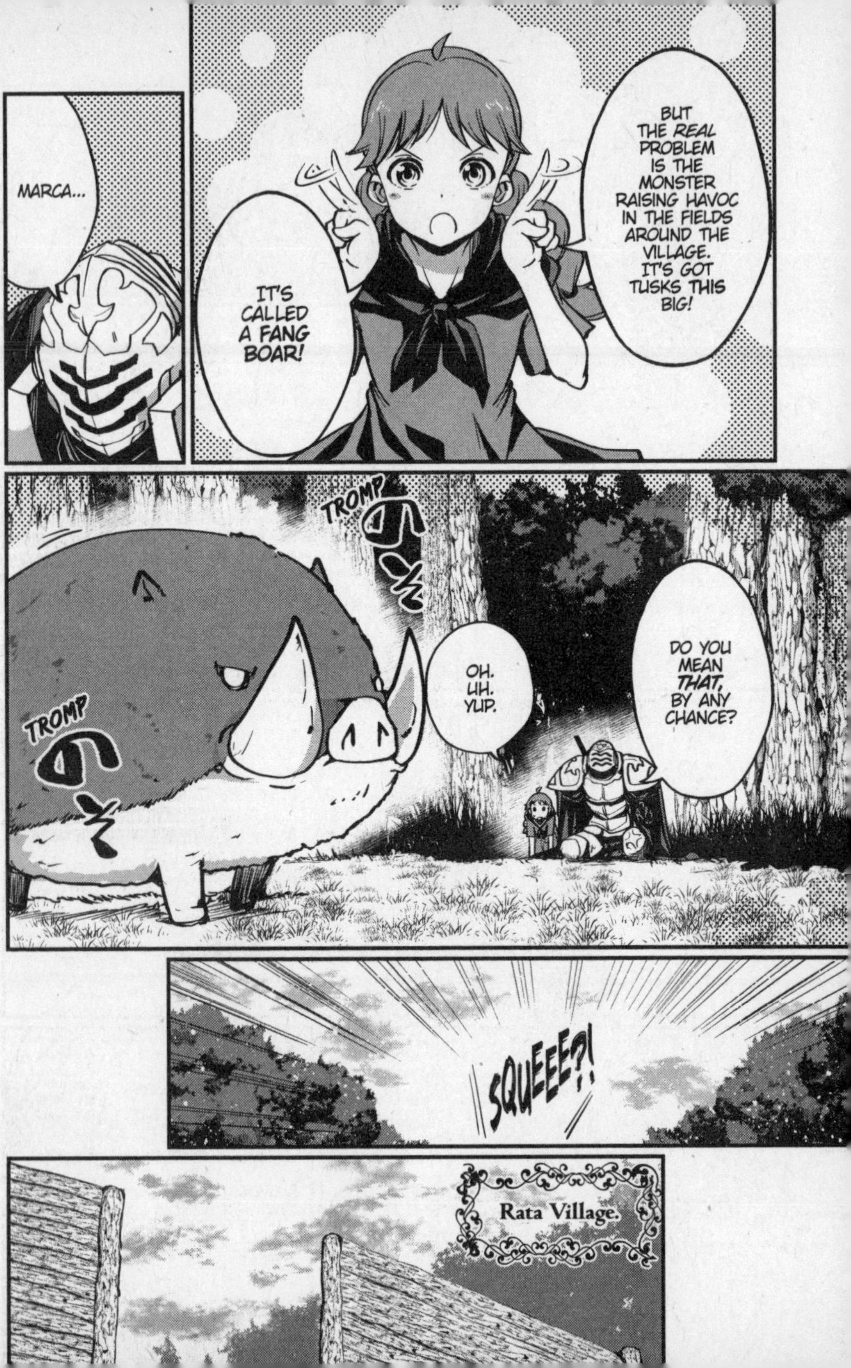
BUT THE *REAL* PROBLEM IS THE MONSTER RAISING HAVOC IN THE FIELDS AROUND THE VILLAGE. IT'S GOT TUSKS THIS BIG!
IT'S CALLED A FANG BOAR!
MARCA...
DO YOU MEAN *THAT,* BY ANY CHANCE?
OH. UH. YUP.
TROMP
TROMP
SQUEEE?!
Rata Village.

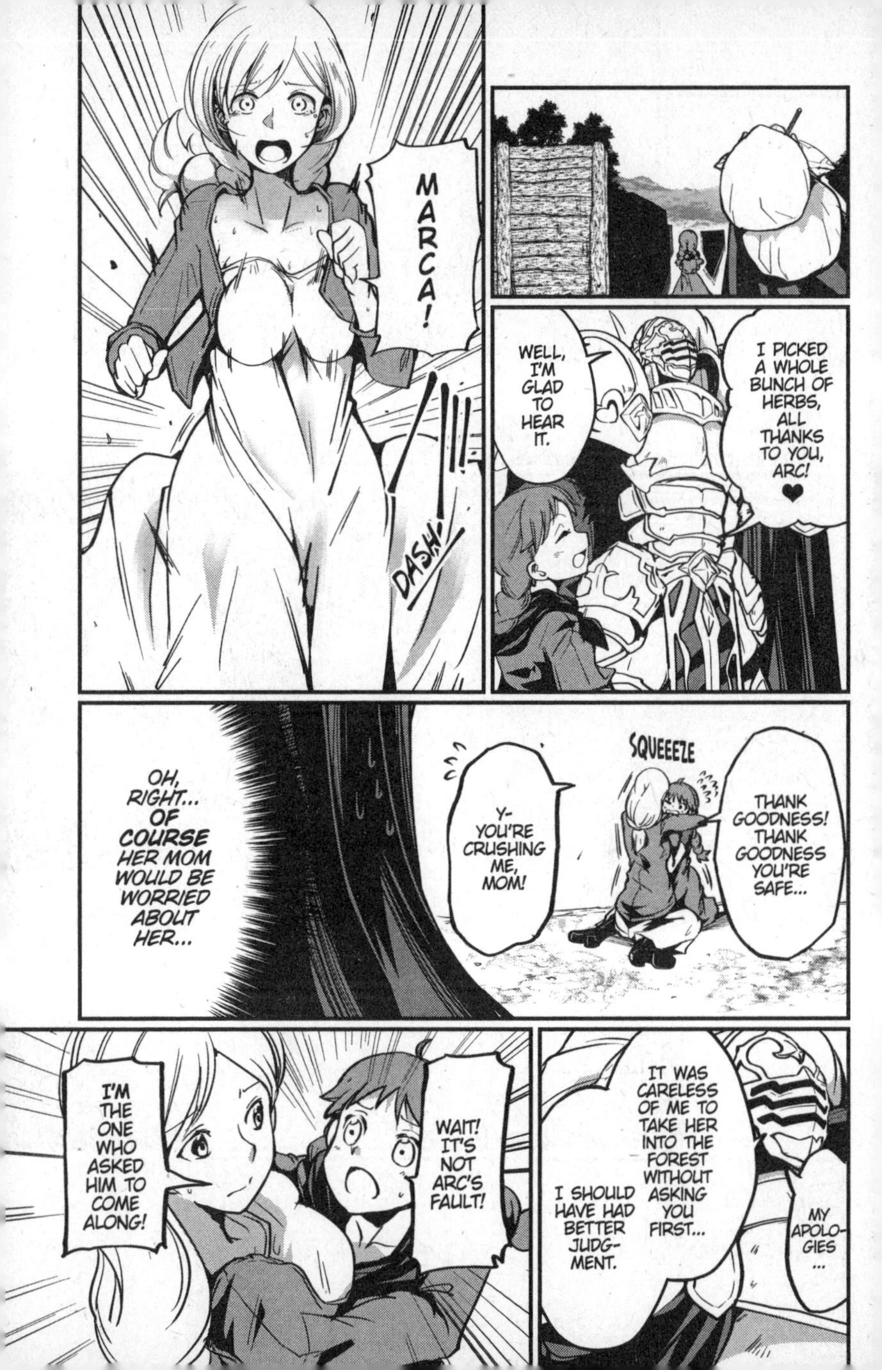
I PICKED A WHOLE BUNCH OF HERBS, ALL THANKS TO YOU, ARC! ♥
WELL, I'M GLAD TO HEAR IT.
MARCA!
DASH!
SQUEEEZE
THANK GOODNESS! THANK GOODNESS YOU'RE SAFE...
Y- YOU'RE CRUSHING ME, MOM!
OH, RIGHT... OF COURSE HER MOM WOULD BE WORRIED ABOUT HER...
MY APOLOGIES...
IT WAS CARELESS OF ME TO TAKE HER INTO THE FOREST WITHOUT ASKING YOU FIRST...
I SHOULD HAVE HAD BETTER JUDGMENT.
WAIT! IT'S NOT ARC'S FAULT!
I'M THE ONE WHO ASKED HIM TO COME ALONG!

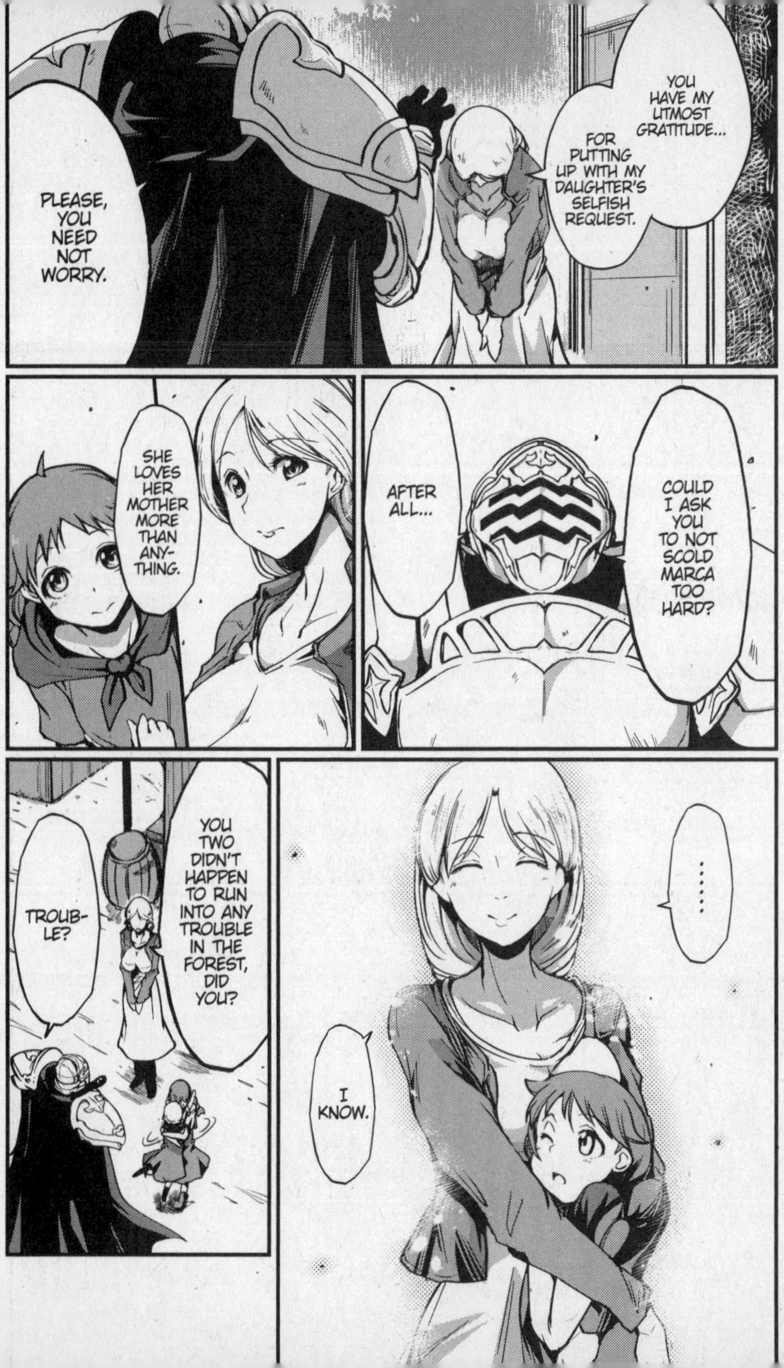
YOU HAVE MY UTMOST GRATITUDE...
FOR PUTTING UP WITH MY DAUGHTER'S SELFISH REQUEST.
PLEASE, YOU NEED NOT WORRY.
COULD I ASK YOU TO NOT SCOLD MARCA TOO HARD?
AFTER ALL...
SHE LOVES HER MOTHER MORE THAN ANY-THING.
......
I KNOW.
YOU TWO DIDN'T HAPPEN TO RUN INTO ANY TROUBLE IN THE FOREST, DID YOU?
TROUB-LE?

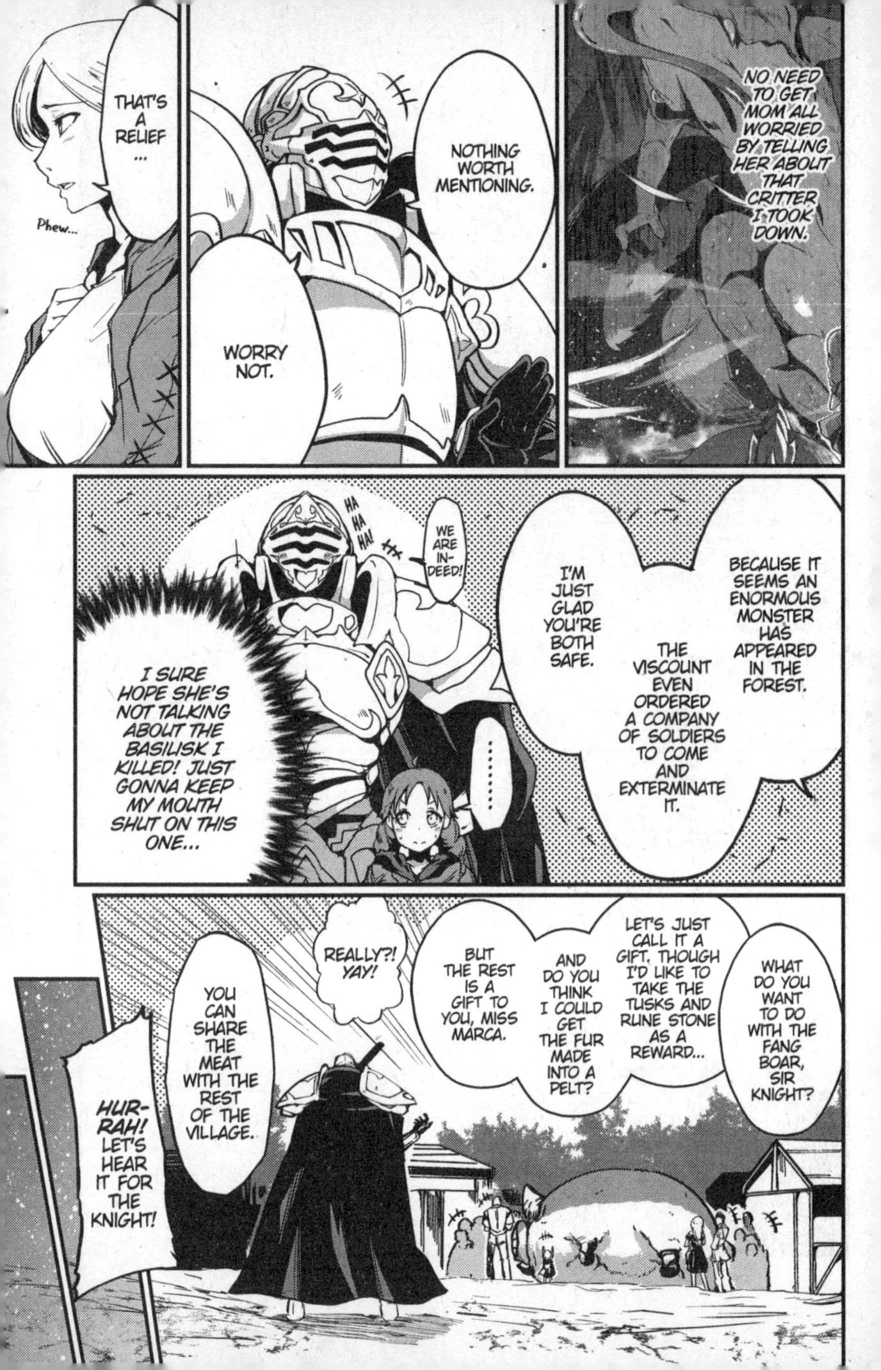
NO NEED TO GET MOM ALL WORRIED BY TELLING HER ABOUT THAT CRITTER I TOOK DOWN.
NOTHING WORTH MENTIONING.
WORRY NOT.
THAT'S A RELIEF...
Phew...
BECAUSE IT SEEMS AN ENORMOUS MONSTER HAS APPEARED IN THE FOREST.
THE VISCOUNT EVEN ORDERED A COMPANY OF SOLDIERS TO COME AND EXTERMINATE IT.
I'M JUST GLAD YOU'RE BOTH SAFE.
WE ARE IN-DEED!
HA HA HA!
......
I SURE HOPE SHE'S NOT TALKING ABOUT THE BASILISK I KILLED! JUST GONNA KEEP MY MOUTH SHUT ON THIS ONE...
WHAT DO YOU WANT TO DO WITH THE FANG BOAR, SIR KNIGHT?
LET'S JUST CALL IT A GIFT, THOUGH I'D LIKE TO TAKE THE TUSKS AND RUNE STONE AS A REWARD...
AND DO YOU THINK I COULD GET THE FUR MADE INTO A PELT?
BUT THE REST IS A GIFT TO YOU, MISS MARCA.
REALLY?! YAY!
YOU CAN SHARE THE MEAT WITH THE REST OF THE VILLAGE.
HUR-RAH! LET'S HEAR IT FOR THE KNIGHT!

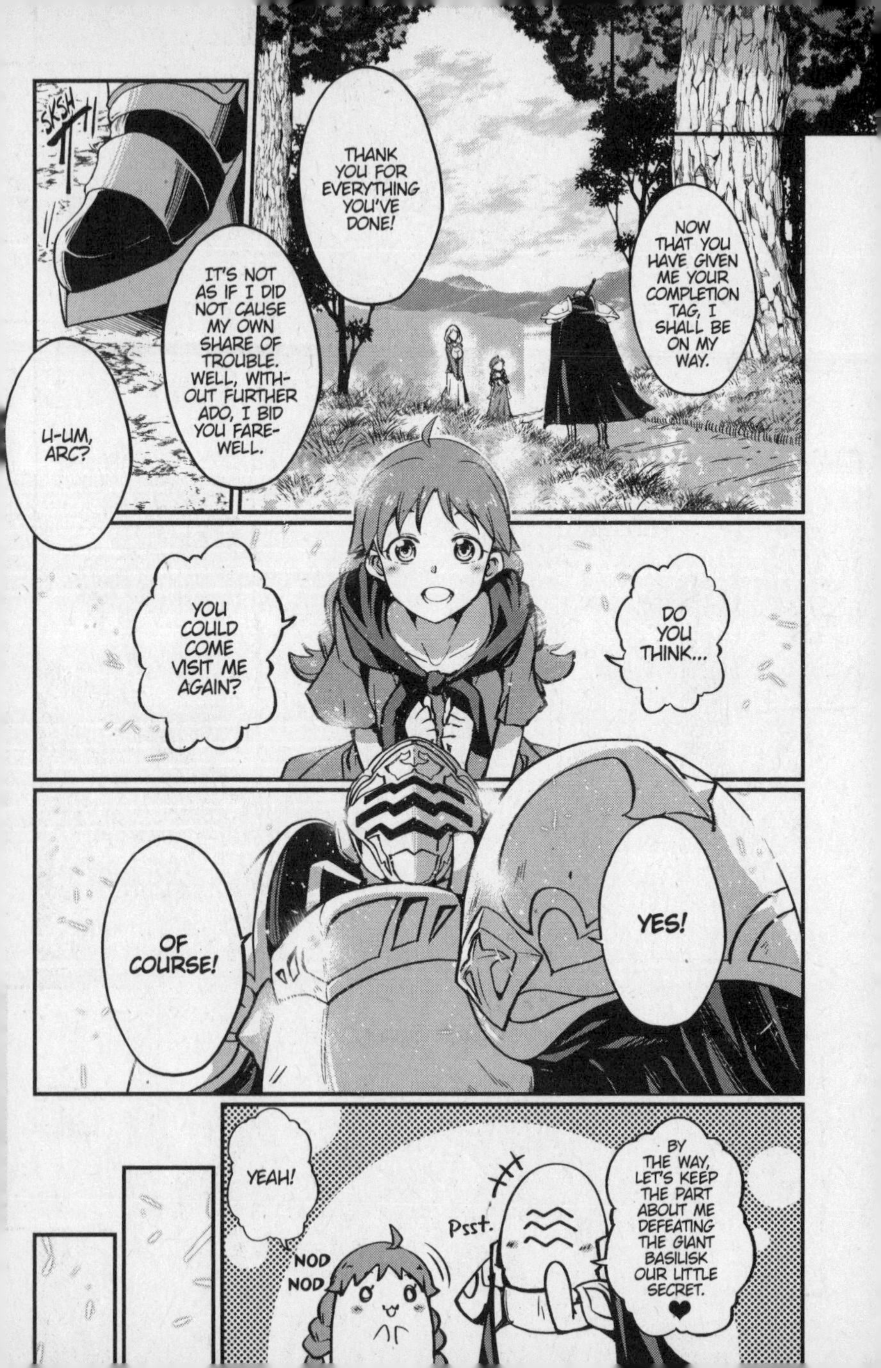
NOW THAT YOU HAVE GIVEN ME YOUR COMPLETION TAG, I SHALL BE ON MY WAY.
THANK YOU FOR EVERYTHING YOU'VE DONE!
IT'S NOT AS IF I DID NOT CAUSE MY OWN SHARE OF TROUBLE. WELL, WITH-OUT FURTHER ADO, I BID YOU FARE-WELL.
SKSH
U-UM, ARC?
DO YOU THINK...
YOU COULD COME VISIT ME AGAIN?
YES!
OF COURSE!
BY THE WAY, LET'S KEEP THE PART ABOUT ME DEFEATING THE GIANT BASILISK OUR LITTLE SECRET. ❤
Psst.
YEAH!
NOD NOD

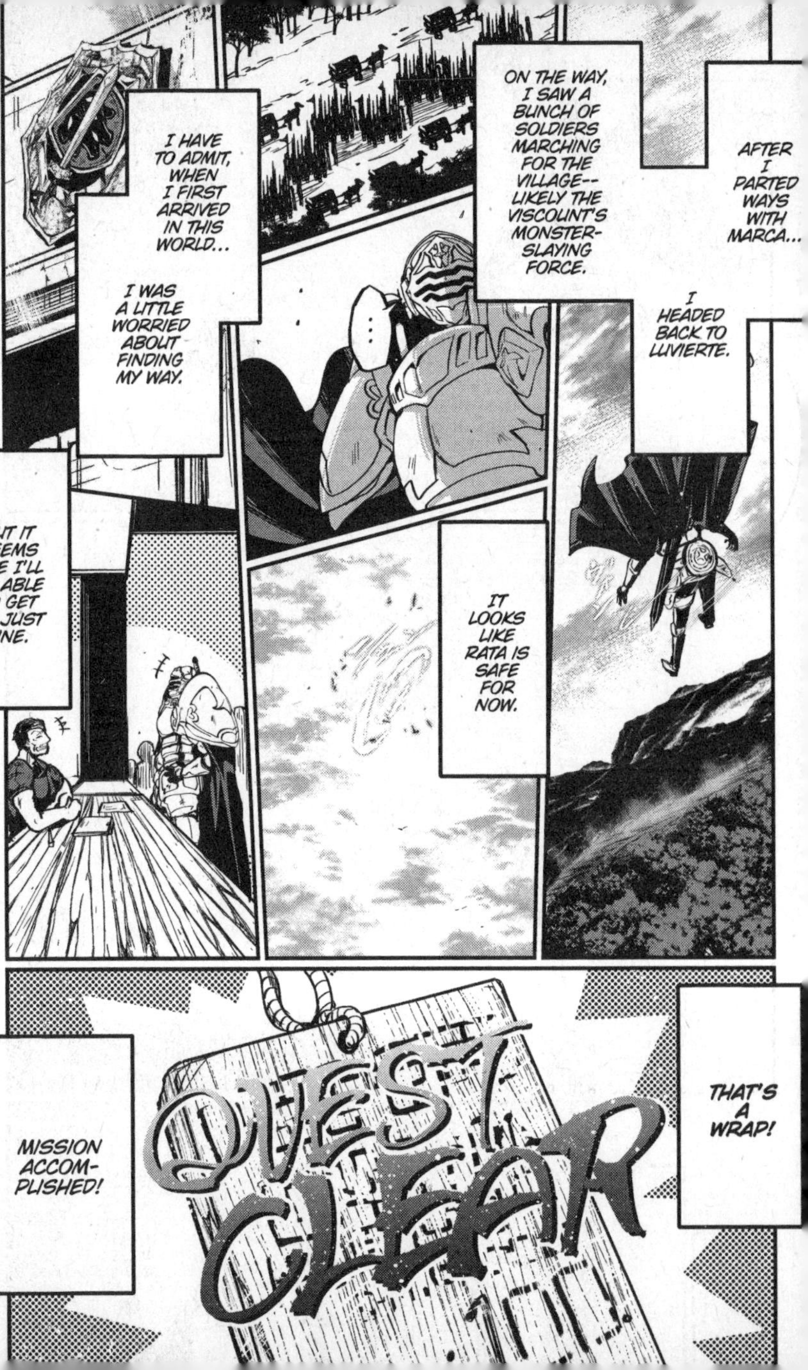

AFTER I PARTED WAYS WITH MARCA...
I HEADED BACK TO LUVIERTE.
ON THE WAY, I SAW A BUNCH OF SOLDIERS MARCHING FOR THE VILLAGE--LIKELY THE VISCOUNT'S MONSTER-SLAYING FORCE.
IT LOOKS LIKE RATA IS SAFE FOR NOW.
I HAVE TO ADMIT, WHEN I FIRST ARRIVED IN THIS WORLD...
I WAS A LITTLE WORRIED ABOUT FINDING MY WAY.
BUT IT SEEMS LIKE I'LL BE ABLE TO GET BY JUST FINE.
THAT'S A WRAP!
QUEST CLEAR
MISSION ACCOM-PLISHED!

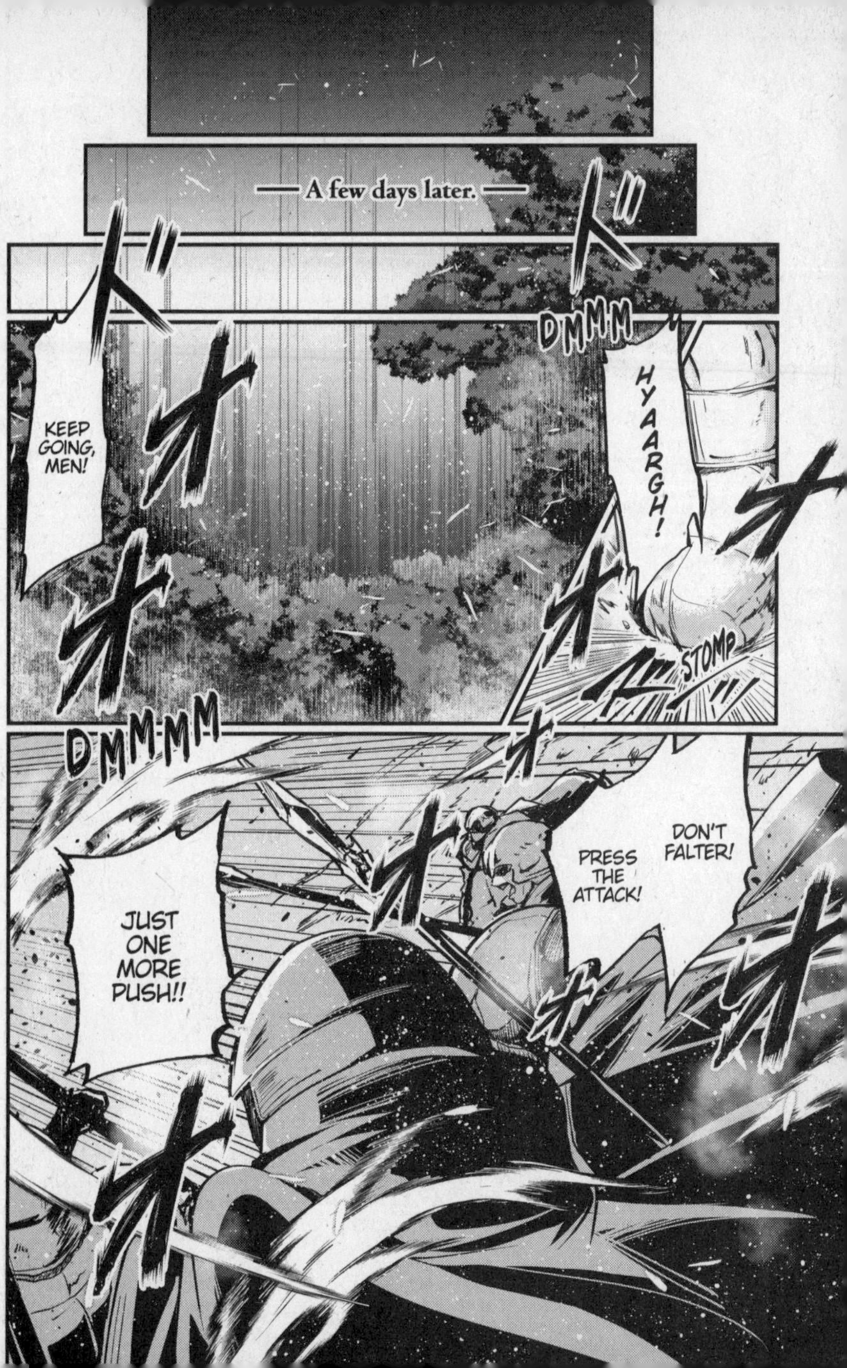
—A few days later.—
DMMM
HYAARGH!
STOMP
KEEP GOING, MEN!
DMMMM
DON'T FALTER!
PRESS THE ATTACK!
JUST ONE MORE PUSH!!

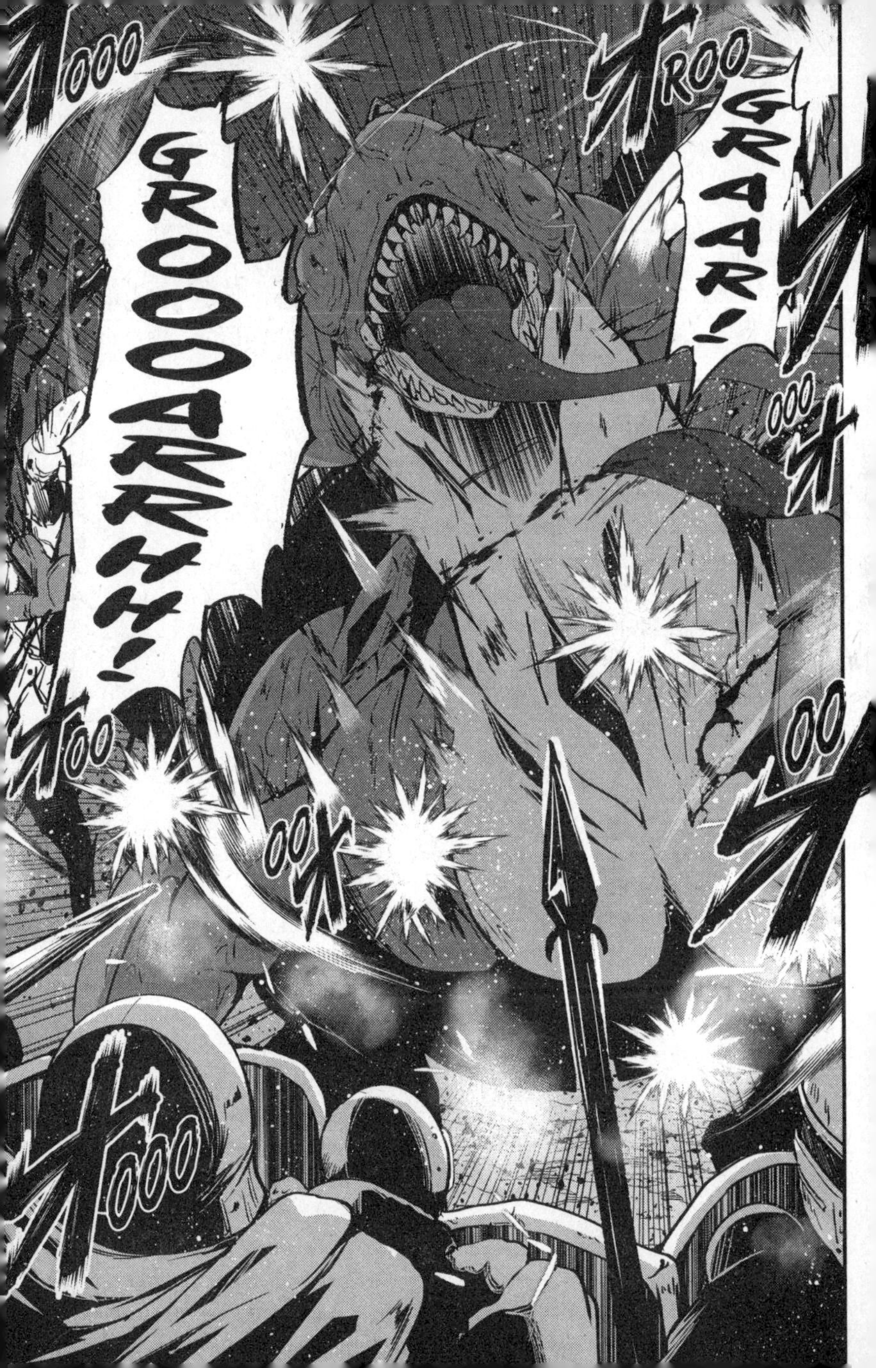
ROO
GRAAR!
OOO
OO
OOO
GROOOARRHH!
OO
OO
OOO

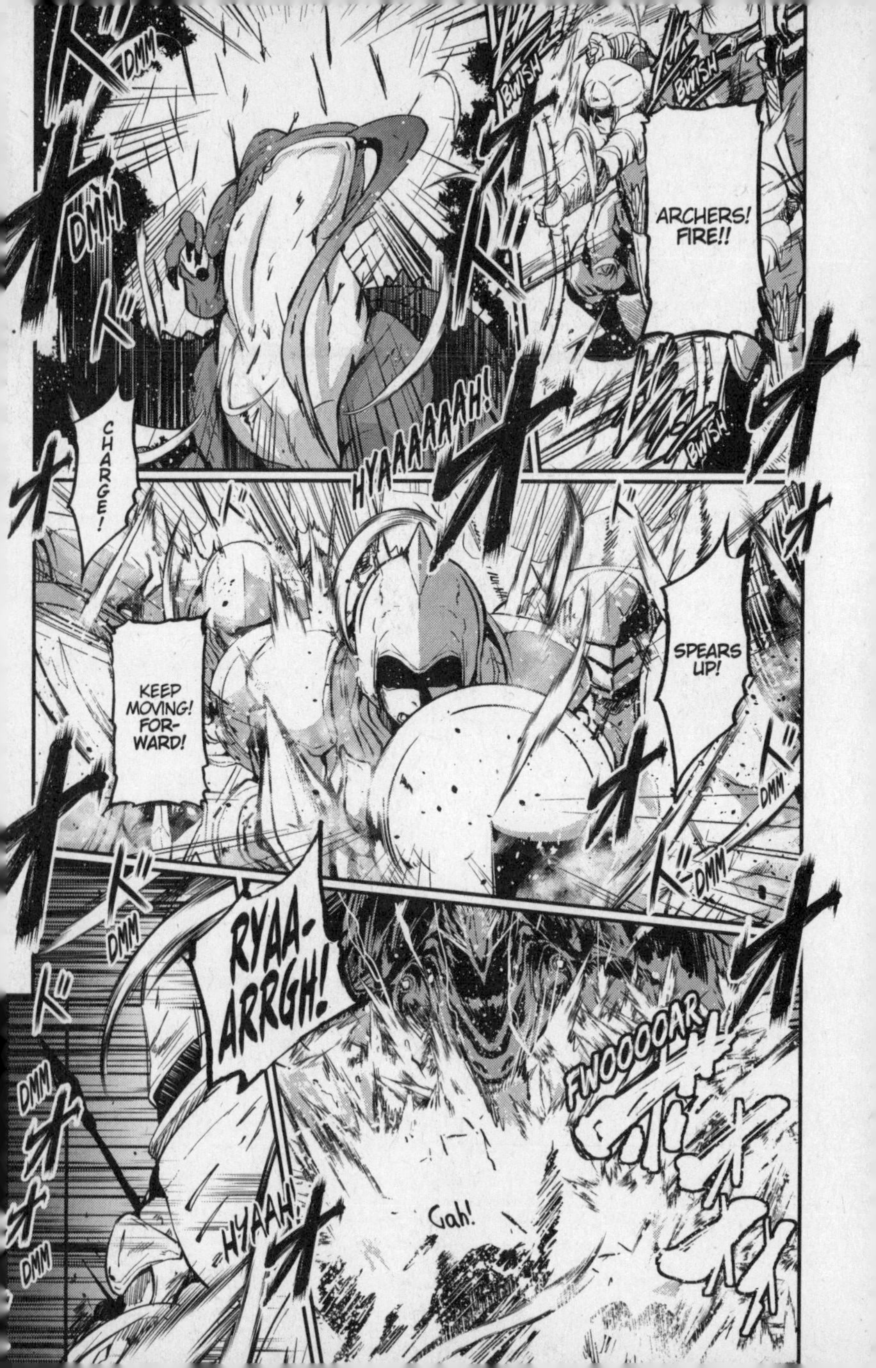
BWISH
BWISH
ARCHERS! FIRE!!
BWISH
HYAAAAAAAH!
DMM
DMM
CHARGE!
SPEARS UP!
DMM
DMM
KEEP MOVING! FOR-WARD!
DMM
FWOOOOAR
RYAA-ARRGH!
Gah!
HYAAH!
DMM
DMM

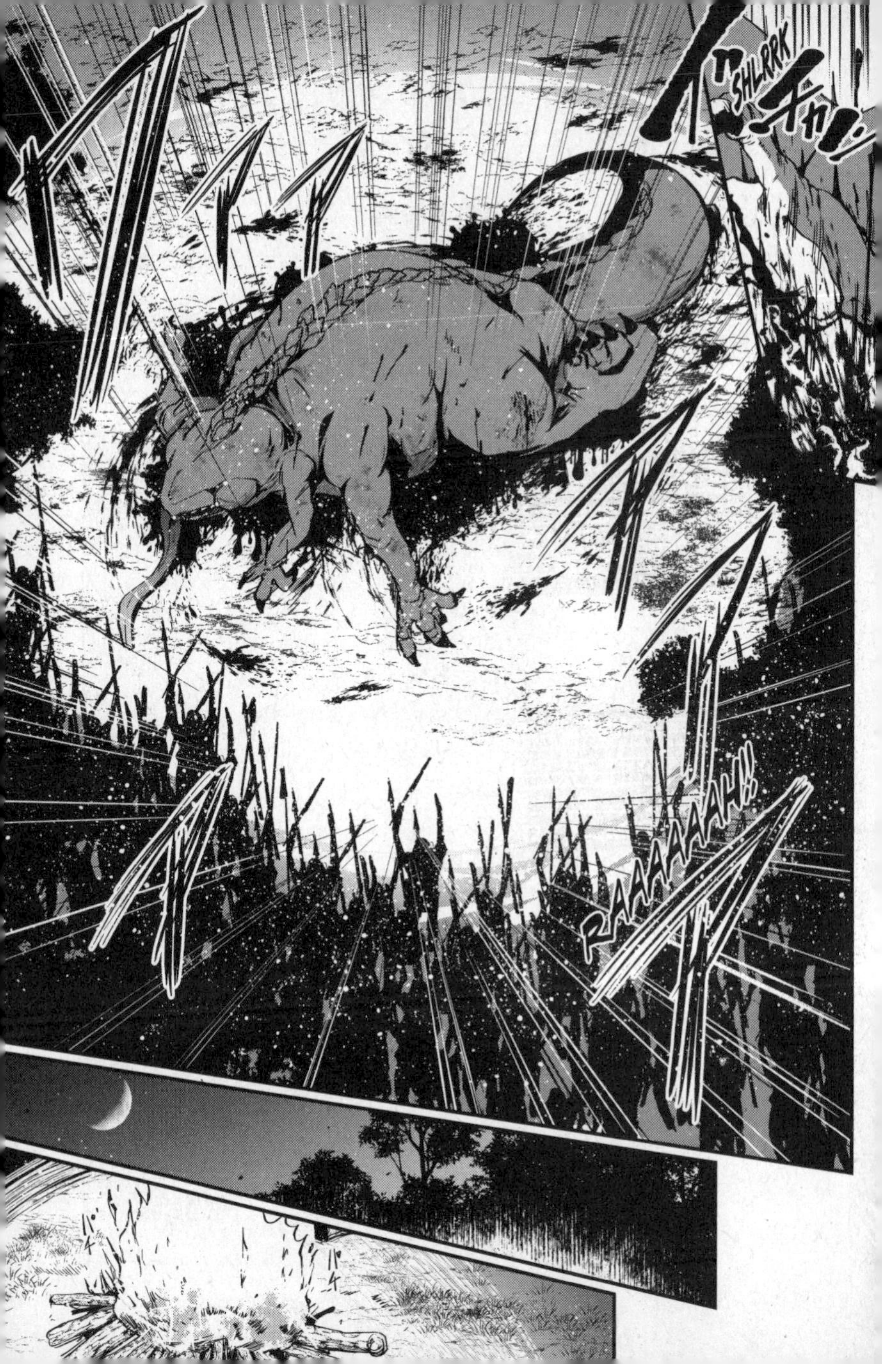
SHLRRK
RAAAAAH!!

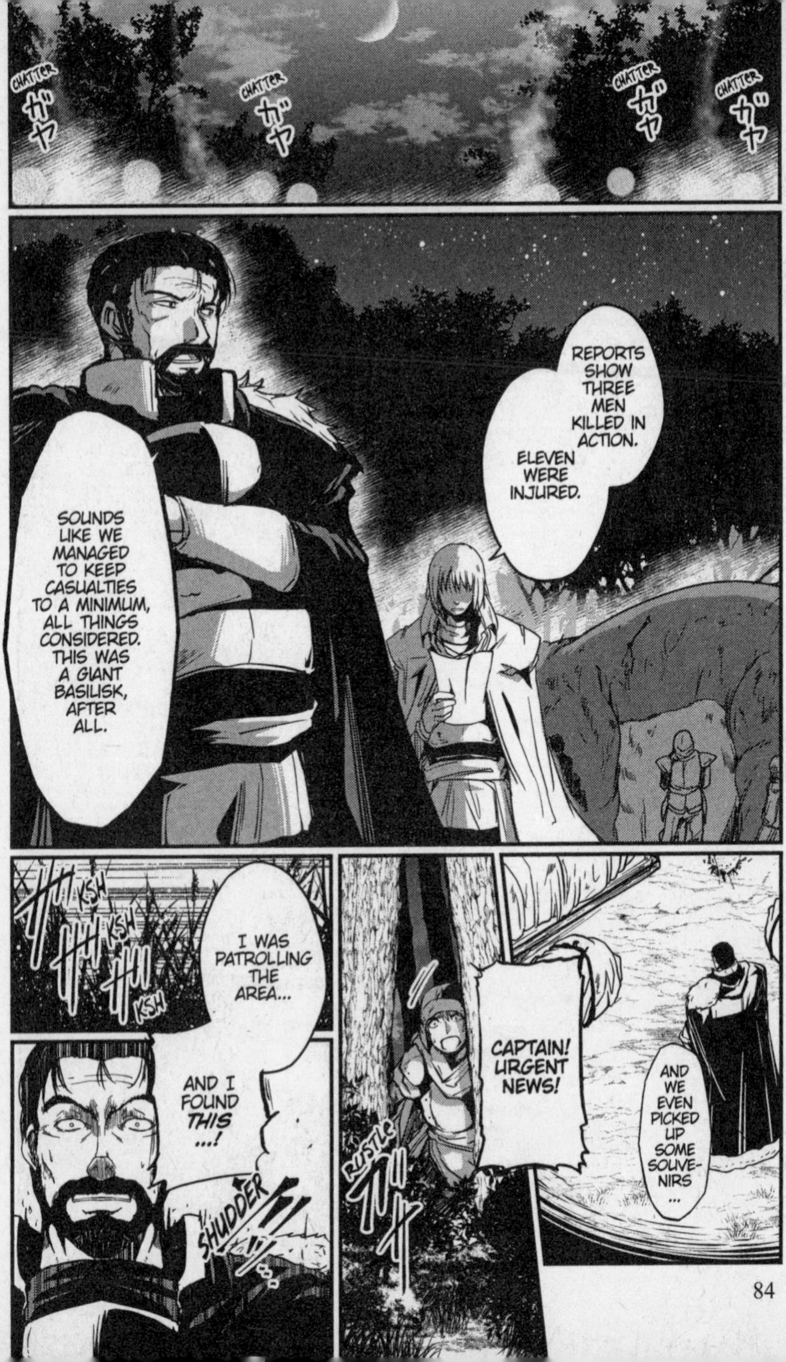

CHATTER
ガヤ
CHATTER
ガヤ
CHATTER
ガヤ
CHATTER
ガヤ
REPORTS SHOW THREE MEN KILLED IN ACTION.
ELEVEN WERE INJURED.
SOUNDS LIKE WE MANAGED TO KEEP CASUALTIES TO A MINIMUM, ALL THINGS CONSIDERED. THIS WAS A GIANT BASILISK, AFTER ALL.
AND WE EVEN PICKED UP SOME SOUVE-NIRS ...
CAPTAIN! URGENT NEWS!
RUSTLE
KSH
KSH
KSH
I WAS PATROLLING THE AREA...
AND I FOUND *THIS* ...!
SHUDDER

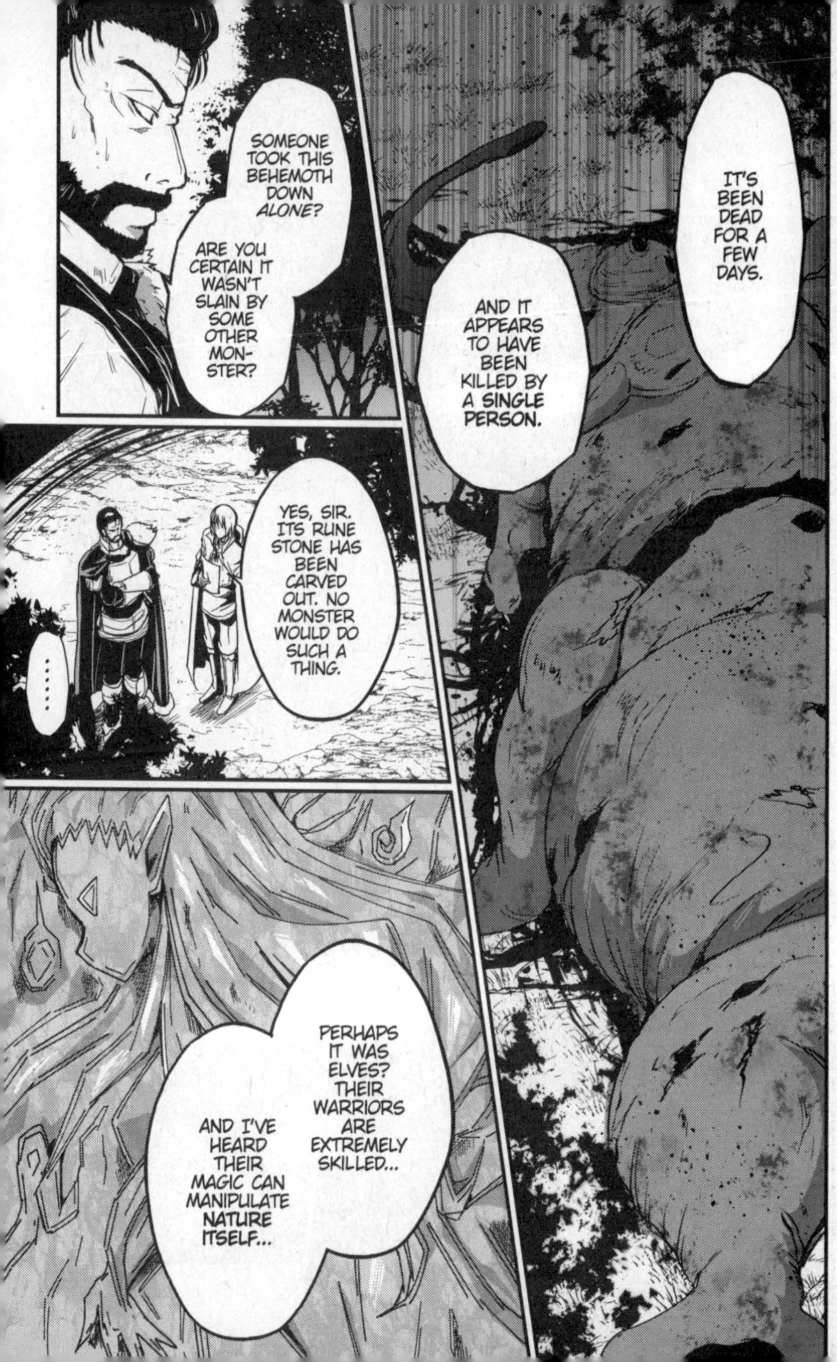
IT'S BEEN DEAD FOR A FEW DAYS.
AND IT APPEARS TO HAVE BEEN KILLED BY A SINGLE PERSON.
SOMEONE TOOK THIS BEHEMOTH DOWN *ALONE?*
ARE YOU CERTAIN IT WASN'T SLAIN BY SOME OTHER MON-STER?
YES, SIR. ITS RUNE STONE HAS BEEN CARVED OUT. NO MONSTER WOULD DO SUCH A THING.
......
PERHAPS IT WAS ELVES? THEIR WARRIORS ARE EXTREMELY SKILLED...
AND I'VE HEARD THEIR MAGIC CAN MANIPULATE NATURE ITSELF...

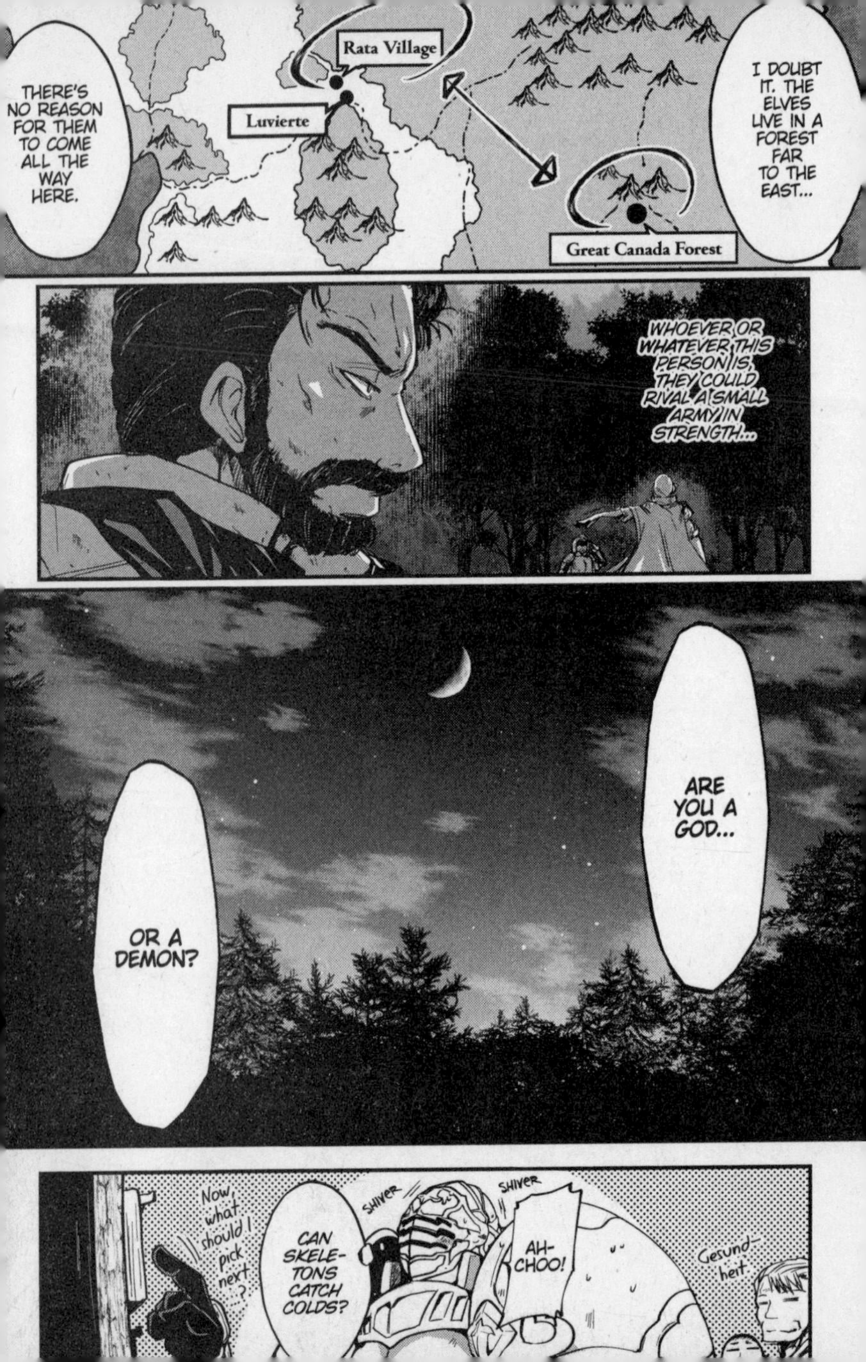

I DOUBT IT. THE ELVES LIVE IN A FOREST FAR TO THE EAST...
Rata Village
Luvierte
Great Canada Forest
THERE'S NO REASON FOR THEM TO COME ALL THE WAY HERE.
WHOEVER OR WHATEVER THIS PERSON IS, THEY COULD RIVAL A SMALL ARMY IN STRENGTH...
ARE YOU A GOD...
OR A DEMON?
Gesundheit
AH-CHOO!
SHIVER
SHIVER
CAN SKELETONS CATCH COLDS?
Now, what should I pick next...?

A Flower Crown from Helina

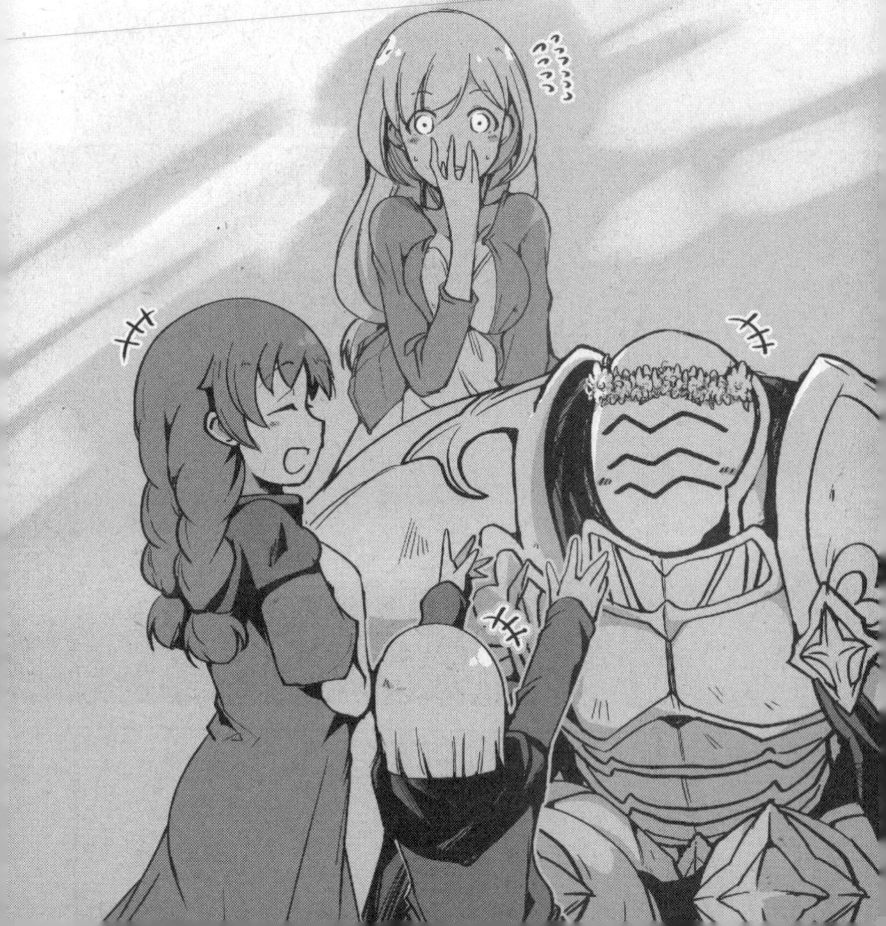

SKELETON KNIGHT IN ANOTHER WORLD

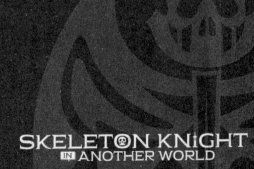

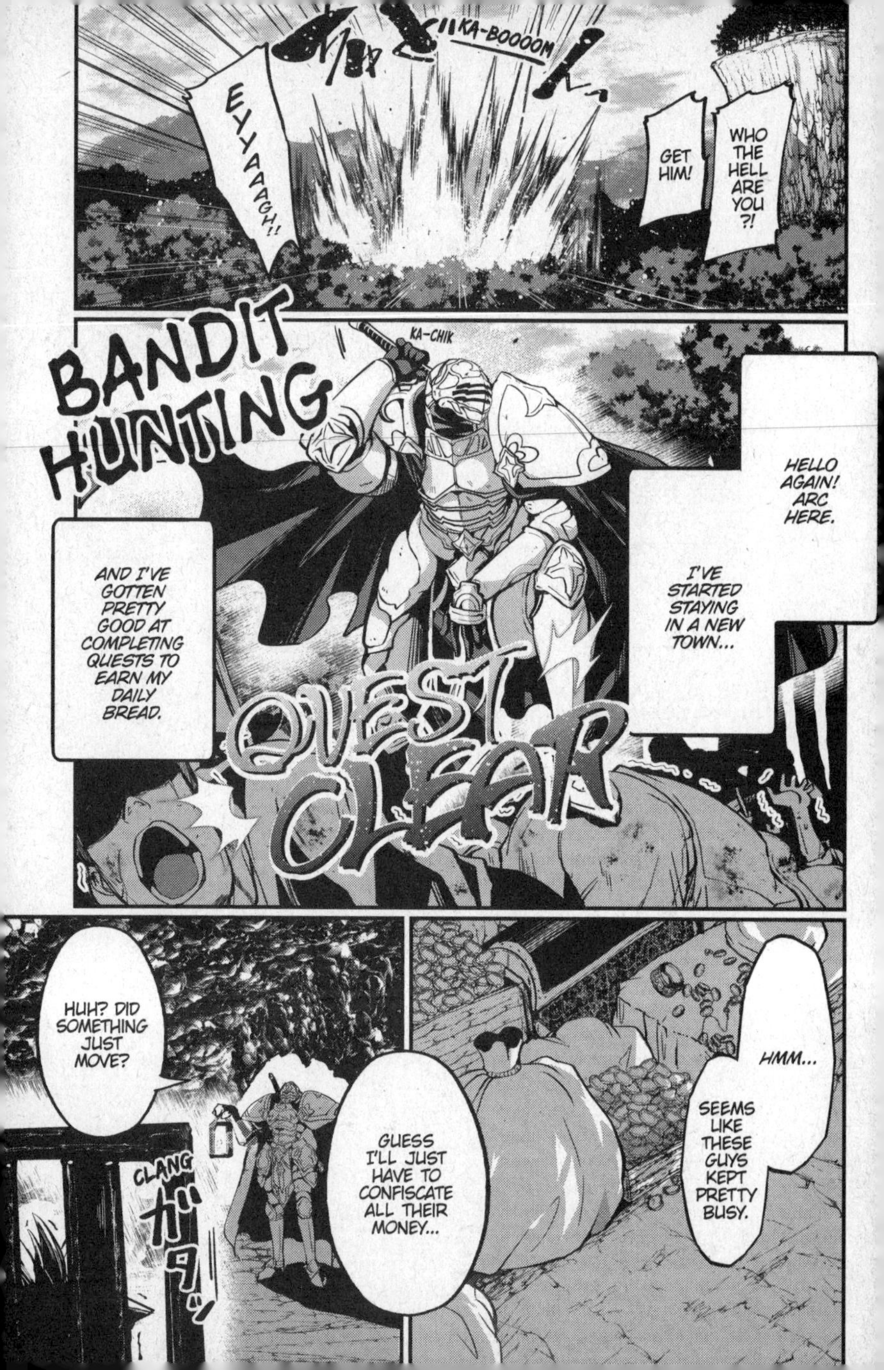
WHO THE HELL ARE YOU?!
GET HIM!
KA-BOOOOM
EYYAAAGH!!
HELLO AGAIN! ARC HERE.
I'VE STARTED STAYING IN A NEW TOWN...
KA-CHIK
BANDIT HUNTING
AND I'VE GOTTEN PRETTY GOOD AT COMPLETING QUESTS TO EARN MY DAILY BREAD.
QUEST CLEAR
HMM...
SEEMS LIKE THESE GUYS KEPT PRETTY BUSY.
GUESS I'LL JUST HAVE TO CONFISCATE ALL THEIR MONEY...
HUH? DID SOMETHING JUST MOVE?
CLANG
ガタッ

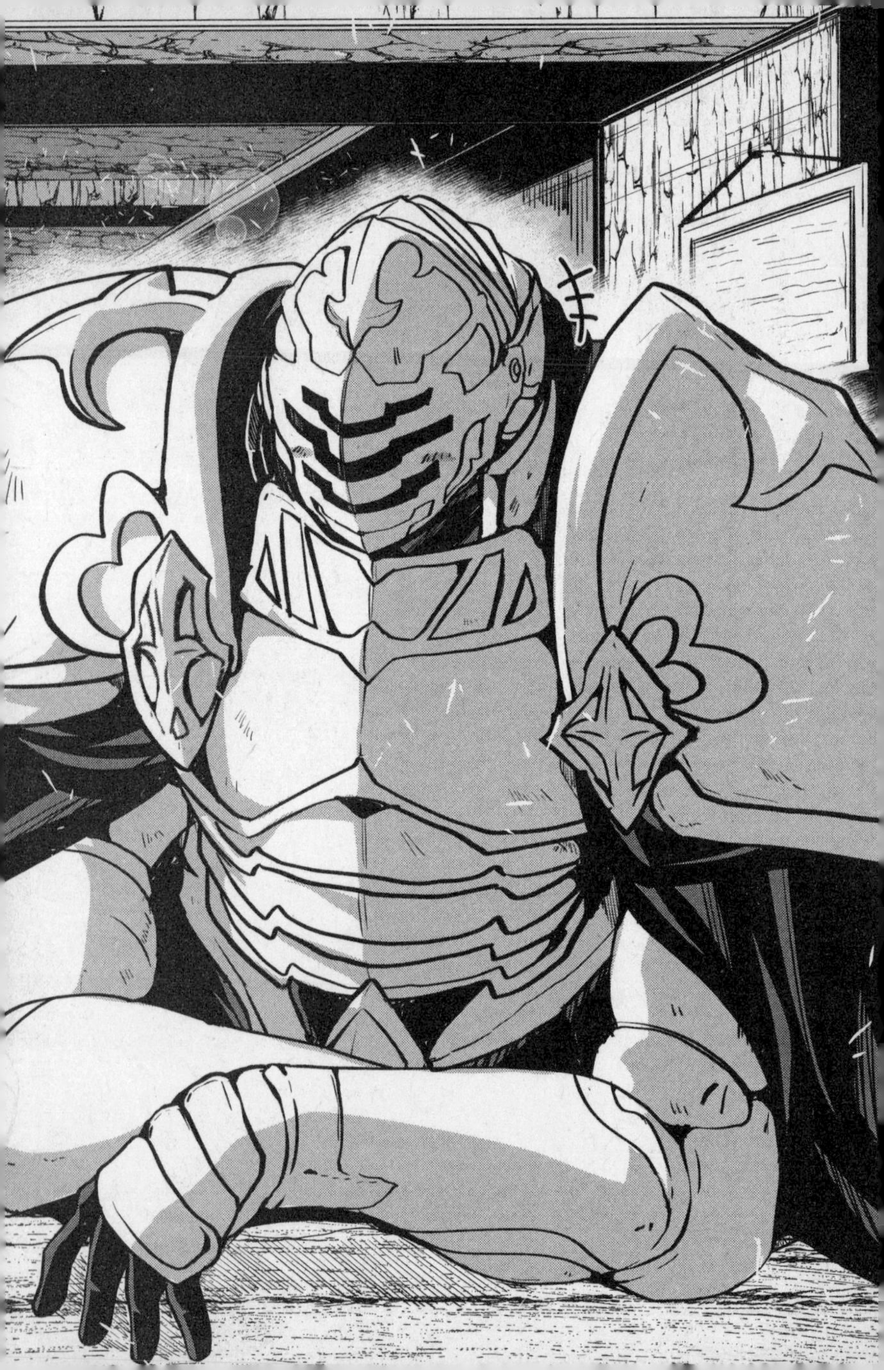

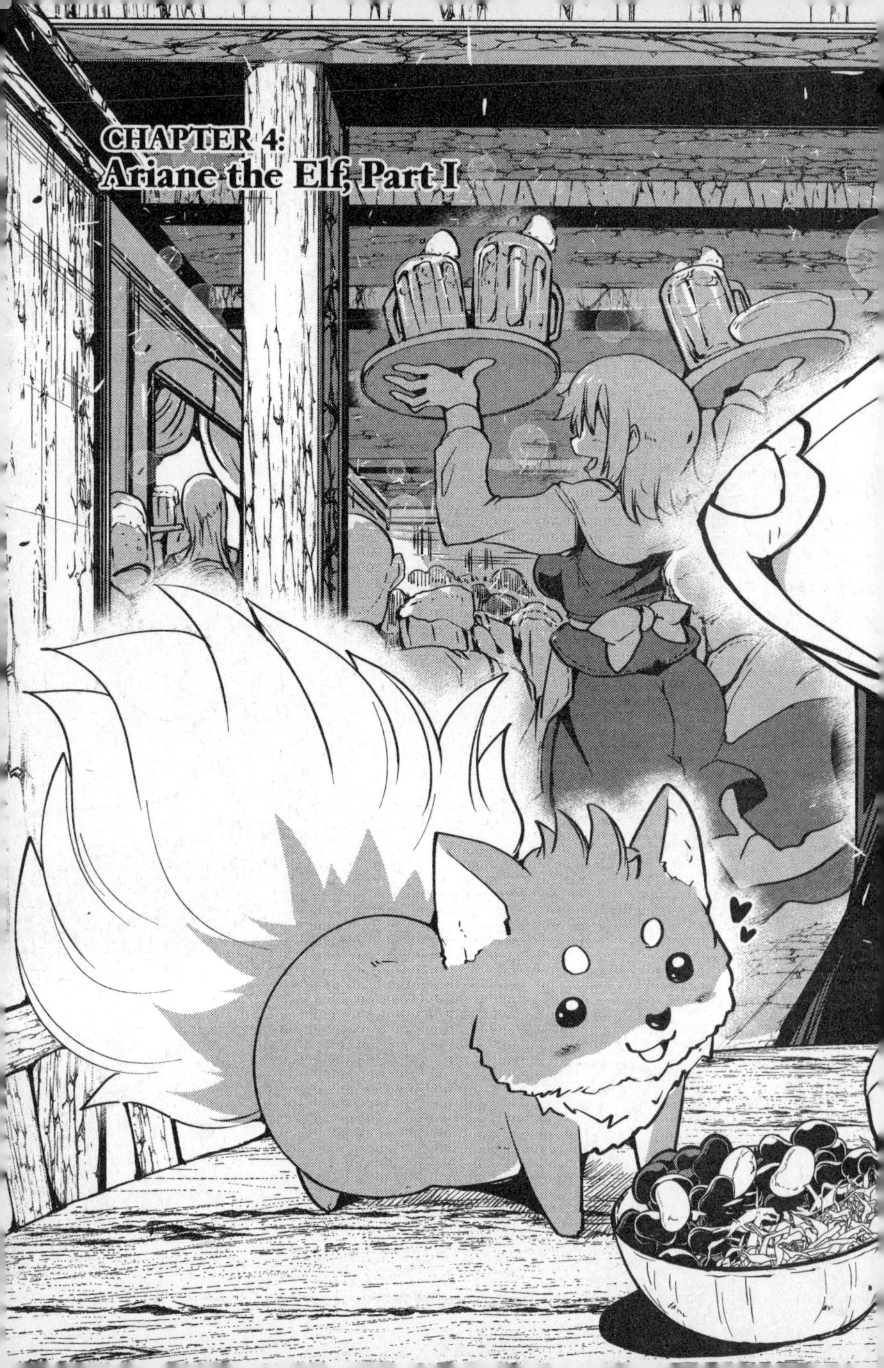
CHAPTER 4:
Ariane the Elf, Part I

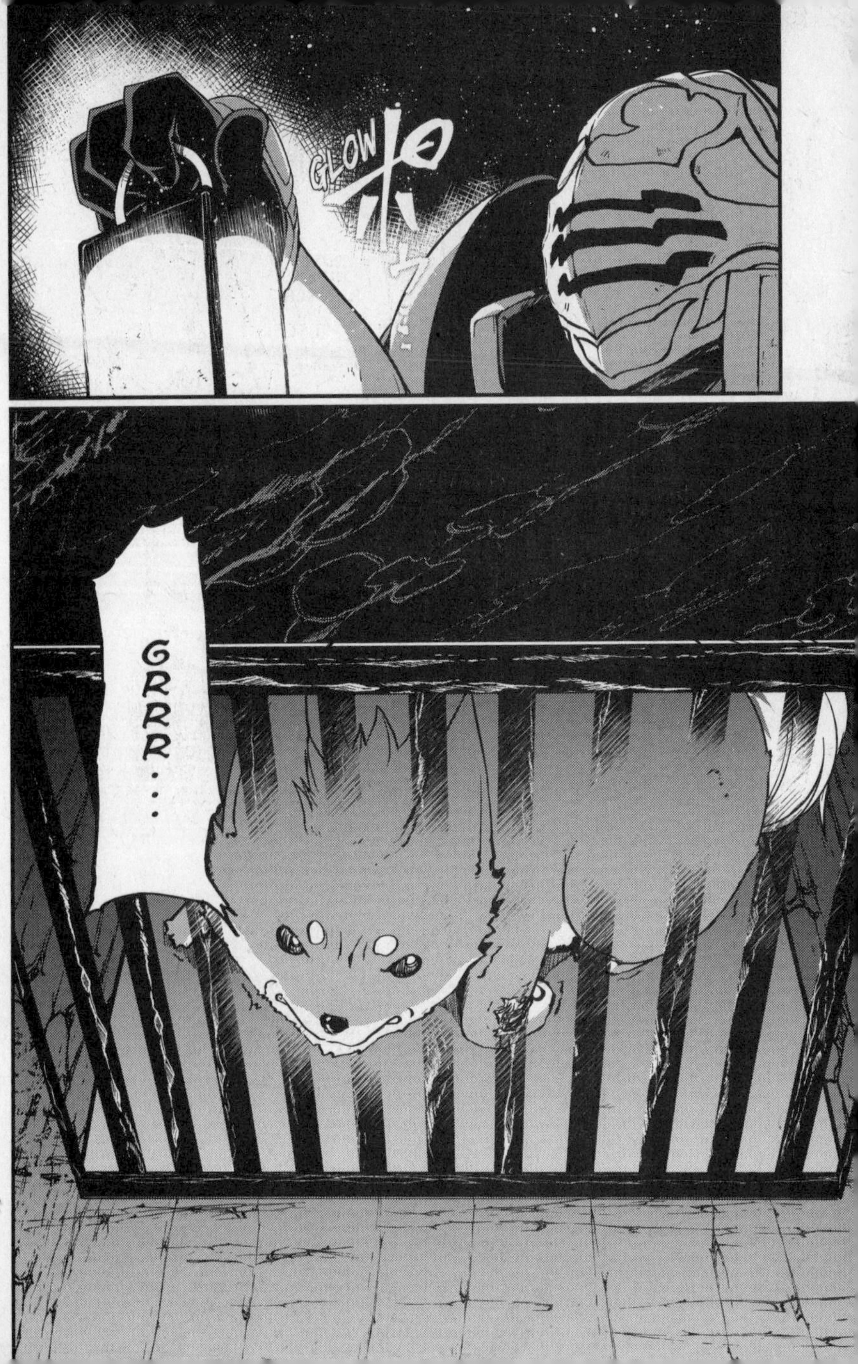
GLOW
GRRR...

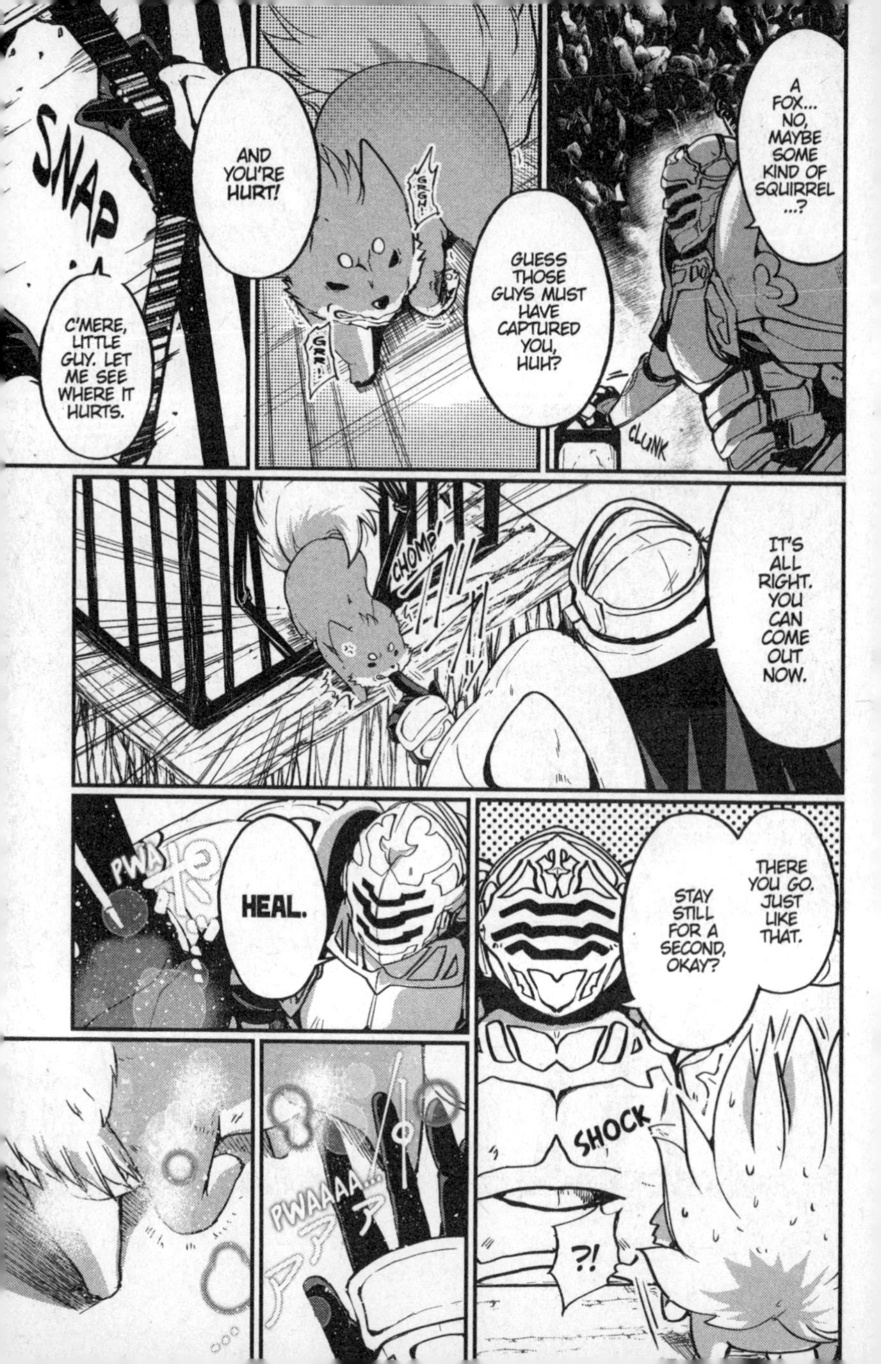
A FOX... NO, MAYBE SOME KIND OF SQUIRREL...?
GUESS THOSE GUYS MUST HAVE CAPTURED YOU, HUH?
CLUNK
AND YOU'RE HURT!
SNAP
C'MERE, LITTLE GUY. LET ME SEE WHERE IT HURTS.
IT'S ALL RIGHT. YOU CAN COME OUT NOW.
CHOMP
THERE YOU GO. JUST LIKE THAT.
STAY STILL FOR A SECOND, OKAY?
HEAL.
PWA
SHOCK
?!
PWAAAA...

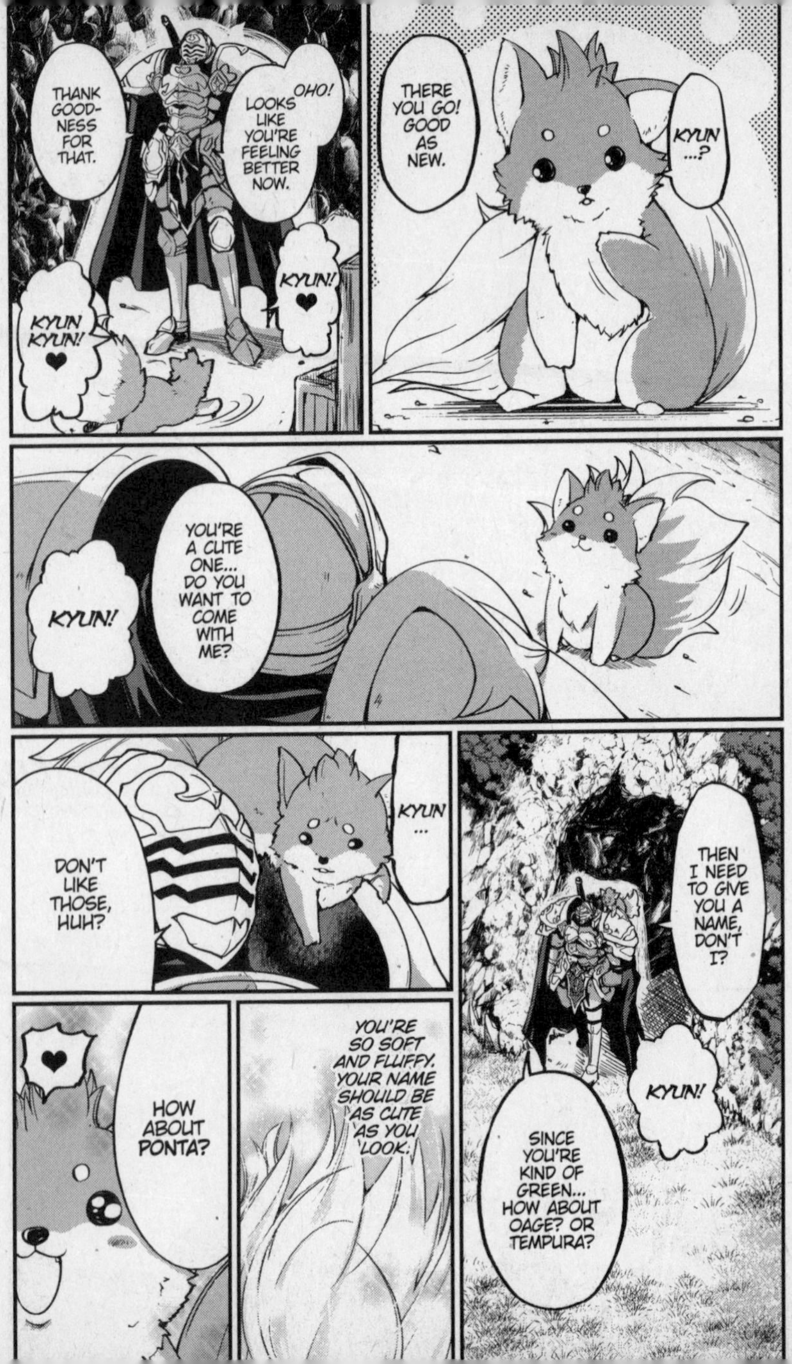
THERE YOU GO! GOOD AS NEW.
KYUN ...?
OHO! LOOKS LIKE YOU'RE FEELING BETTER NOW.
KYUN! ❤
THANK GOOD-NESS FOR THAT.
KYUN KYUN! ❤
YOU'RE A CUTE ONE... DO YOU WANT TO COME WITH ME?
KYUN!
THEN I NEED TO GIVE YOU A NAME, DON'T I?
KYUN!
SINCE YOU'RE KIND OF GREEN... HOW ABOUT OAGE? OR TEMPURA?
KYUN ...
DON'T LIKE THOSE, HUH?
YOU'RE SO SOFT AND FLUFFY. YOUR NAME SHOULD BE AS CUTE AS YOU LOOK.
HOW ABOUT PONTA?
❤

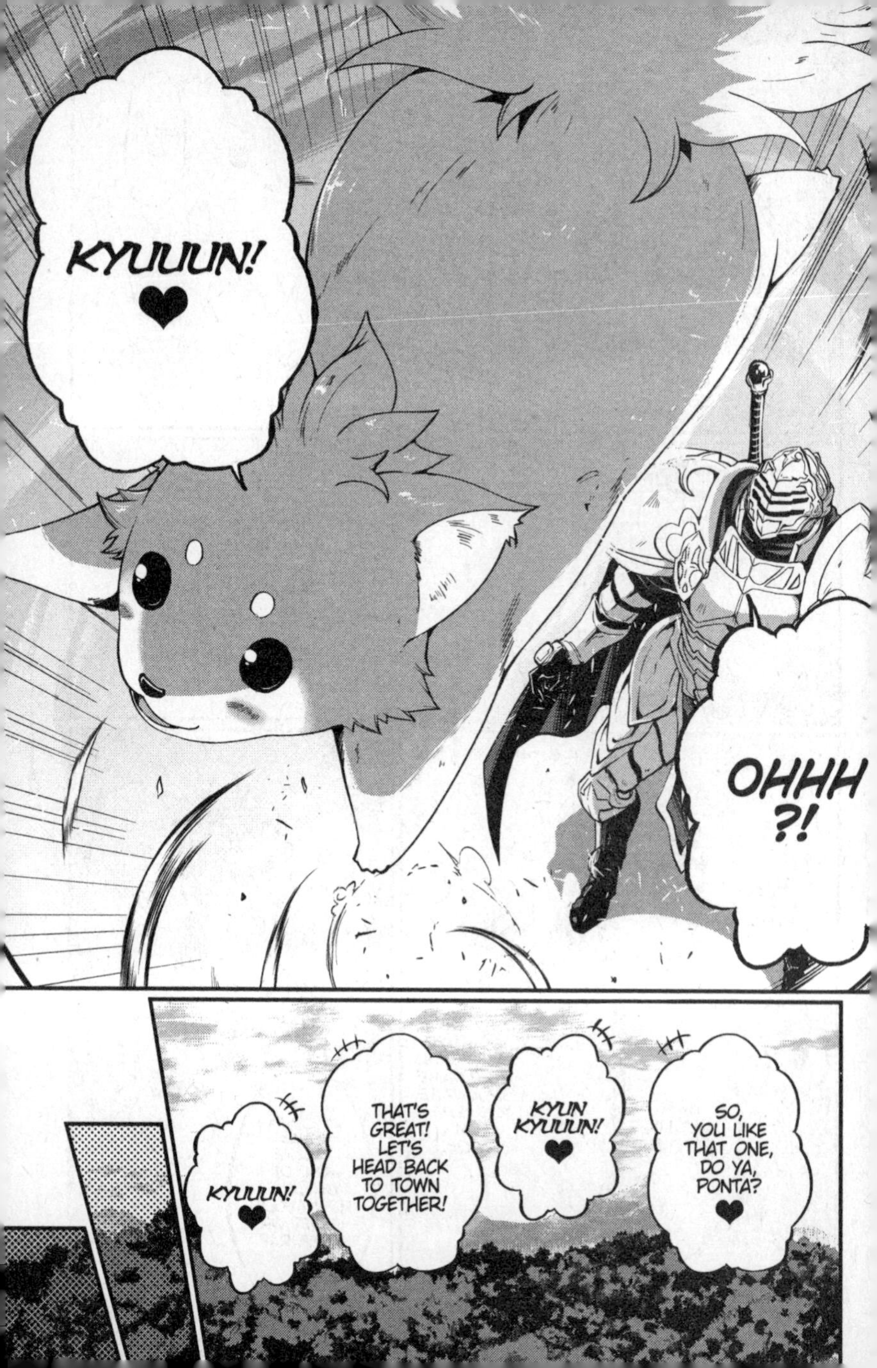
KYUUUN! ❤
OHHH ?!
SO, YOU LIKE THAT ONE, DO YA, PONTA? ❤
KYUN KYUUUN! ❤
THAT'S GREAT! LET'S HEAD BACK TO TOWN TOGETHER!
KYUUUN! ❤

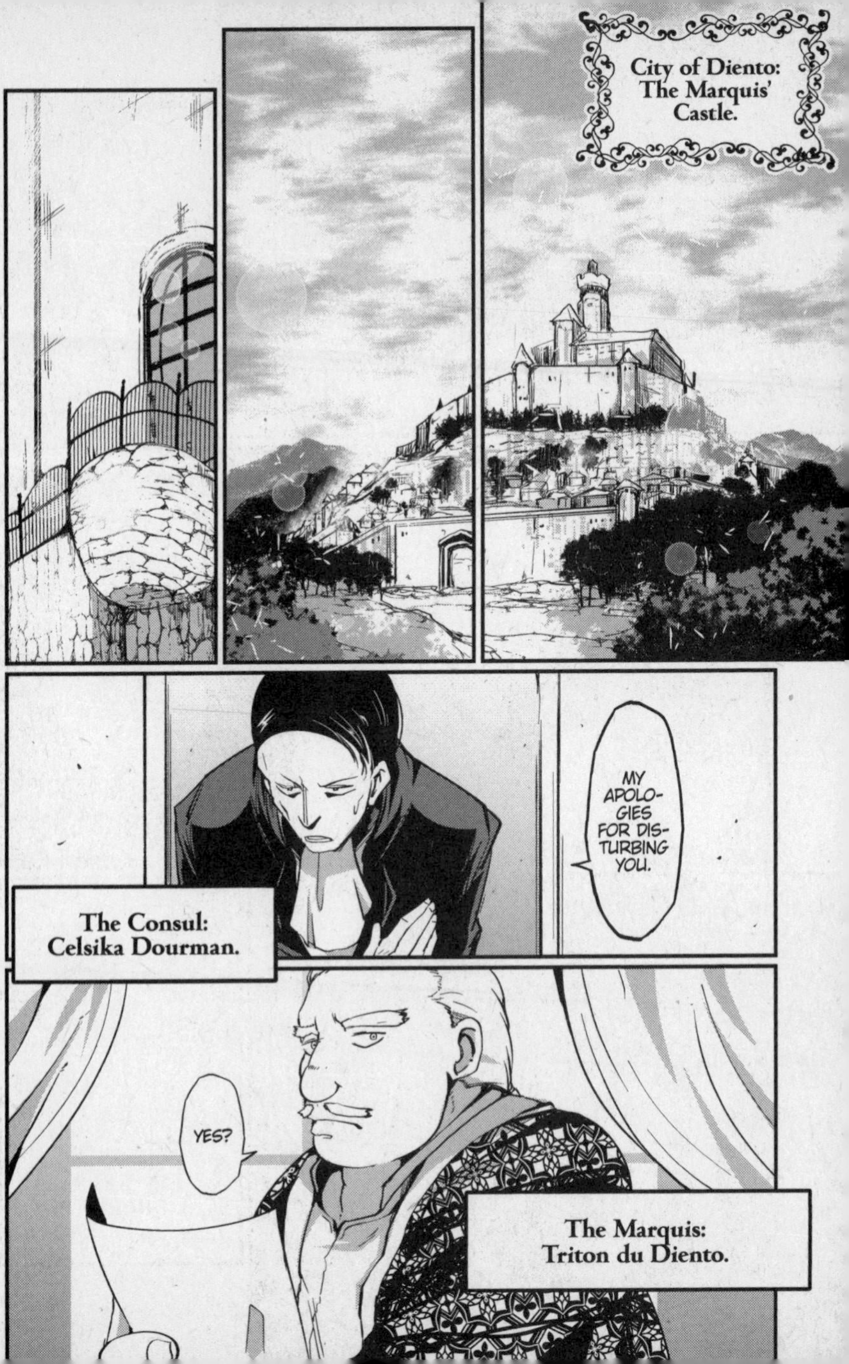
City of Diento: The Marquis' Castle.
MY APOLOGIES FOR DISTURBING YOU.
The Consul: Celsika Dourman.
YES?
The Marquis: Triton du Diento.

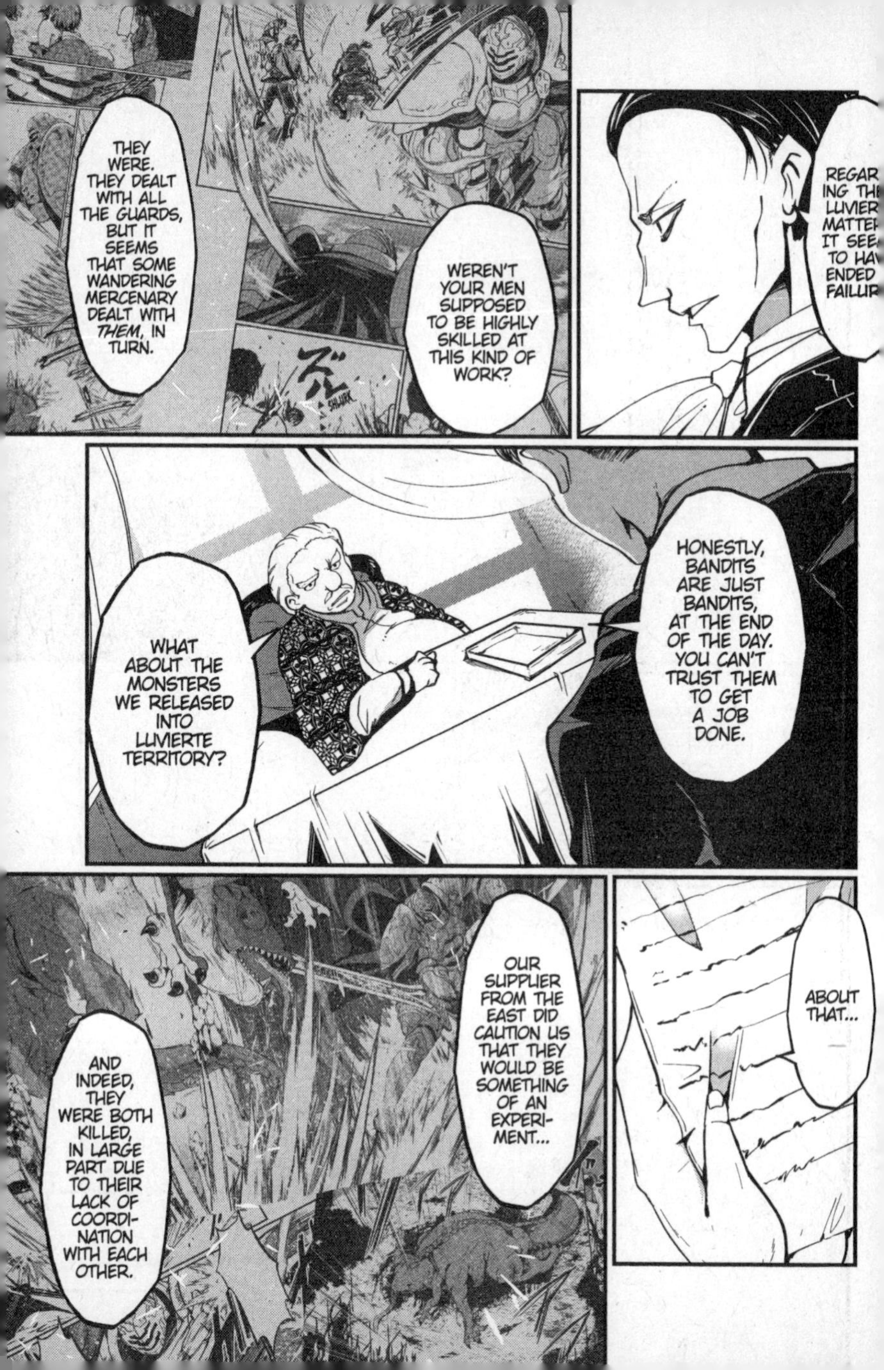
REGAR ING TH LUVIER MATTE IT SEE TO HAV ENDED FAILUR
WEREN'T YOUR MEN SUPPOSED TO BE HIGHLY SKILLED AT THIS KIND OF WORK?
THEY WERE. THEY DEALT WITH ALL THE GUARDS, BUT IT SEEMS THAT SOME WANDERING MERCENARY DEALT WITH *THEM*, IN TURN.
HONESTLY, BANDITS ARE JUST BANDITS, AT THE END OF THE DAY. YOU CAN'T TRUST THEM TO GET A JOB DONE.
WHAT ABOUT THE MONSTERS WE RELEASED INTO LUVIERTE TERRITORY?
ABOUT THAT...
OUR SUPPLIER FROM THE EAST DID CAUTION US THAT THEY WOULD BE SOMETHING OF AN EXPERI-MENT...
AND INDEED, THEY WERE BOTH KILLED, IN LARGE PART DUE TO THEIR LACK OF COORDI-NATION WITH EACH OTHER.

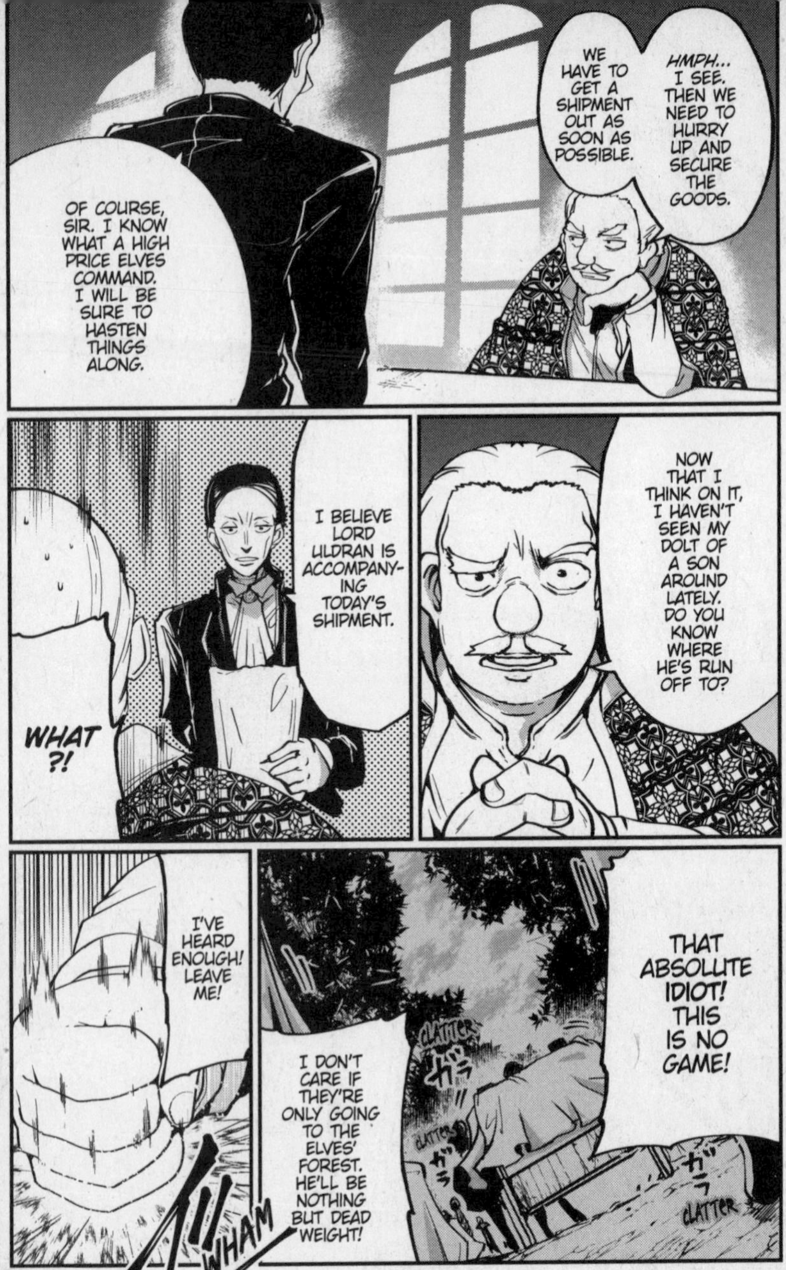
HMPH... I SEE. THEN WE NEED TO HURRY UP AND SECURE THE GOODS.
WE HAVE TO GET A SHIPMENT OUT AS SOON AS POSSIBLE.
OF COURSE, SIR. I KNOW WHAT A HIGH PRICE ELVES COMMAND. I WILL BE SURE TO HASTEN THINGS ALONG.
NOW THAT I THINK ON IT, I HAVEN'T SEEN MY DOLT OF A SON AROUND LATELY. DO YOU KNOW WHERE HE'S RUN OFF TO?
I BELIEVE LORD ULDRAN IS ACCOMPANYING TODAY'S SHIPMENT.
WHAT?!
THAT ABSOLUTE IDIOT! THIS IS NO GAME!
CLATTER
CLATTER
CLATTER
I DON'T CARE IF THEY'RE ONLY GOING TO THE ELVES' FOREST. HE'LL BE NOTHING BUT DEAD WEIGHT!
I'VE HEARD ENOUGH! LEAVE ME!
WHAM

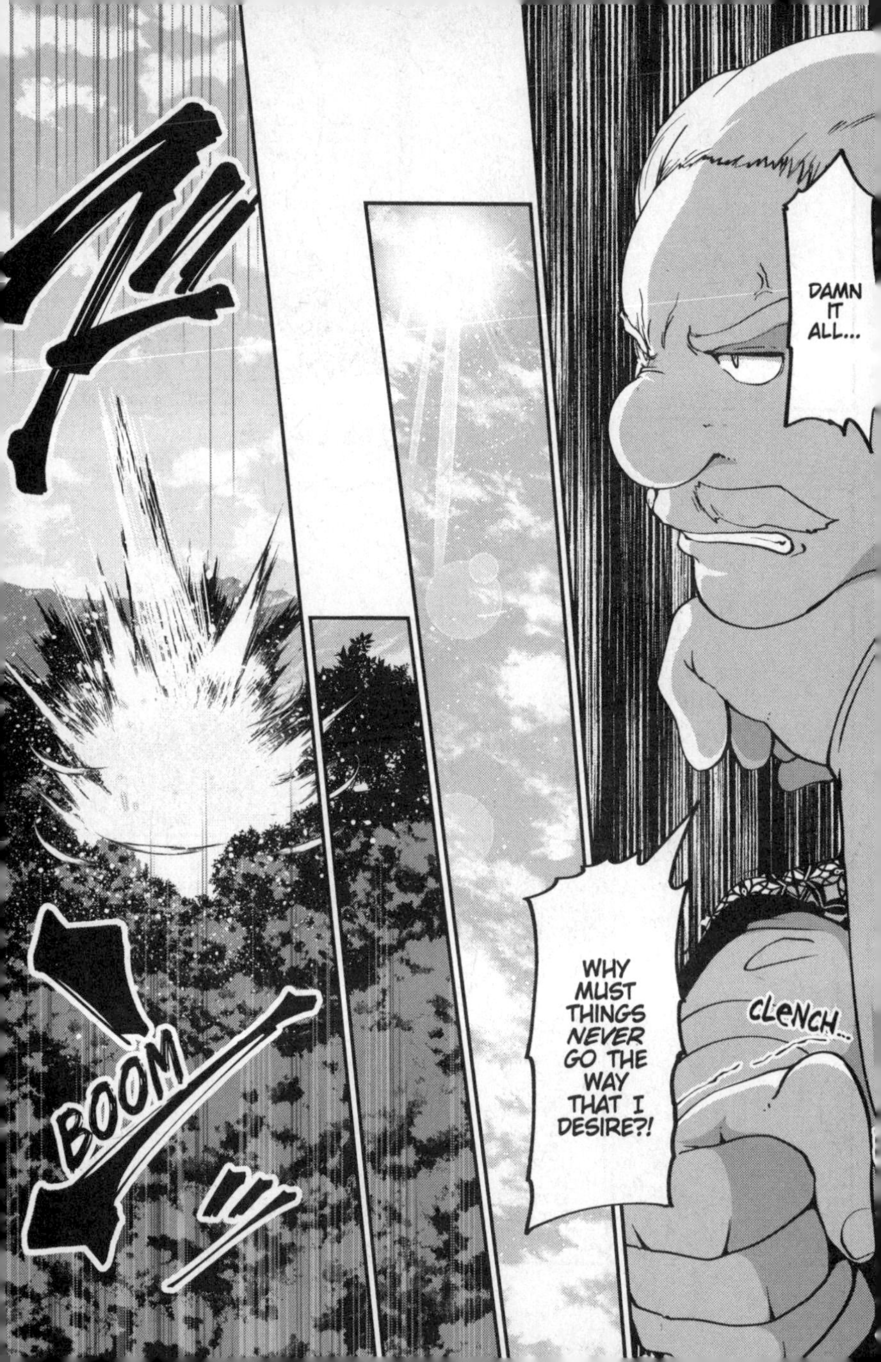
DAMN IT ALL...
WHY MUST THINGS *NEVER* GO THE WAY THAT I DESIRE?!
CLENCH...
BOOM

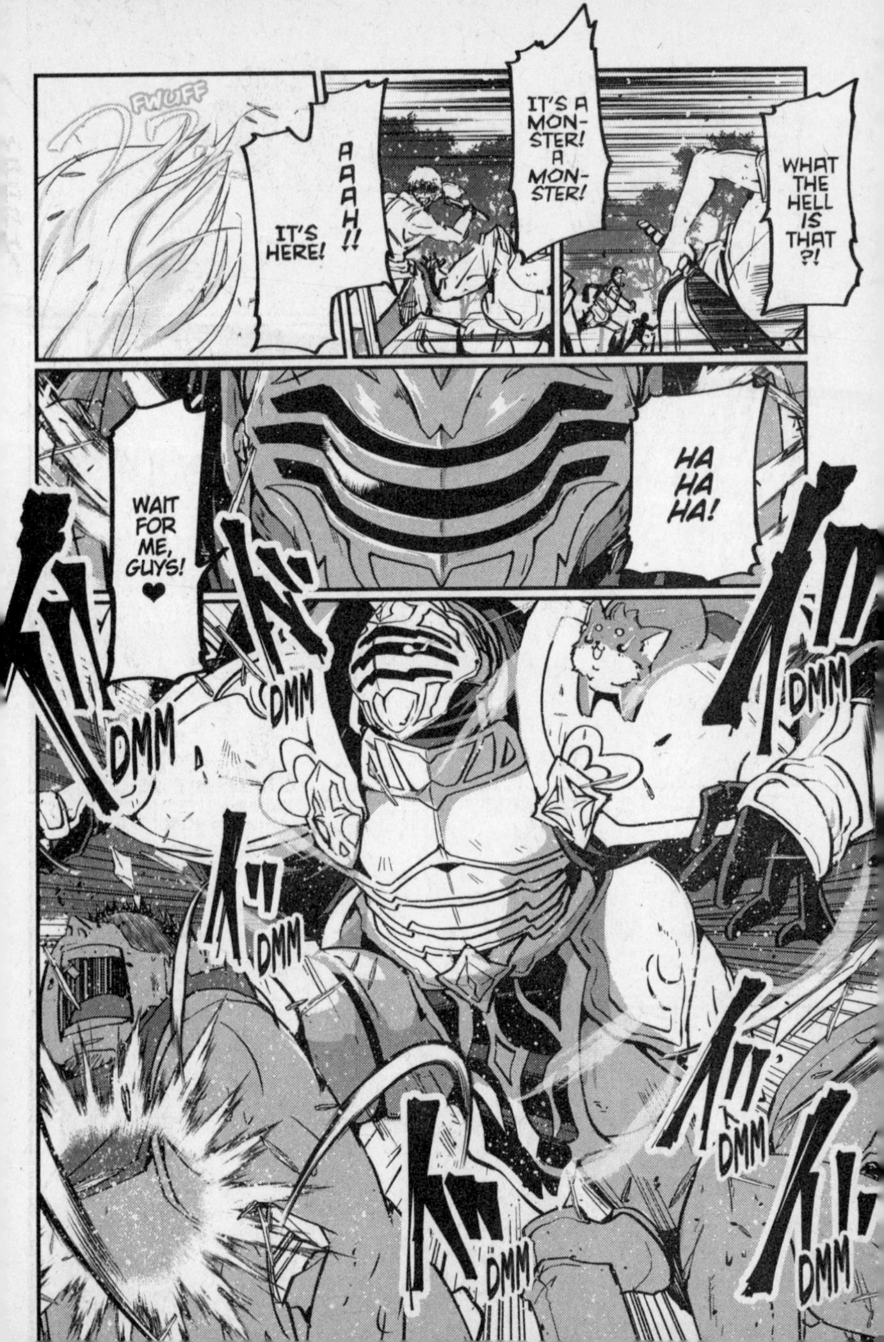
WHAT THE HELL IS THAT?!
IT'S A MONSTER! A MONSTER!
AAAAH!!
IT'S HERE!
FWUFF
HA HA HA!
WAIT FOR ME, GUYS! ❤
DMM
DMM
DMM
DMM
DMM
DMM
DMM
DMM

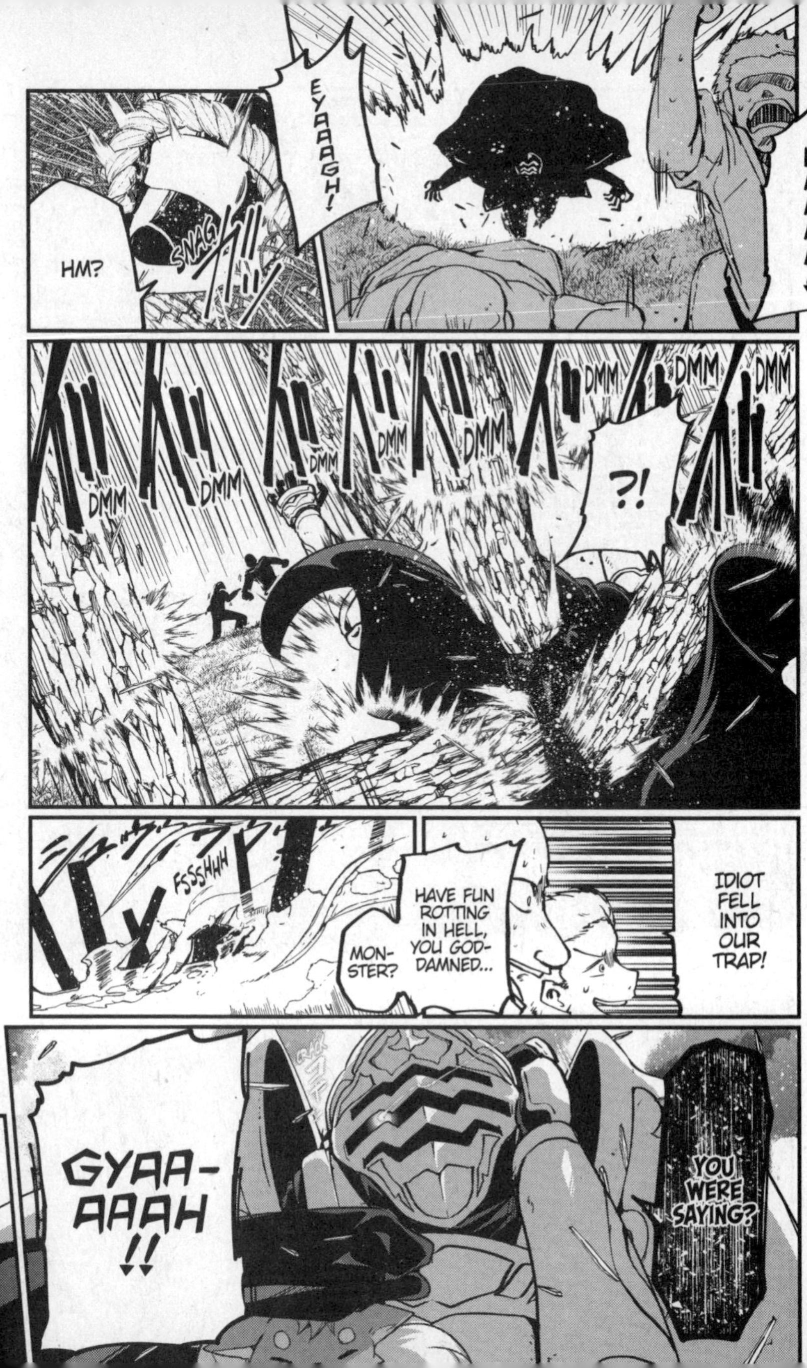
WAAAAH!
EYAAAGH!
SNAG
HM?
DMM DMM DMM
DMM DMM DMM DMM DMM
?!
IDIOT FELL INTO OUR TRAP!
HAVE FUN ROTTING IN HELL, YOU GOD-DAMNED...
MON-STER?
FSSSHHH
YOU WERE SAYING?
CRACK
GYAA-AAAH!!

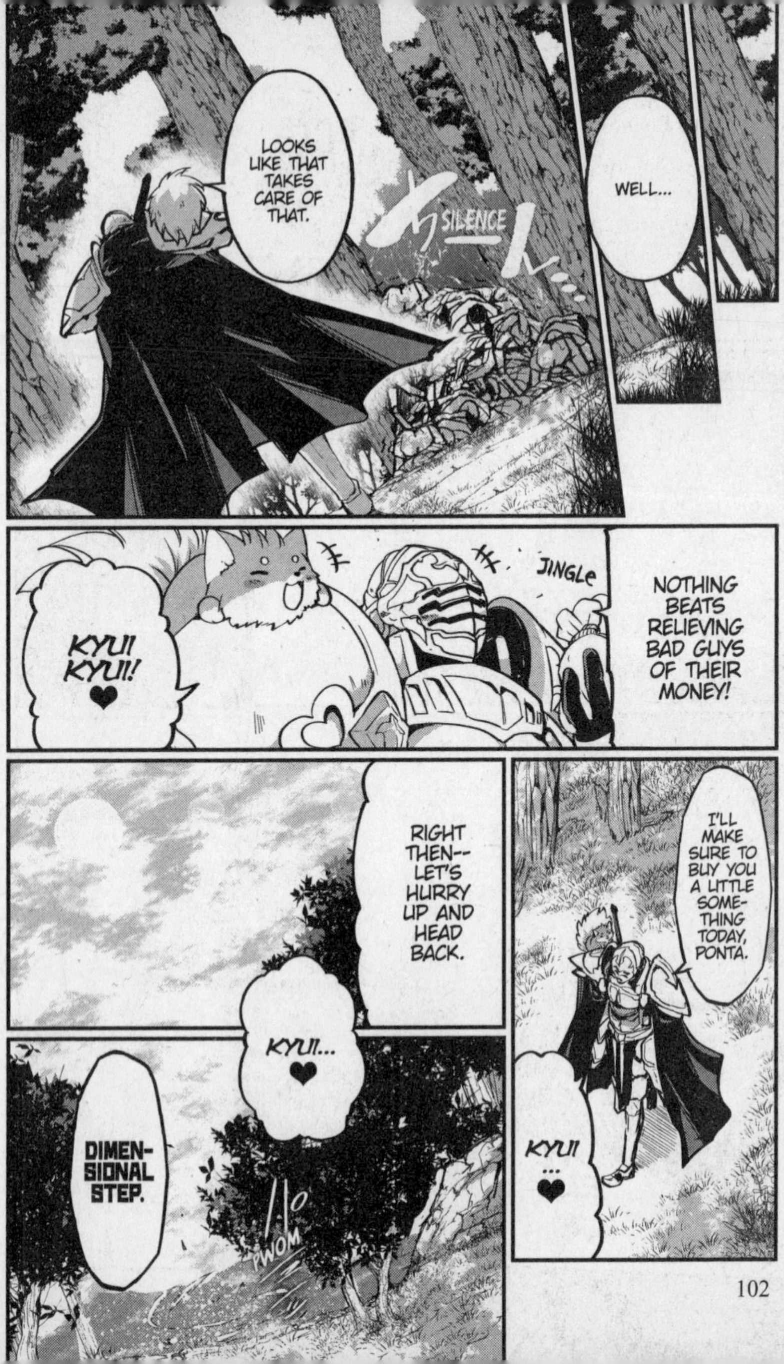
WELL...
LOOKS LIKE THAT TAKES CARE OF THAT.
SILENCE
NOTHING BEATS RELIEVING BAD GUYS OF THEIR MONEY!
JINGLE
KYU! KYU! ♥
I'LL MAKE SURE TO BUY YOU A LITTLE SOME-THING TODAY, PONTA.
KYU! ... ♥
RIGHT THEN-- LET'S HURRY UP AND HEAD BACK.
KYU!... ♥
DIMEN-SIONAL STEP.
PWOM

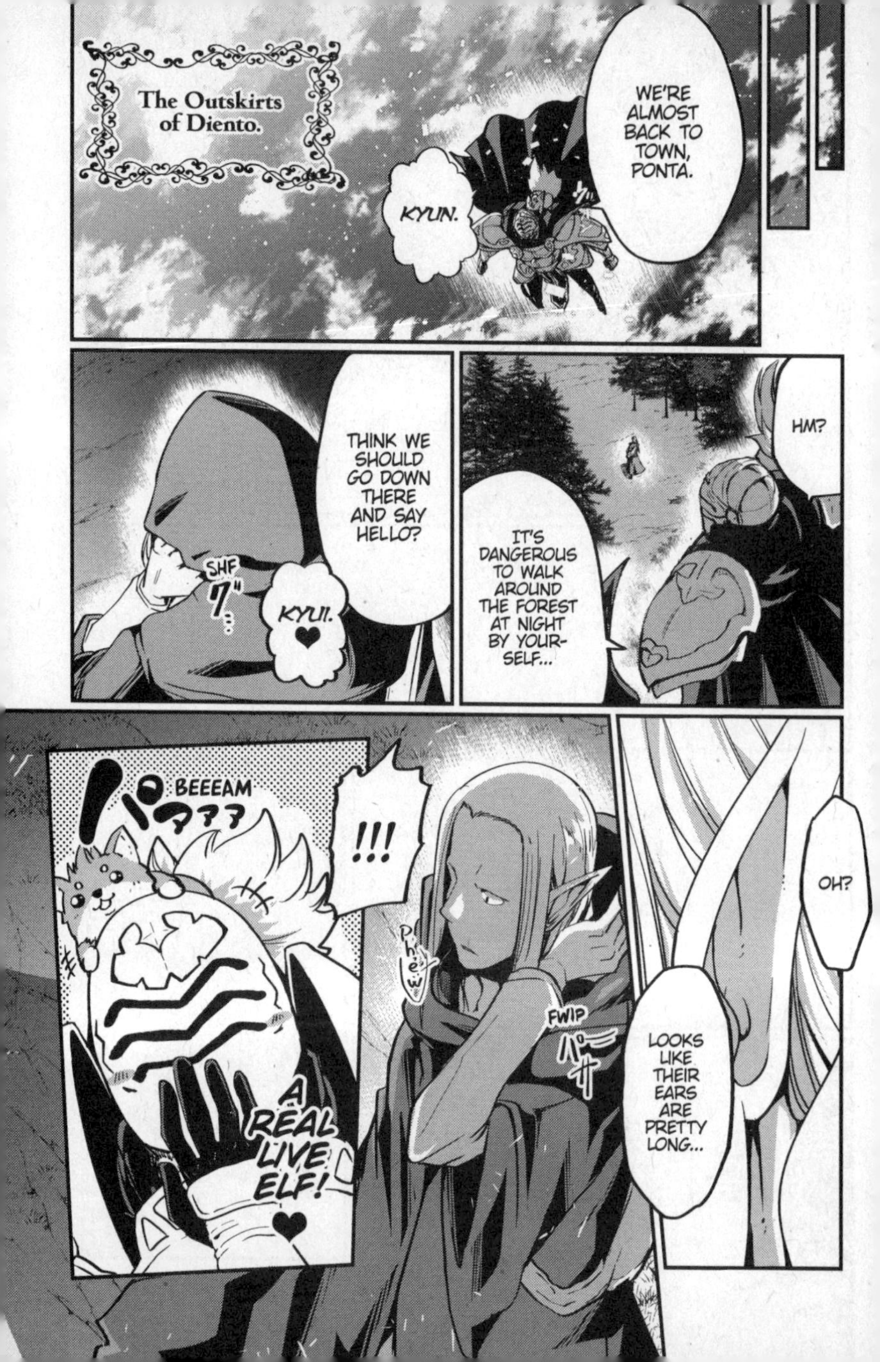
WE'RE ALMOST BACK TO TOWN, PONTA.
The Outskirts of Diento.
KYUN.
HM?
IT'S DANGEROUS TO WALK AROUND THE FOREST AT NIGHT BY YOUR-SELF...
THINK WE SHOULD GO DOWN THERE AND SAY HELLO?
SHF
KYUI. ♥
OH?
LOOKS LIKE THEIR EARS ARE PRETTY LONG...
!!!
Phew
FWIP
BEEEAM
A REAL LIVE ELF! ♥

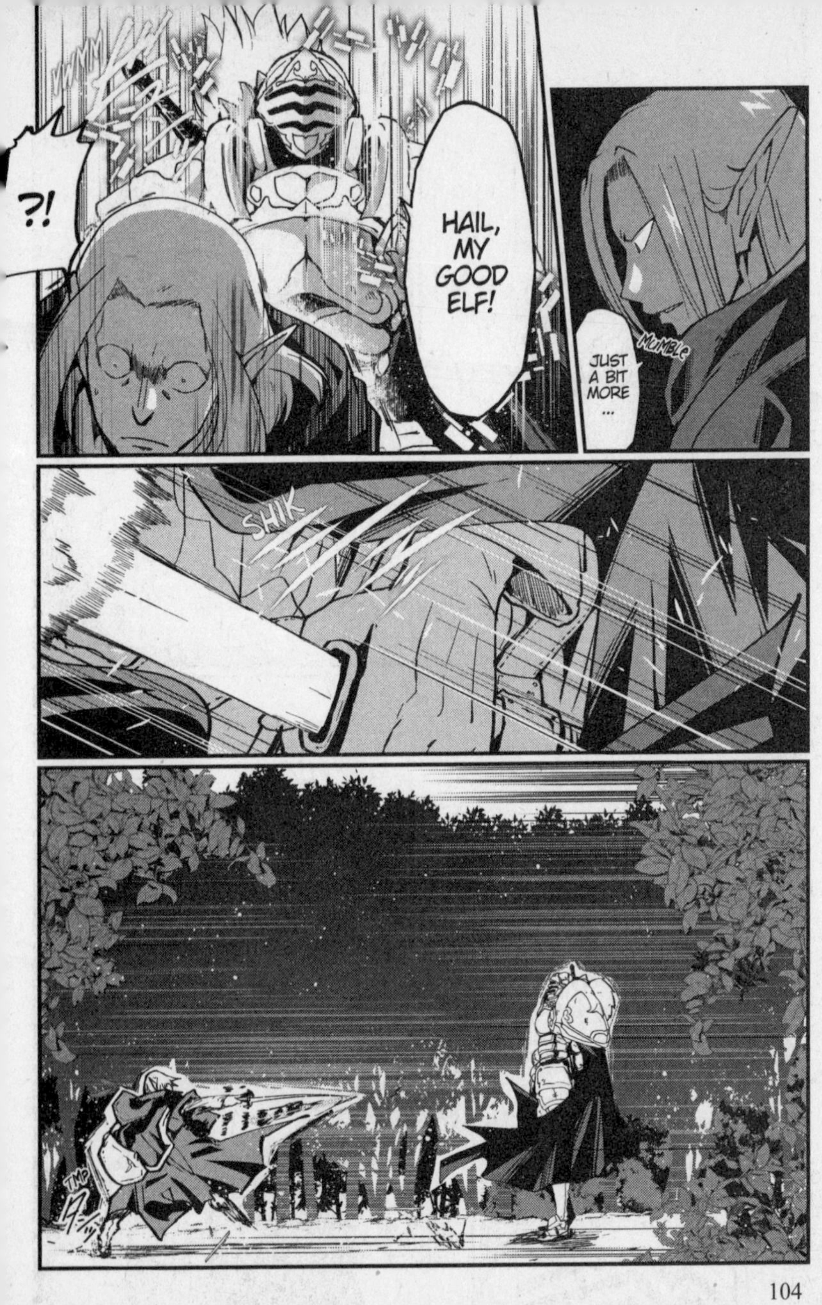
MUMBLE
JUST A BIT MORE ...
HAIL, MY GOOD ELF!
?!
VWMM
SHIK
TMP

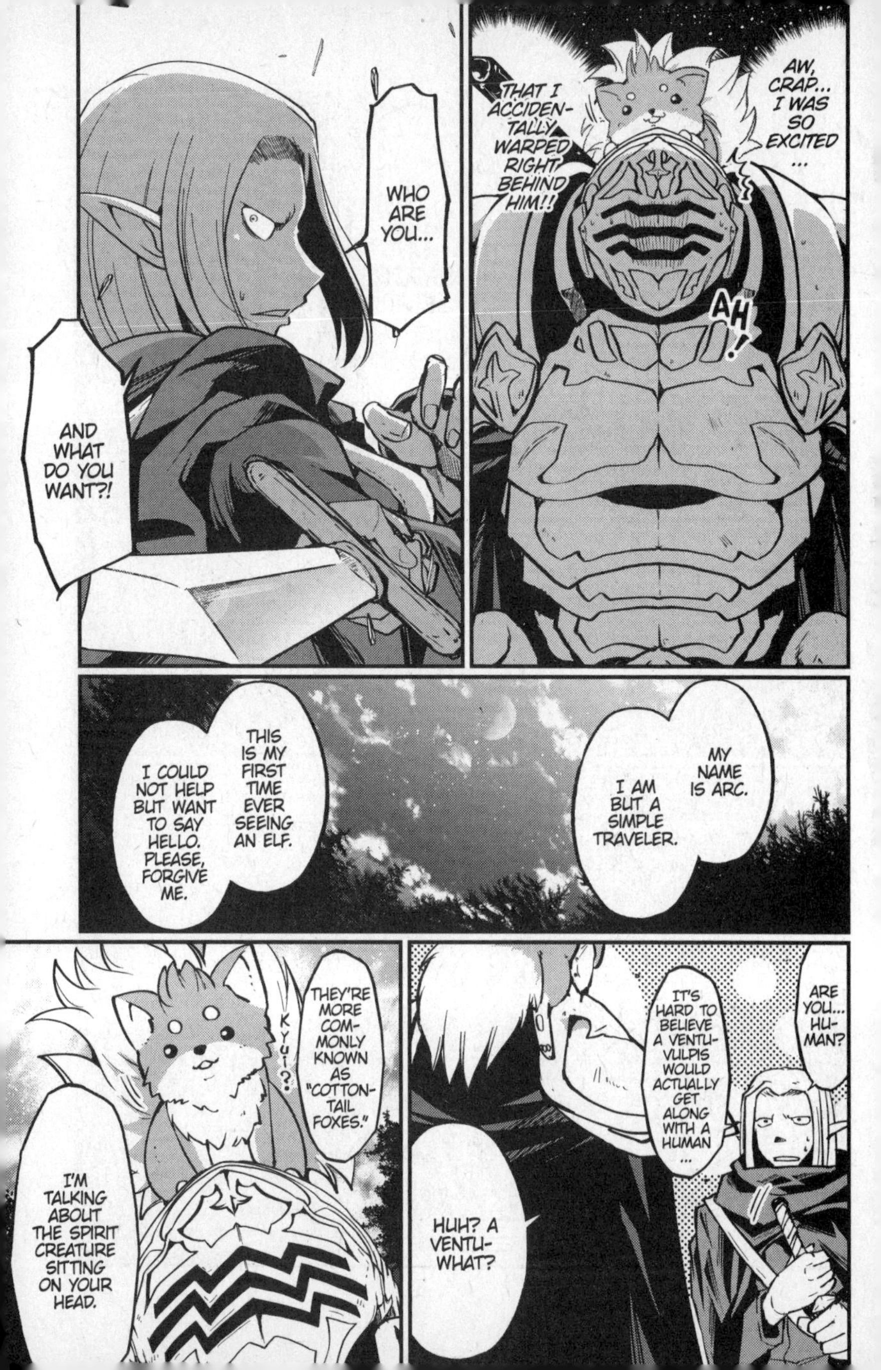
AW, CRAP... I WAS SO EXCITED...
THAT I ACCIDENTALLY WARPED RIGHT BEHIND HIM!!
AH!
WHO ARE YOU...
AND WHAT DO YOU WANT?!
MY NAME IS ARC.
I AM BUT A SIMPLE TRAVELER.
THIS IS MY FIRST TIME EVER SEEING AN ELF.
I COULD NOT HELP BUT WANT TO SAY HELLO. PLEASE, FORGIVE ME.
ARE YOU... HUMAN?
IT'S HARD TO BELIEVE A VENTUVULPIS WOULD ACTUALLY GET ALONG WITH A HUMAN...
HUH? A VENTU-WHAT?
THEY'RE MORE COMMONLY KNOWN AS "COTTONTAIL FOXES."
KYU!?
I'M TALKING ABOUT THE SPIRIT CREATURE SITTING ON YOUR HEAD.

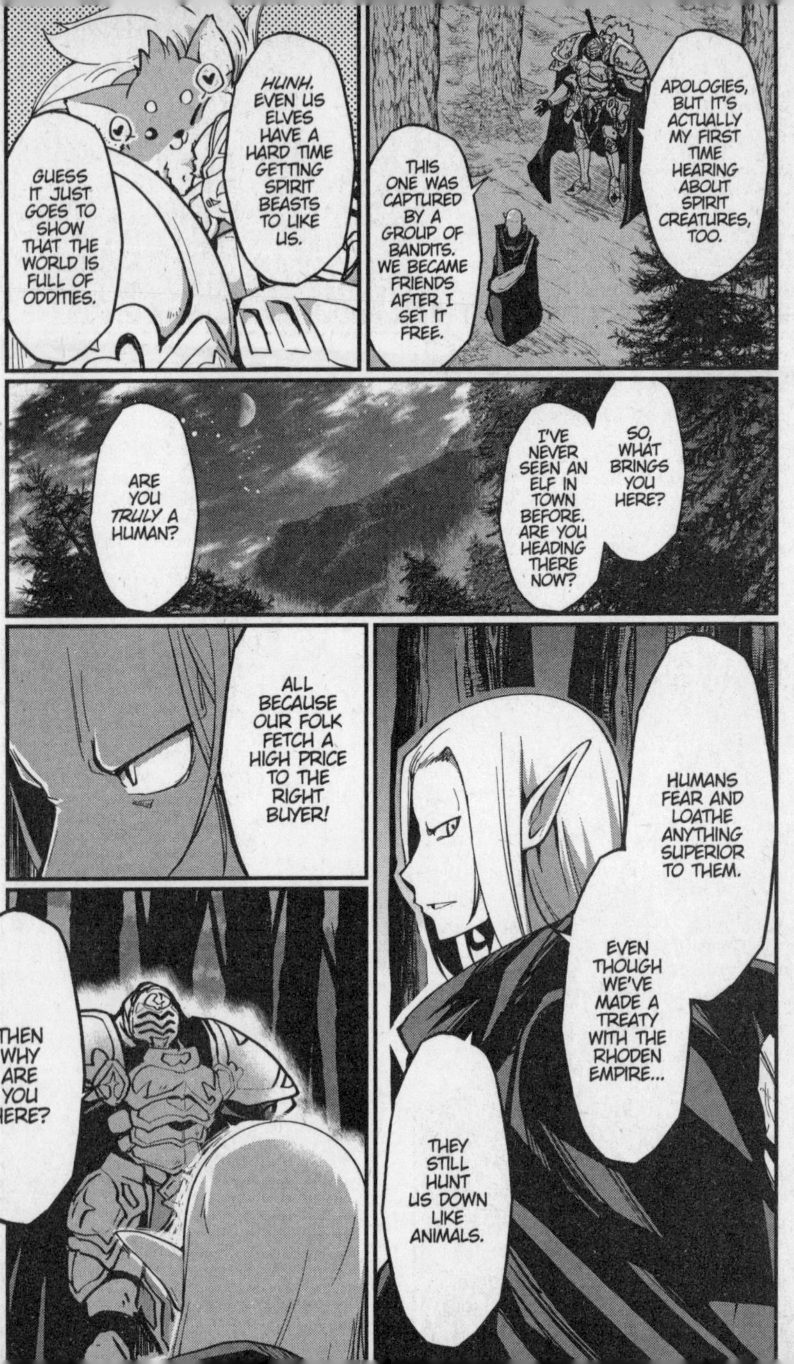
APOLOGIES, BUT IT'S ACTUALLY MY FIRST TIME HEARING ABOUT SPIRIT CREATURES, TOO.
THIS ONE WAS CAPTURED BY A GROUP OF BANDITS. WE BECAME FRIENDS AFTER I SET IT FREE.
HUNH. EVEN US ELVES HAVE A HARD TIME GETTING SPIRIT BEASTS TO LIKE US.
GUESS IT JUST GOES TO SHOW THAT THE WORLD IS FULL OF ODDITIES.
SO, WHAT BRINGS YOU HERE?
I'VE NEVER SEEN AN ELF IN TOWN BEFORE. ARE YOU HEADING THERE NOW?
ARE YOU *TRULY* A HUMAN?
HUMANS FEAR AND LOATHE ANYTHING SUPERIOR TO THEM.
EVEN THOUGH WE'VE MADE A TREATY WITH THE RHODEN EMPIRE...
THEY STILL HUNT US DOWN LIKE ANIMALS.
ALL BECAUSE OUR FOLK FETCH A HIGH PRICE TO THE RIGHT BUYER!
THEN WHY ARE YOU HERE?

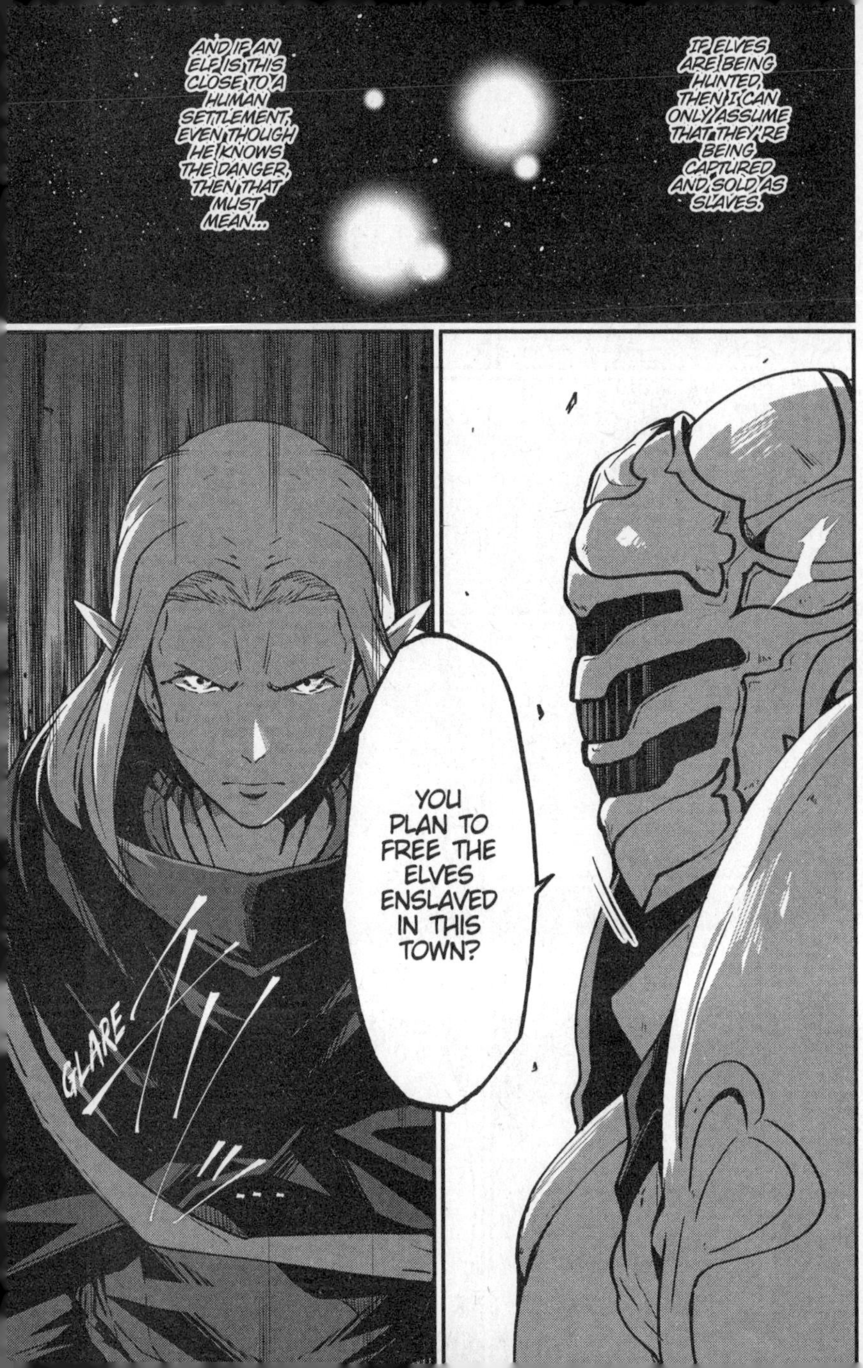
IF ELVES ARE BEING HUNTED, THEN I CAN ONLY ASSUME THAT THEY'RE BEING CAPTURED AND SOLD AS SLAVES.
AND IF AN ELF IS THIS CLOSE TO A HUMAN SETTLEMENT, EVEN THOUGH HE KNOWS THE DANGER, THEN THAT MUST MEAN...
YOU PLAN TO FREE THE ELVES ENSLAVED IN THIS TOWN?
GLARE
...

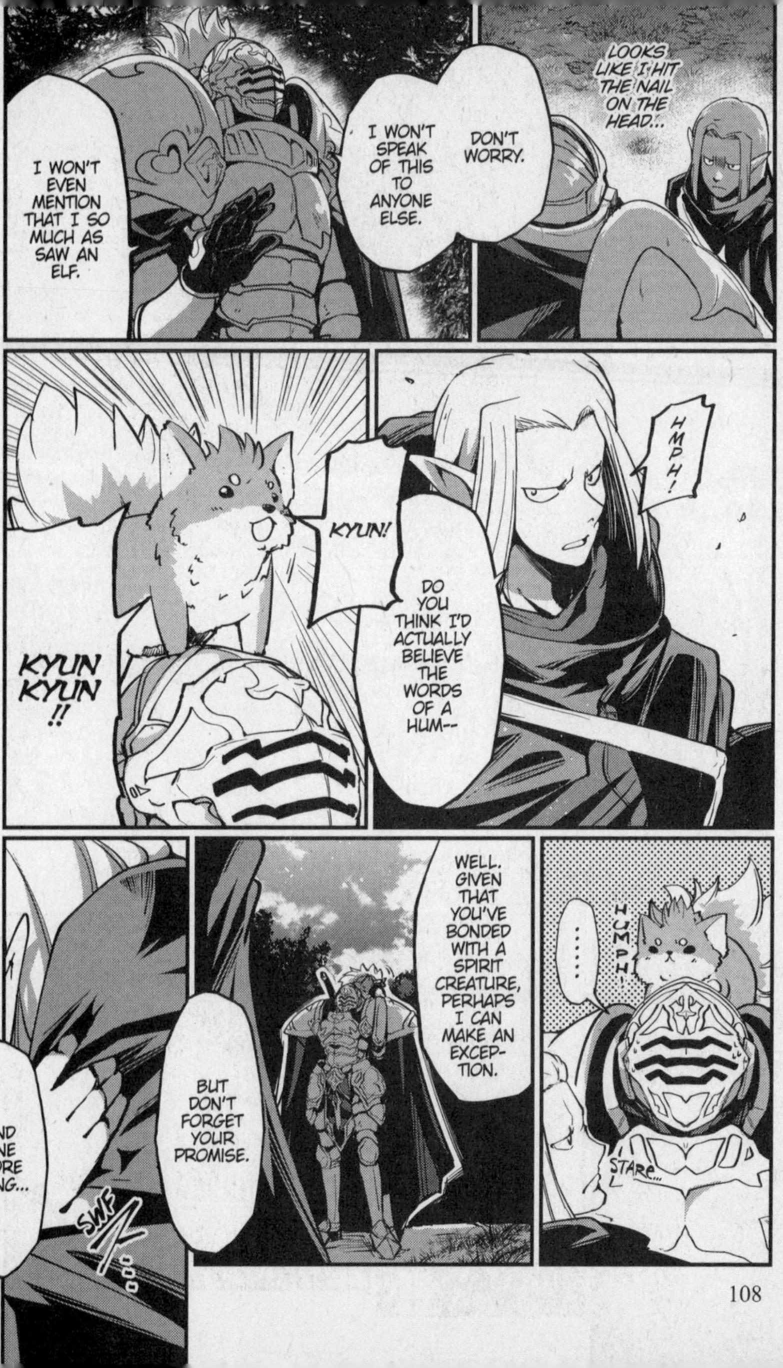
LOOKS LIKE I HIT THE NAIL ON THE HEAD...
DON'T WORRY.
I WON'T SPEAK OF THIS TO ANYONE ELSE.
I WON'T EVEN MENTION THAT I SO MUCH AS SAW AN ELF.
HMPH!
DO YOU THINK I'D ACTUALLY BELIEVE THE WORDS OF A HUM--
KYUN!
KYUN KYUN!!
HUMPH!
......
STARE...
WELL. GIVEN THAT YOU'VE BONDED WITH A SPIRIT CREATURE, PERHAPS I CAN MAKE AN EXCEP-TION.
BUT DON'T FORGET YOUR PROMISE.
AND ONE MORE THING...
SWF

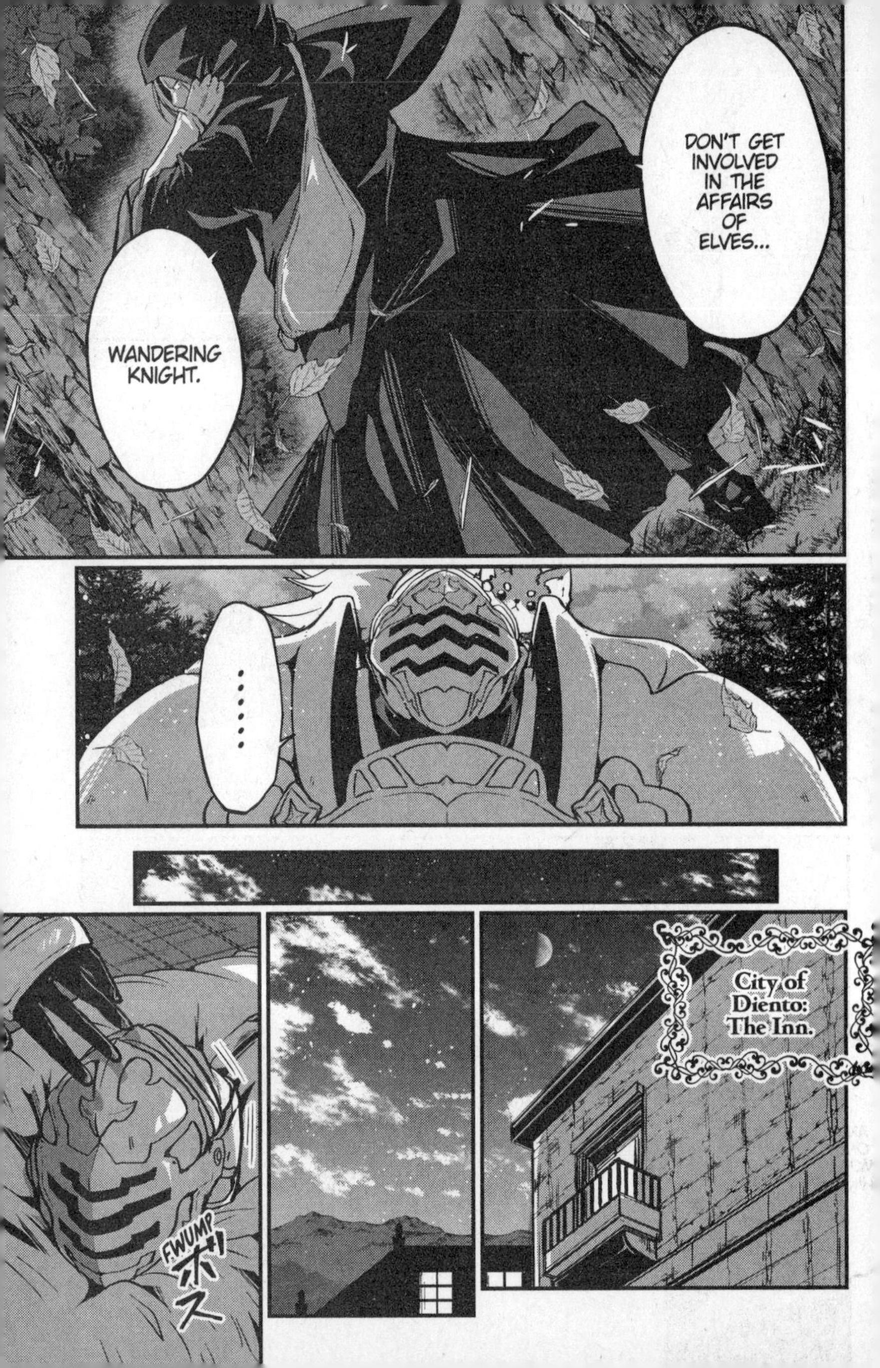
DON'T GET INVOLVED IN THE AFFAIRS OF ELVES...
WANDERING KNIGHT.
......
City of Diento: The Inn.
FWUMP!
ボス

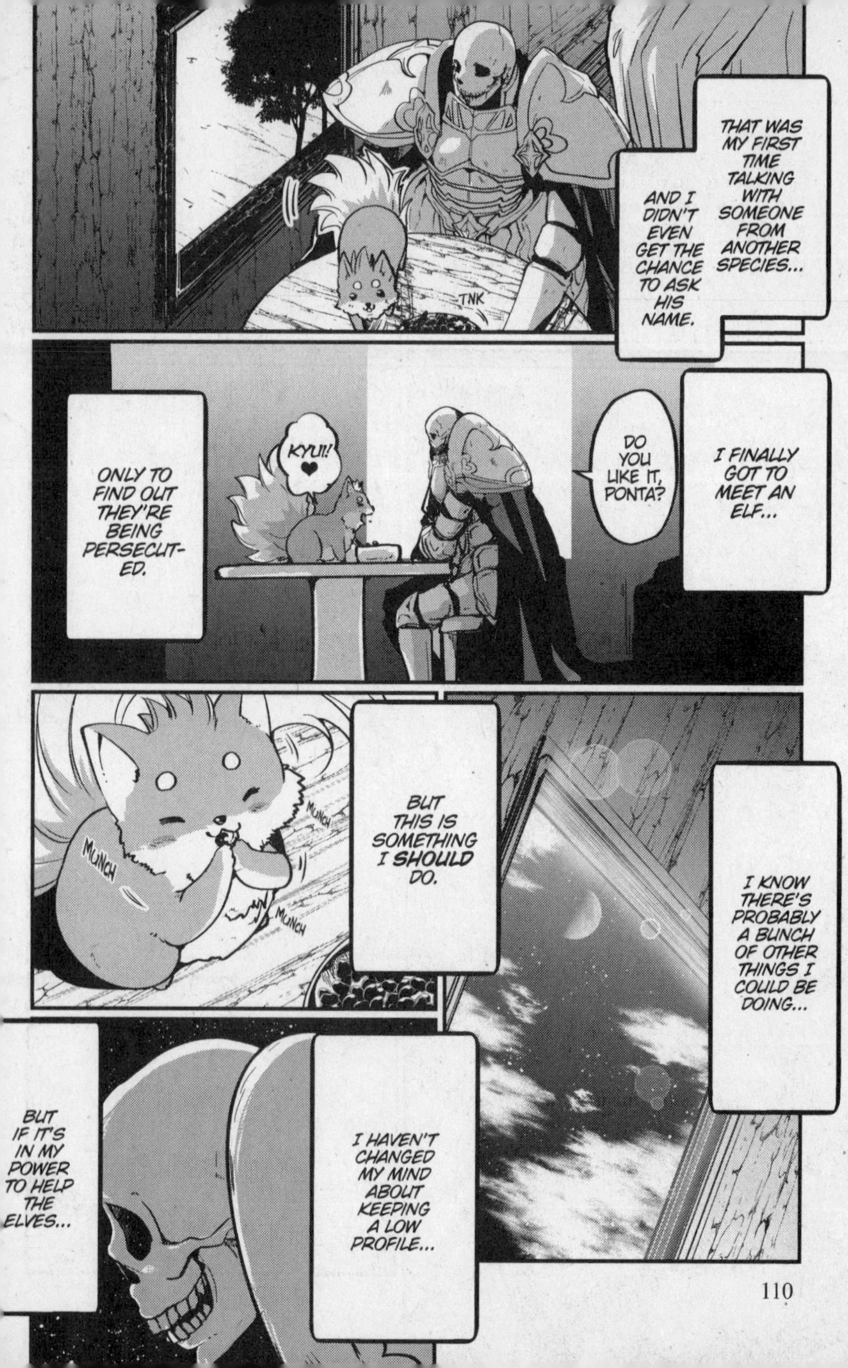
THAT WAS MY FIRST TIME TALKING WITH SOMEONE FROM ANOTHER SPECIES...
AND I DIDN'T EVEN GET THE CHANCE TO ASK HIS NAME.
TNK
I FINALLY GOT TO MEET AN ELF...
DO YOU LIKE IT, PONTA?
KYU!! ♥
ONLY TO FIND OUT THEY'RE BEING PERSECUTED.
I KNOW THERE'S PROBABLY A BUNCH OF OTHER THINGS I COULD BE DOING...
BUT THIS IS SOMETHING I SHOULD DO.
MUNCH
MUNCH
MUNCH
I HAVEN'T CHANGED MY MIND ABOUT KEEPING A LOW PROFILE...
BUT IF IT'S IN MY POWER TO HELP THE ELVES...

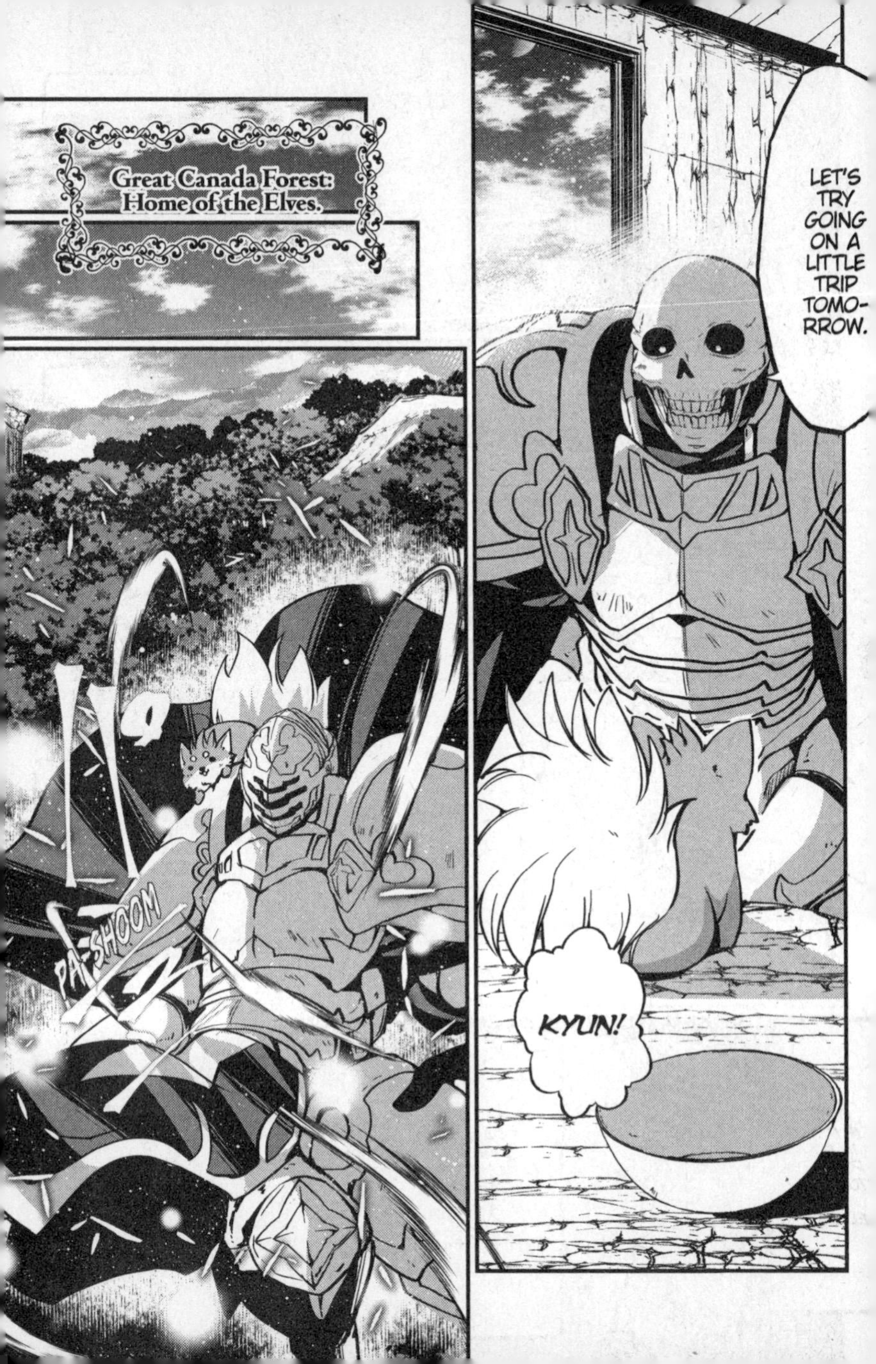
LET'S TRY GOING ON A LITTLE TRIP TOMORROW.
KYUN!
Great Canada Forest: Home of the Elves.
PA-SHOOM

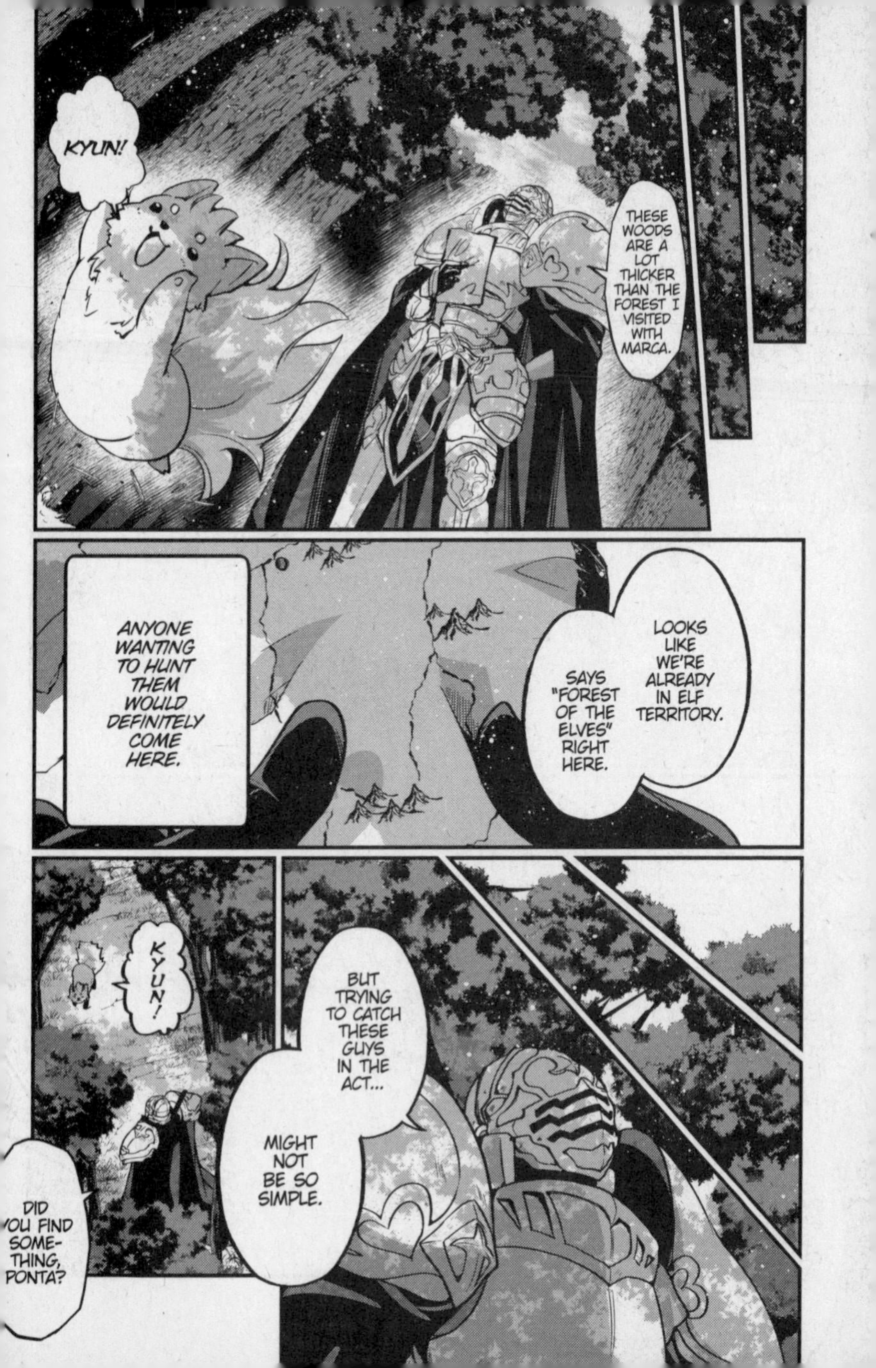
THESE WOODS ARE A LOT THICKER THAN THE FOREST I VISITED WITH MARCA.
KYUN!
LOOKS LIKE WE'RE ALREADY IN ELF TERRITORY.
SAYS "FOREST OF THE ELVES" RIGHT HERE.
ANYONE WANTING TO HUNT THEM WOULD DEFINITELY COME HERE.
BUT TRYING TO CATCH THESE GUYS IN THE ACT...
MIGHT NOT BE SO SIMPLE.
KYUN!
DID OU FIND SOMETHING, PONTA?

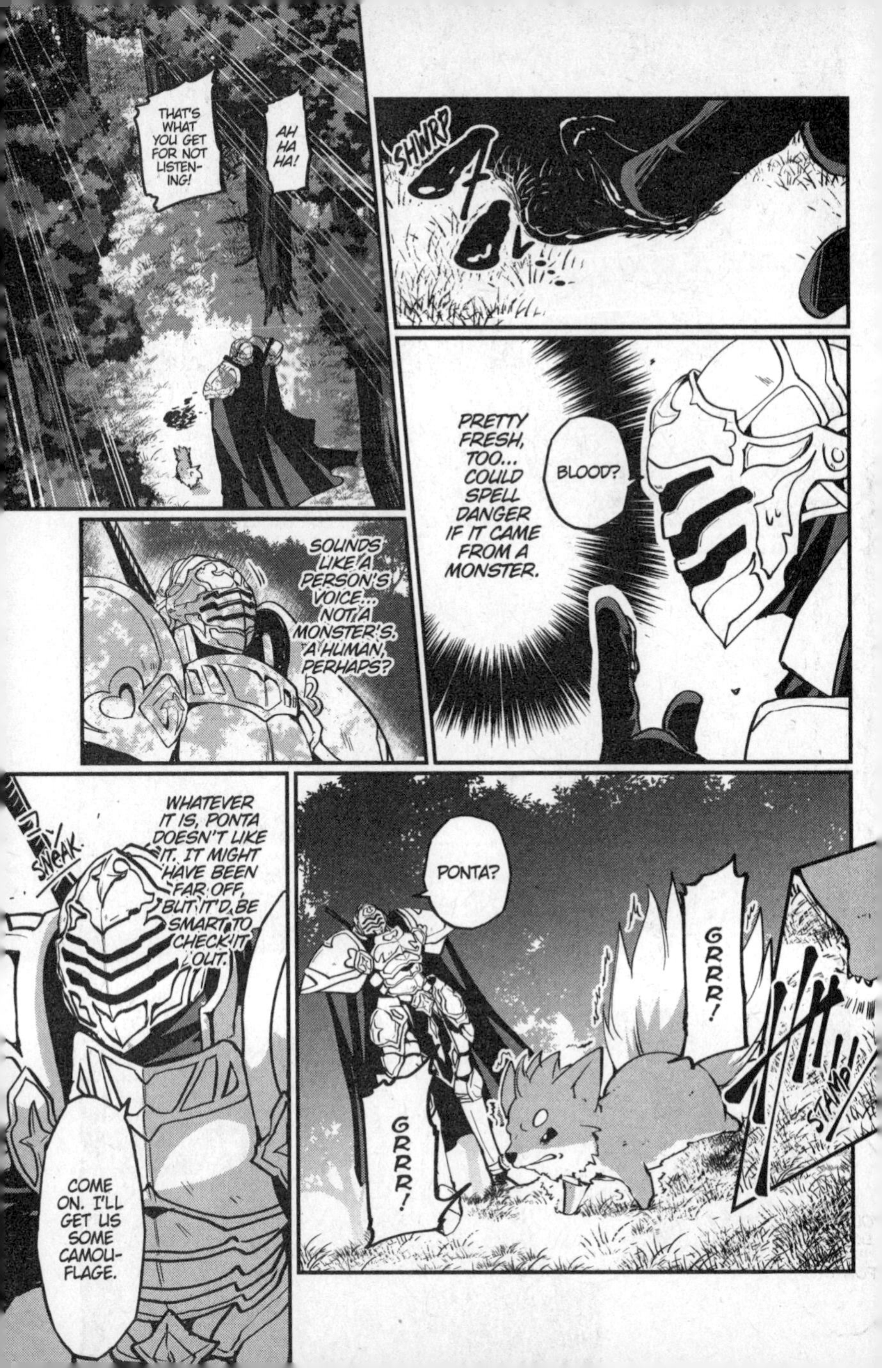
SHWRP
BLOOD?
PRETTY FRESH, TOO... COULD SPELL DANGER IF IT CAME FROM A MONSTER.
AH HA HA!
THAT'S WHAT YOU GET FOR NOT LISTENING!
SOUNDS LIKE A PERSON'S VOICE... NOT A MONSTER'S. A HUMAN, PERHAPS?
PONTA?
GRRR!
STAMP!
GRRR!
SNEAK
WHATEVER IT IS, PONTA DOESN'T LIKE IT. IT MIGHT HAVE BEEN FAR OFF, BUT IT'D BE SMART TO CHECK IT OUT.
COME ON. I'LL GET US SOME CAMOUFLAGE.

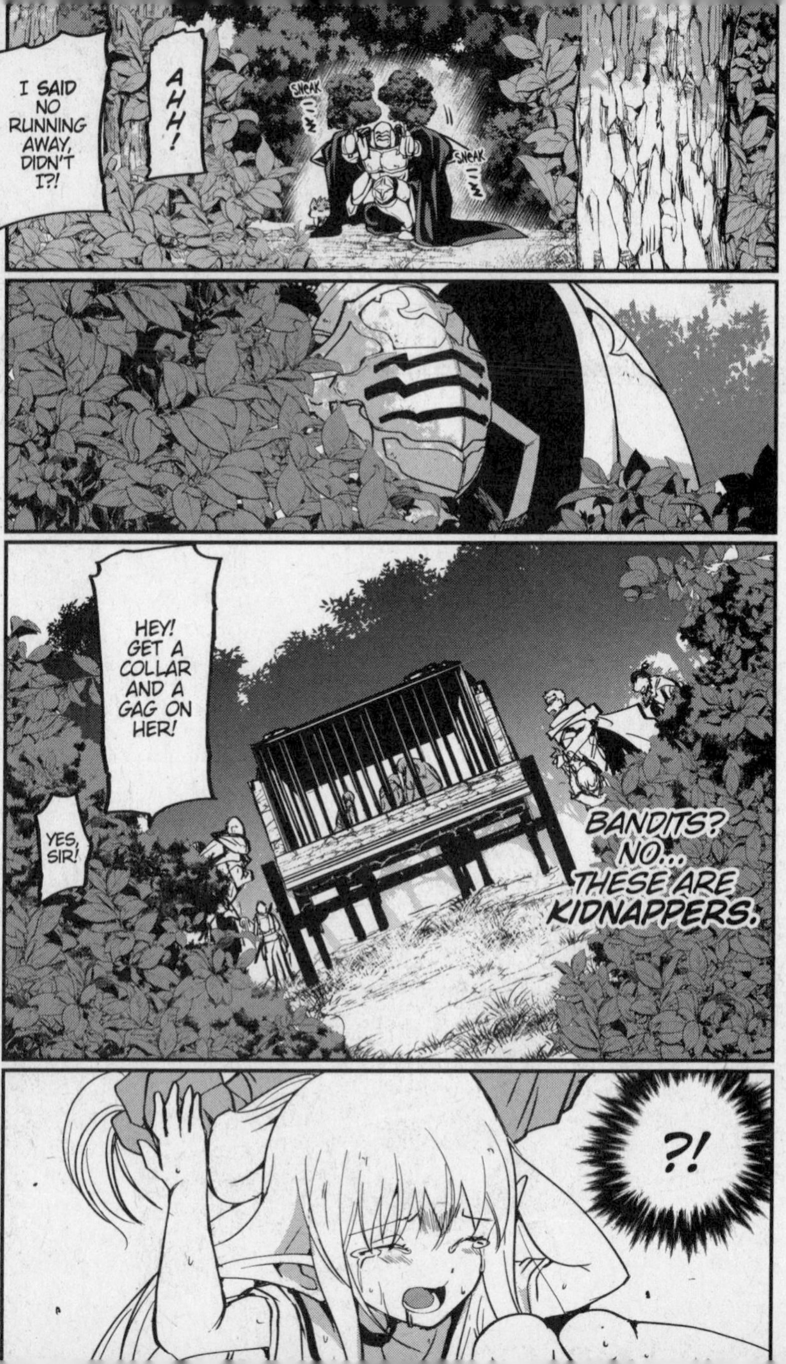
AHH!
I SAID NO RUNNING AWAY, DIDN'T I?!
SNEAK
SNEAK
BANDITS? NO... THESE ARE KIDNAPPERS.
HEY! GET A COLLAR AND A GAG ON HER!
YES, SIR!
?!

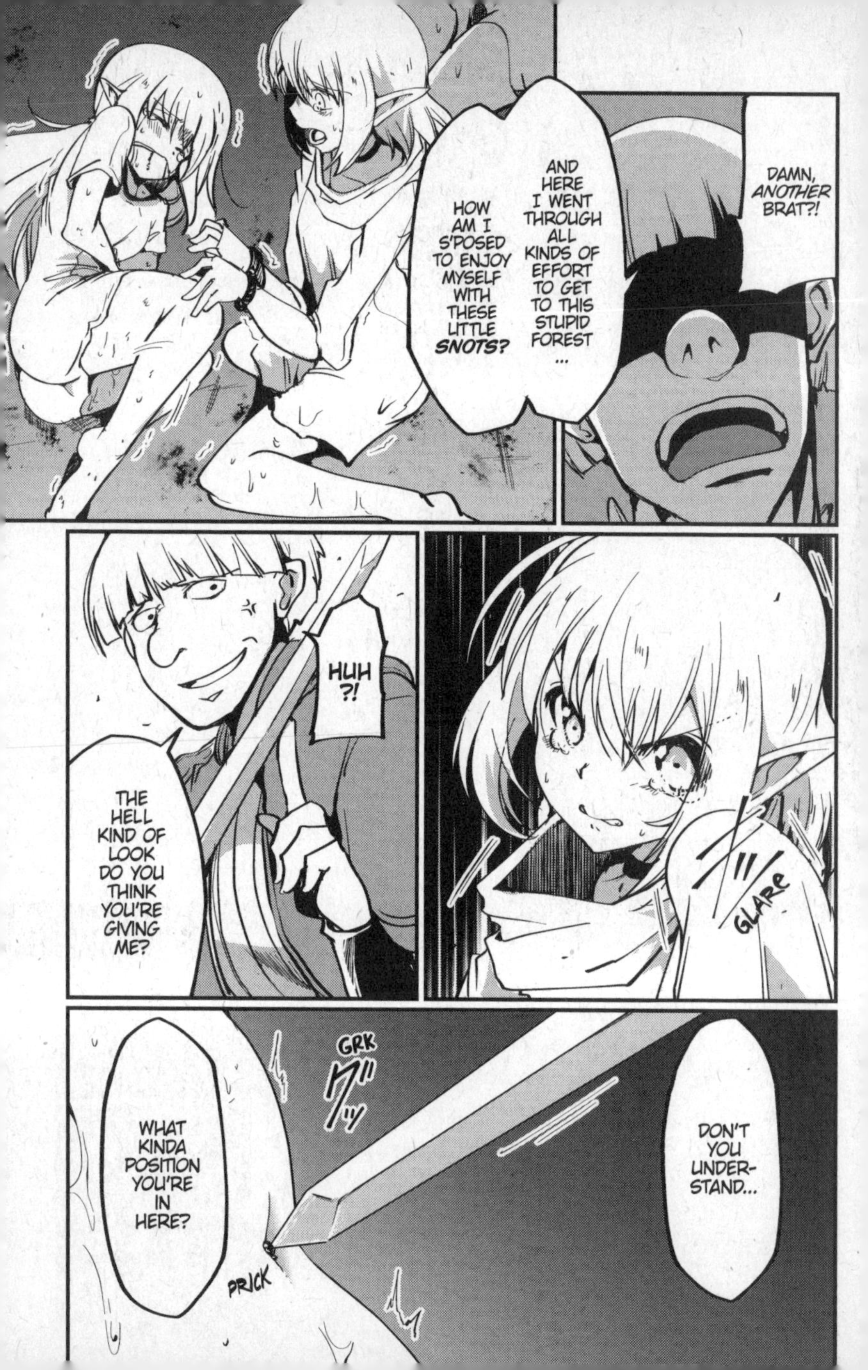
DAMN, ANOTHER BRAT?!
AND HERE I WENT THROUGH ALL KINDS OF EFFORT TO GET TO THIS STUPID FOREST ...
HOW AM I S'POSED TO ENJOY MYSELF WITH THESE LITTLE SNOTS?
GLARE
HUH ?!
THE HELL KIND OF LOOK DO YOU THINK YOU'RE GIVING ME?
DON'T YOU UNDER-STAND...
GRK
WHAT KINDA POSITION YOU'RE IN HERE?
PRICK

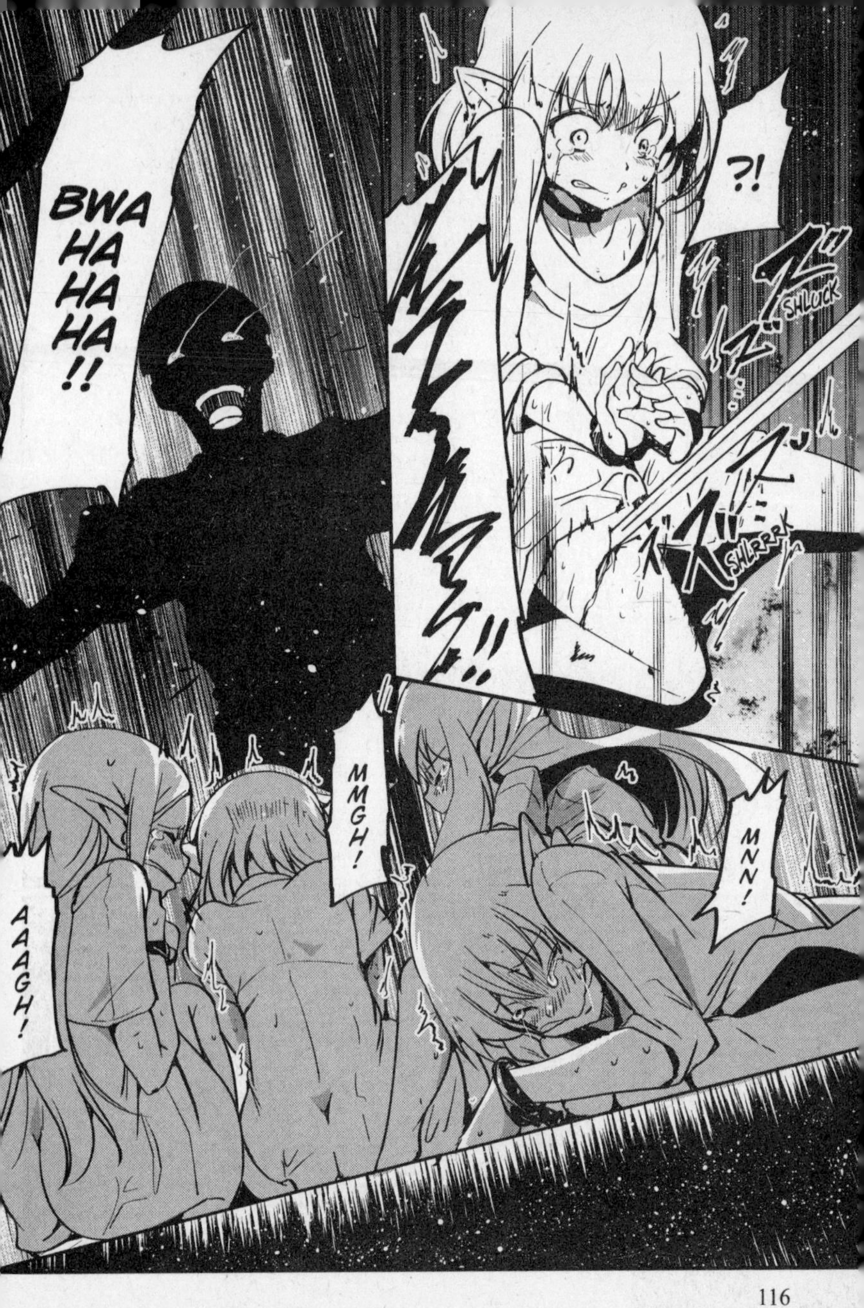
?!
SHLUCK
SHRRRK
BWA HA HA HA!!
MNN!
MMGH!
AAAGH!

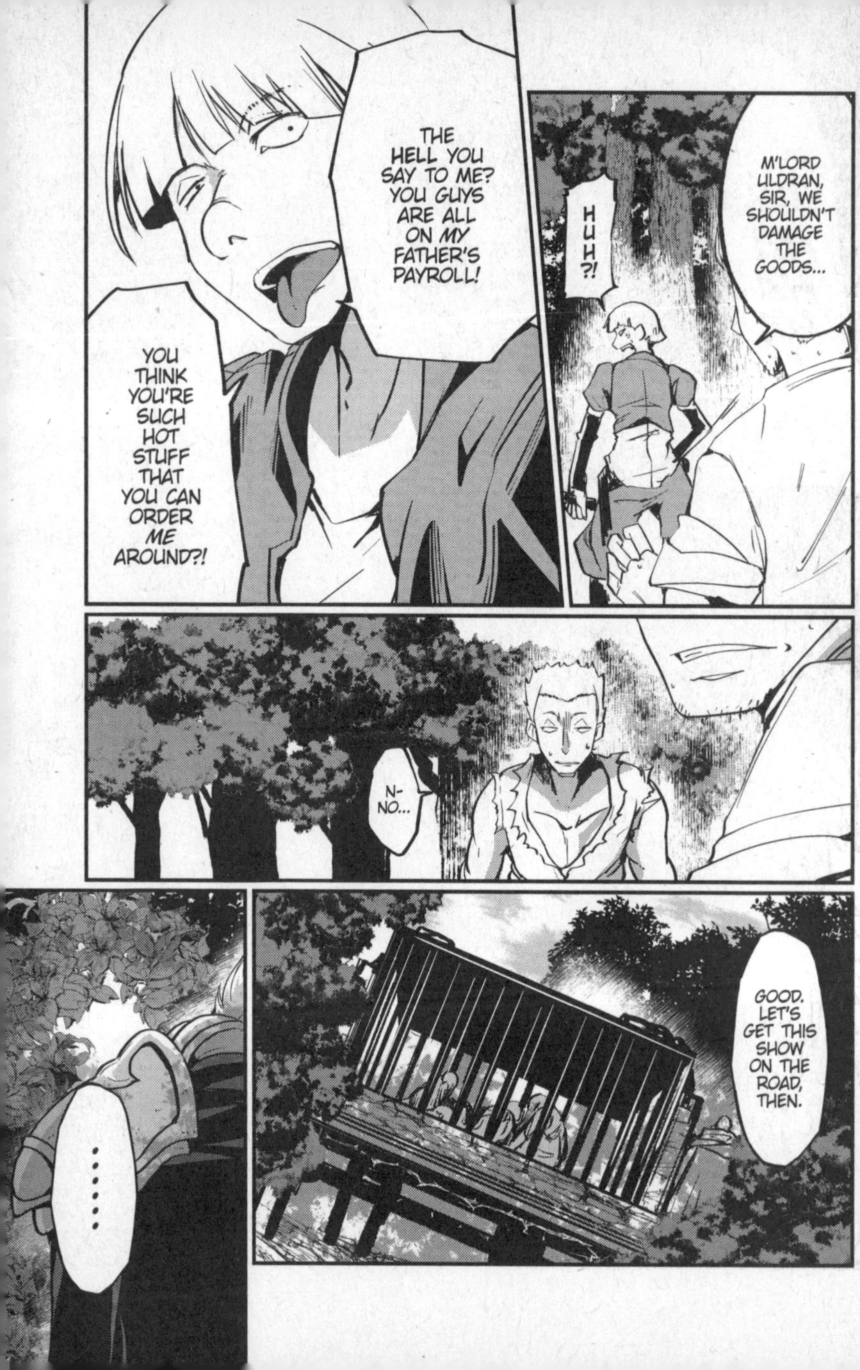
M'LORD ULDRAN, SIR, WE SHOULDN'T DAMAGE THE GOODS...
HUH?!
THE HELL YOU SAY TO ME? YOU GUYS ARE ALL ON MY FATHER'S PAYROLL!
YOU THINK YOU'RE SUCH HOT STUFF THAT YOU CAN ORDER ME AROUND?!
N-NO...
GOOD. LET'S GET THIS SHOW ON THE ROAD, THEN.
......

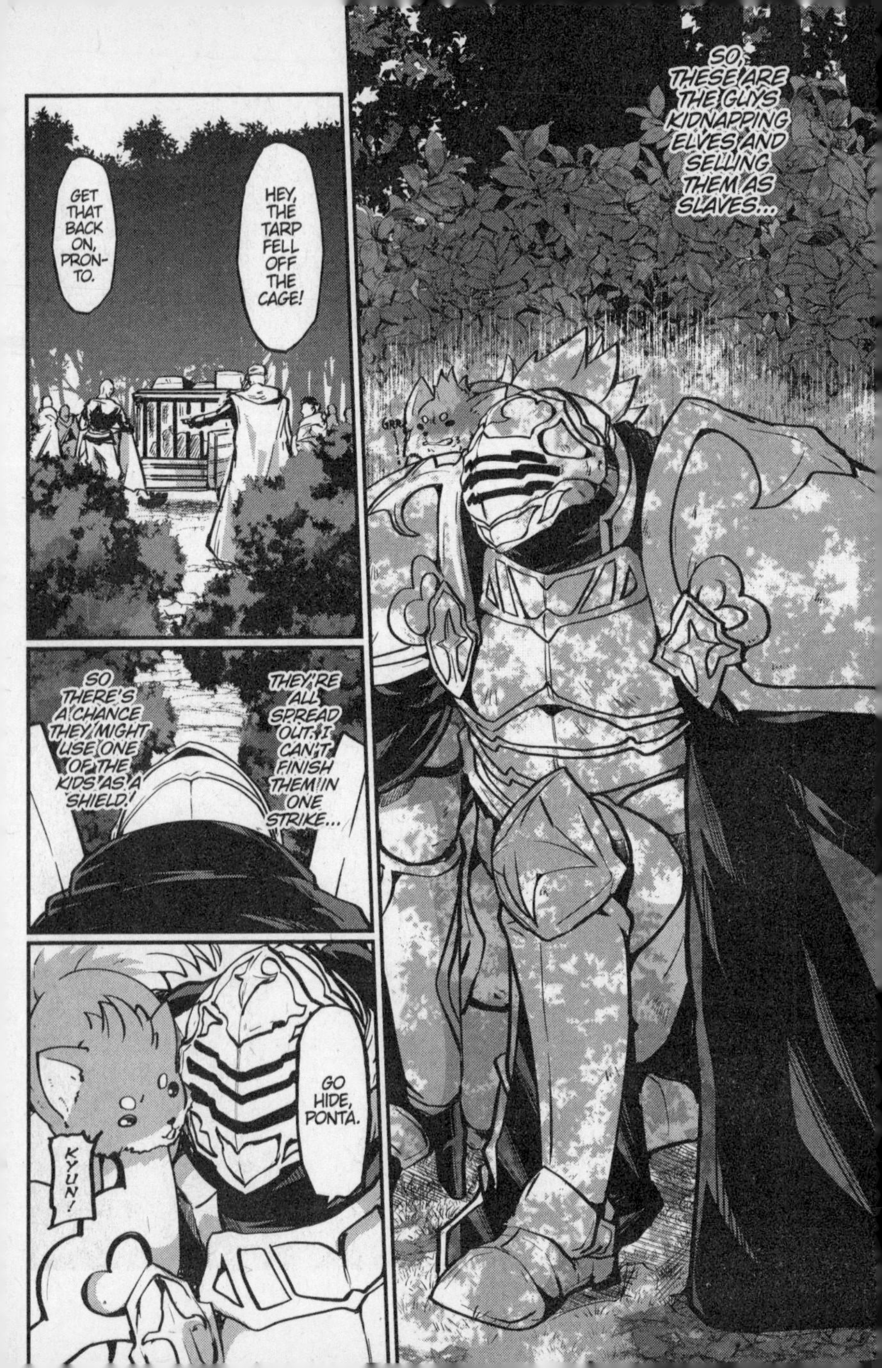
SO, THESE ARE THE GUYS KIDNAPPING ELVES AND SELLING THEM AS SLAVES...
GRR
HEY, THE TARP FELL OFF THE CAGE!
GET THAT BACK ON, PRONTO.
THEY'RE ALL SPREAD OUT. I CAN'T FINISH THEM IN ONE STRIKE...
SO THERE'S A CHANCE THEY MIGHT USE ONE OF THE KIDS AS A SHIELD!
GO HIDE, PONTA.
KYUN!

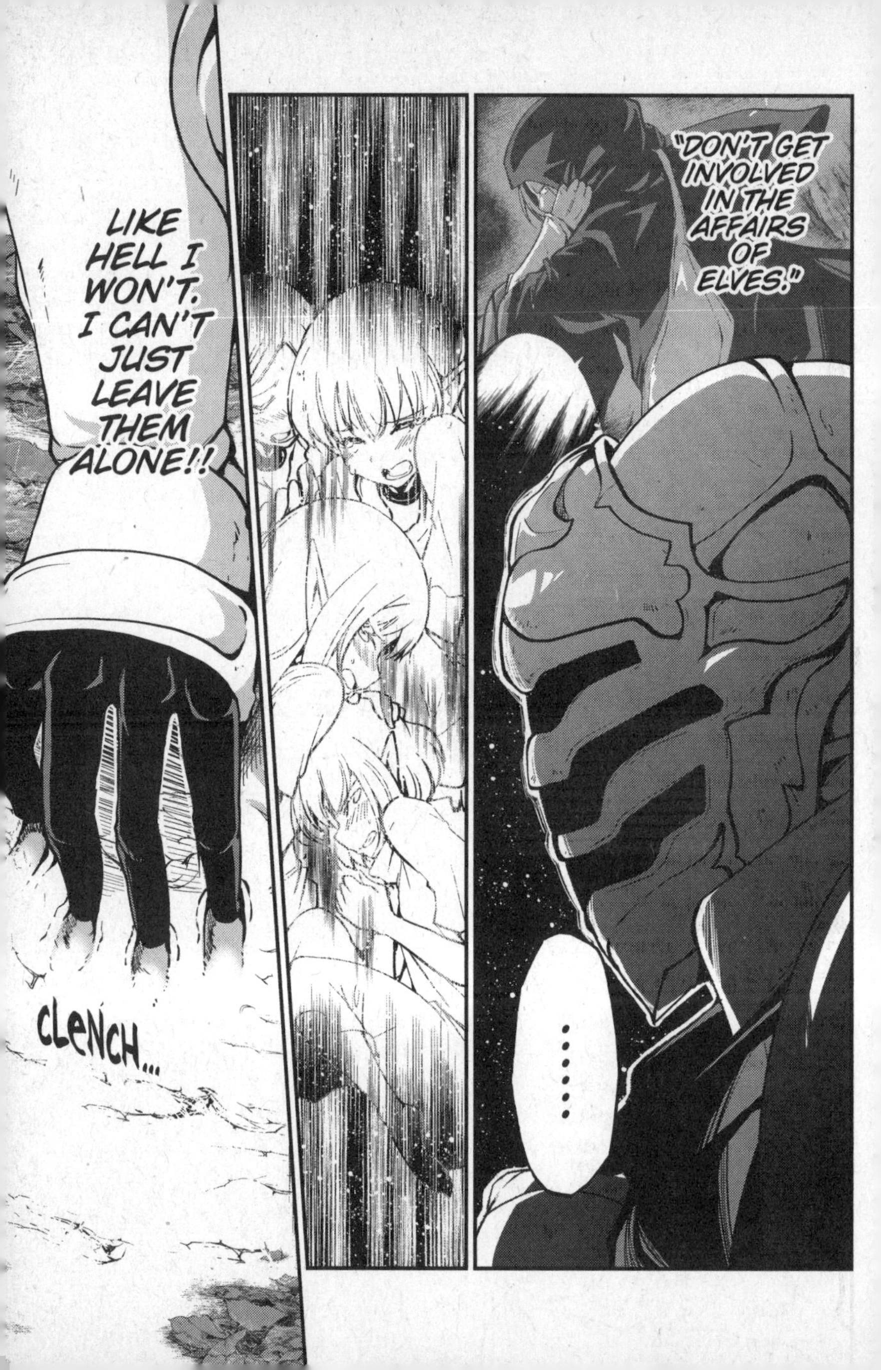
"DON'T GET INVOLVED IN THE AFFAIRS OF ELVES."
......
LIKE HELL I WON'T. I CAN'T JUST LEAVE THEM ALONE!!
CLENCH...

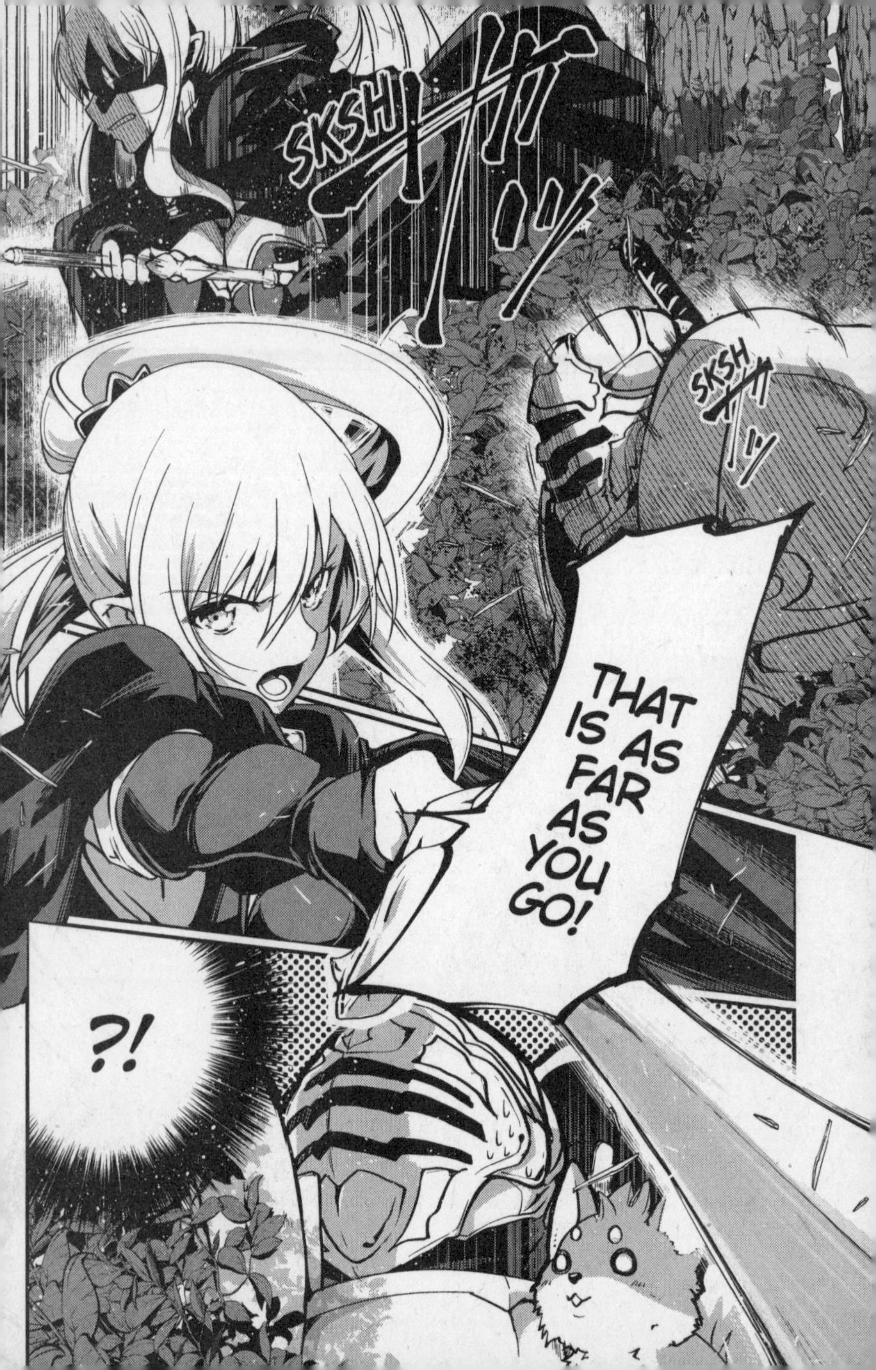
SKSH
SKSH
THAT IS AS FAR AS YOU GO!
?!

Ponta's Favorite Food

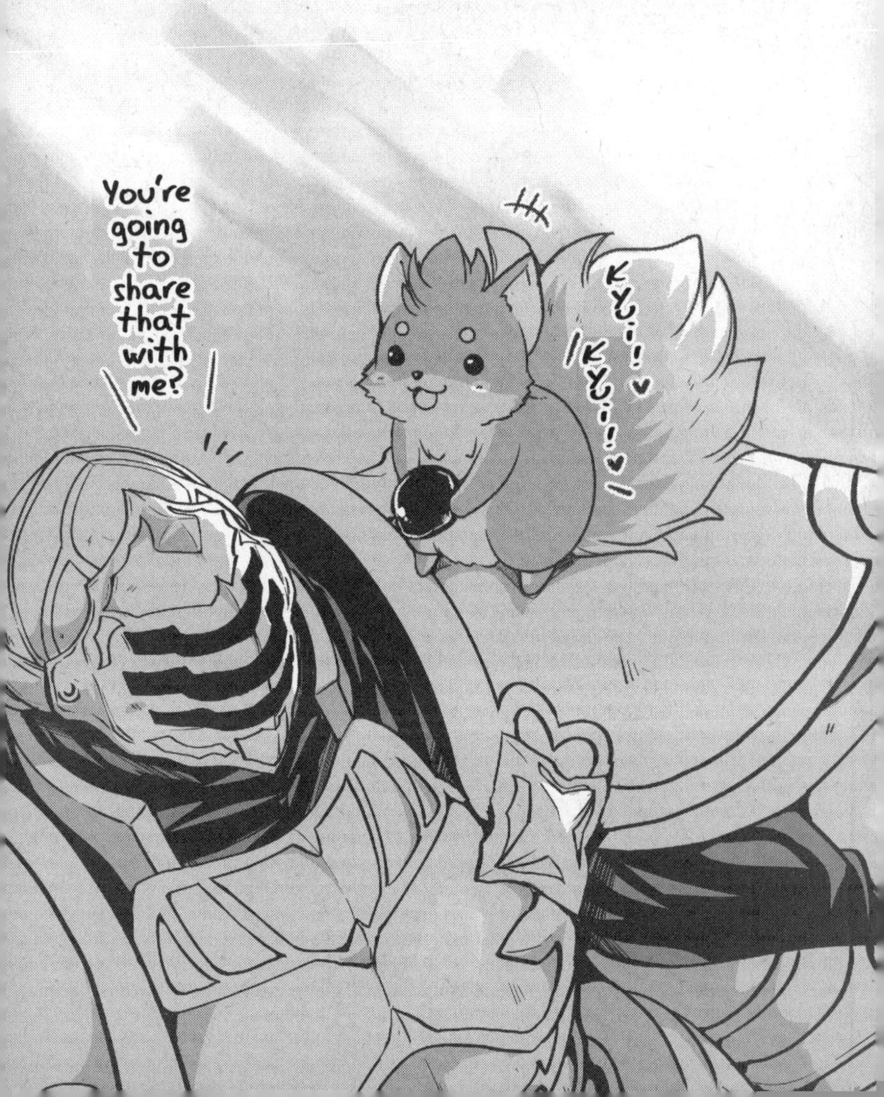

Kyu~!♥ Kyu~!♥
You're going to share that with me?

SKELETON KNIGHT IN ANOTHER WORLD

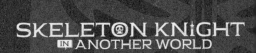

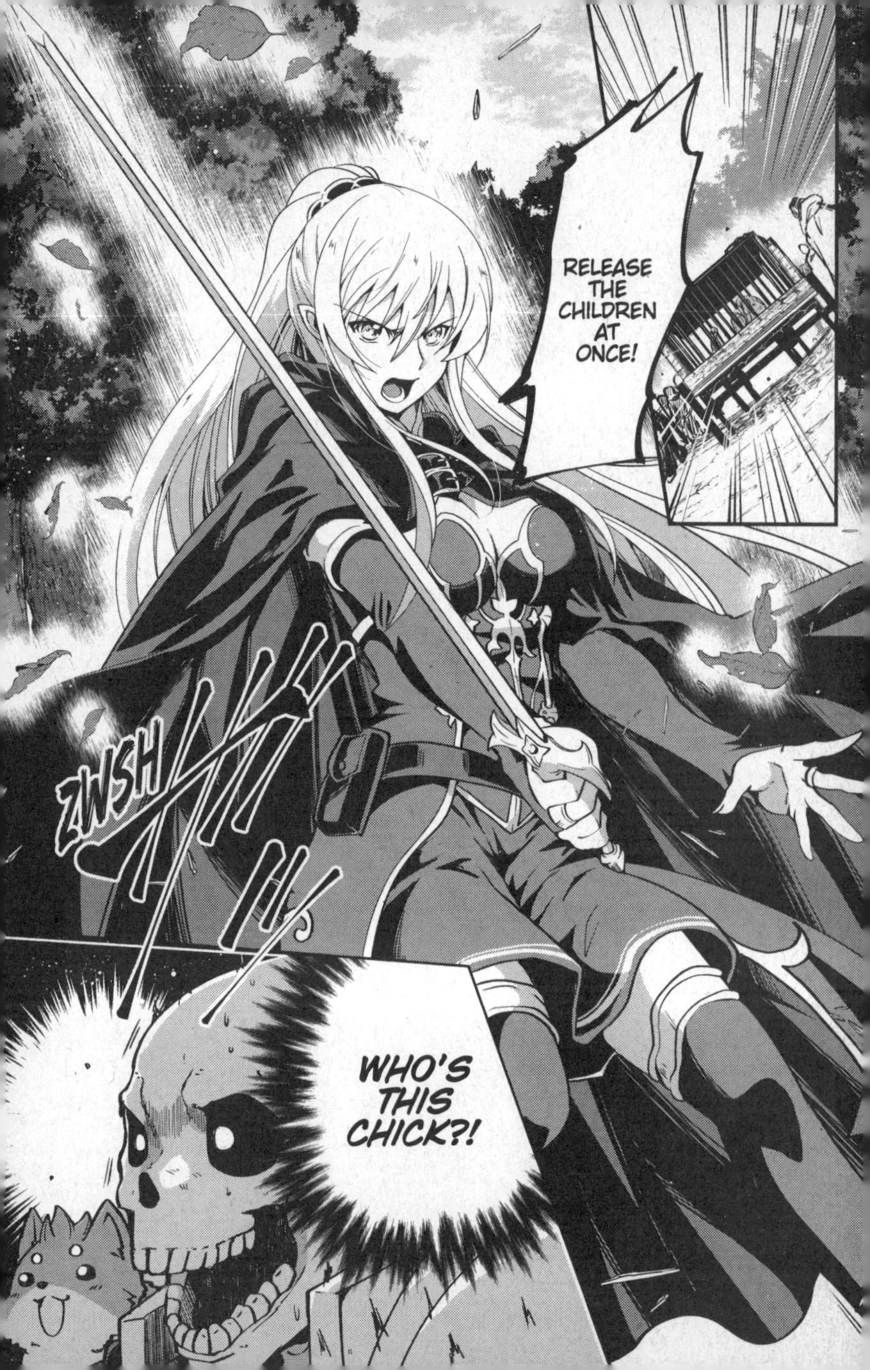
RELEASE THE CHILDREN AT ONCE!
ZWSH
WHO'S THIS CHICK?!

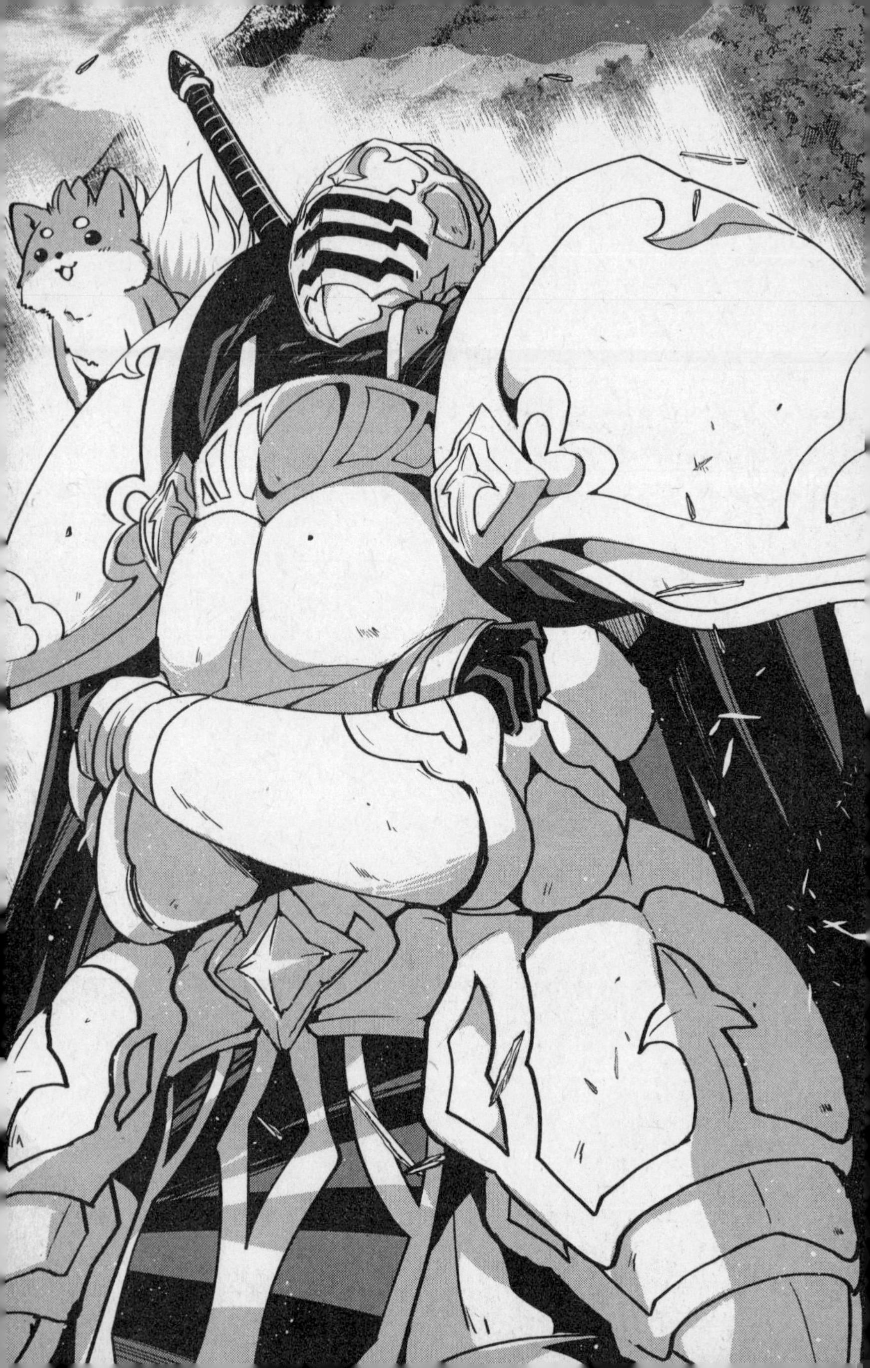

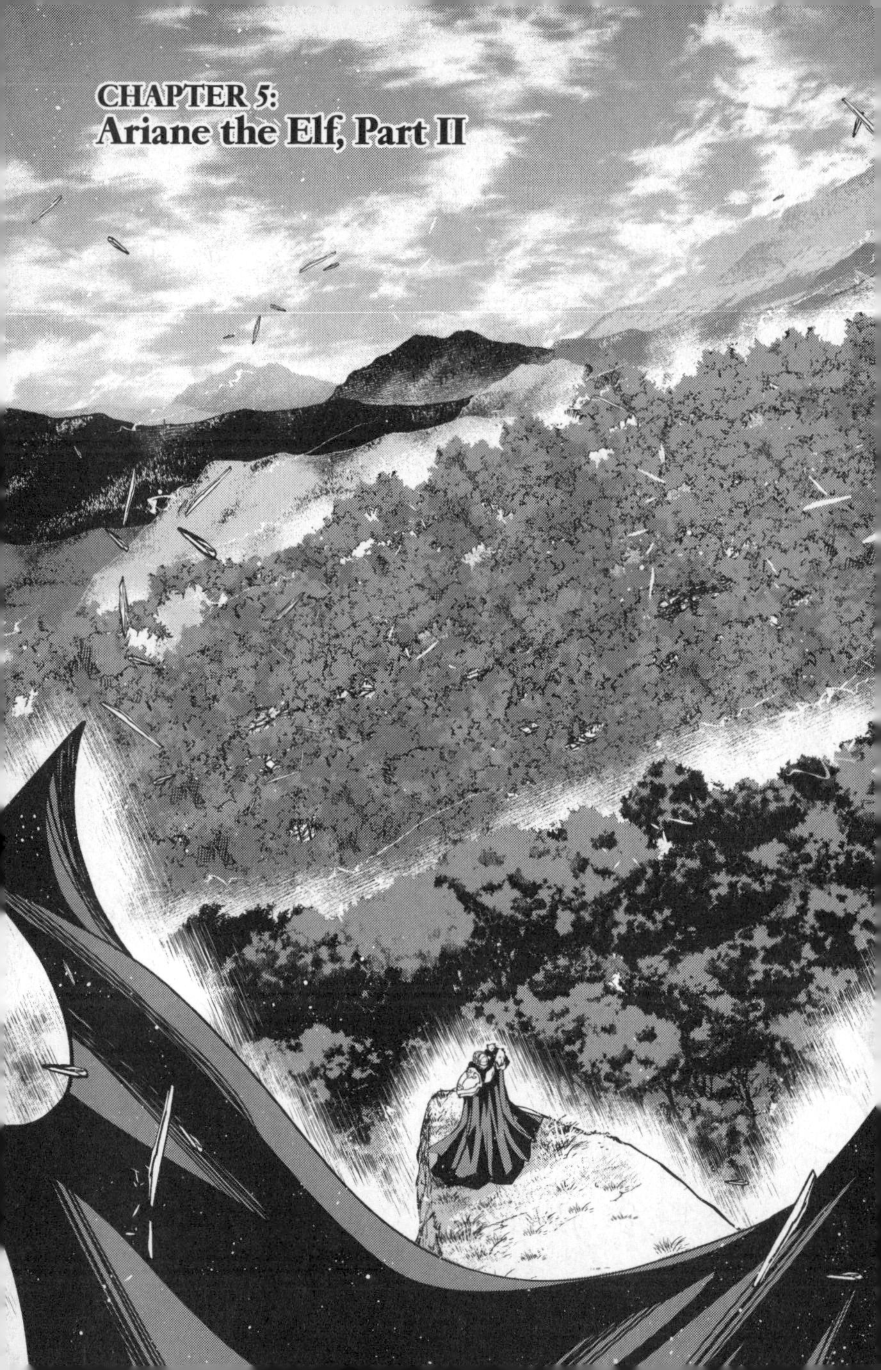
CHAPTER 5:
Ariane the Elf, Part II

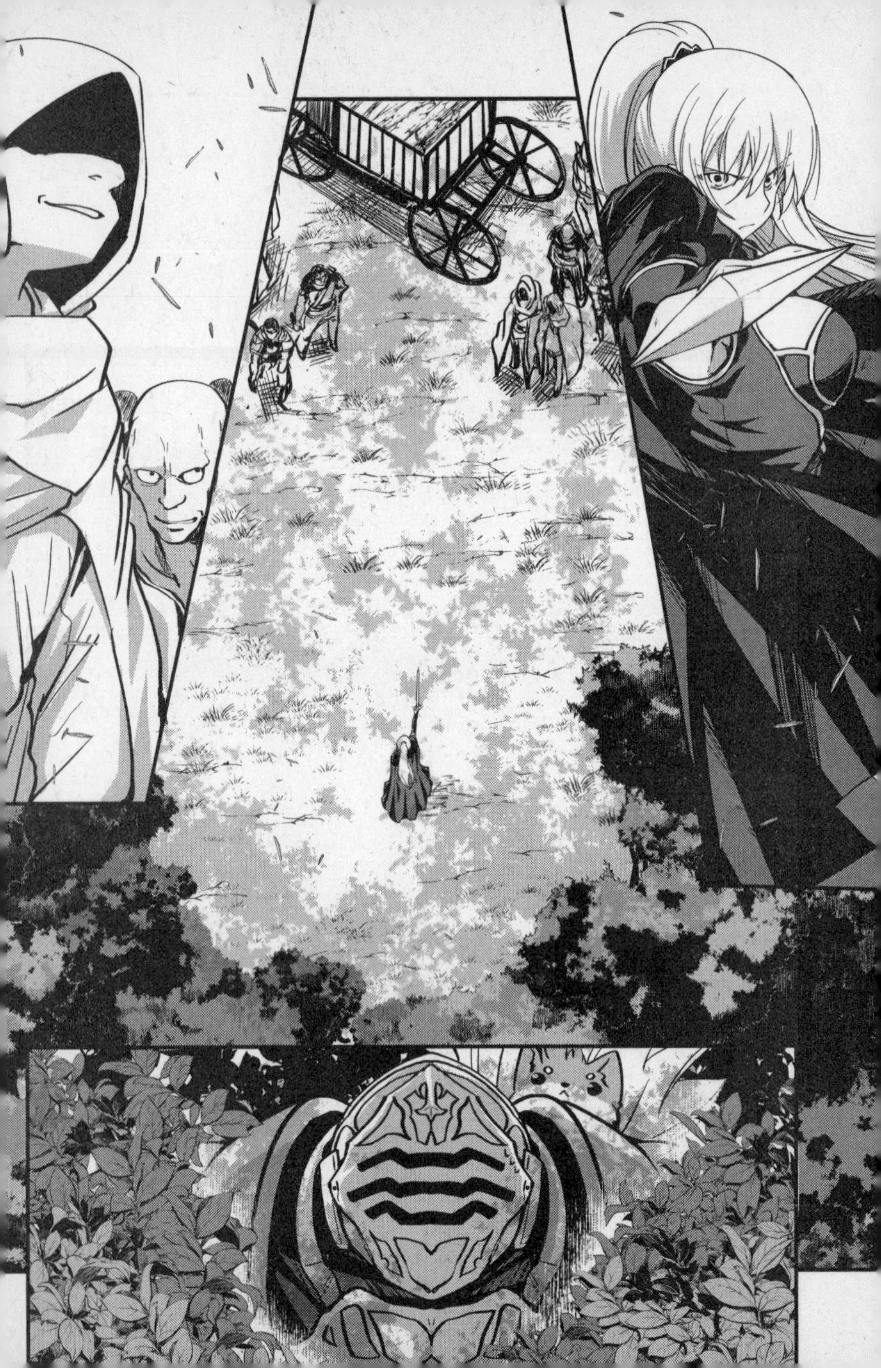

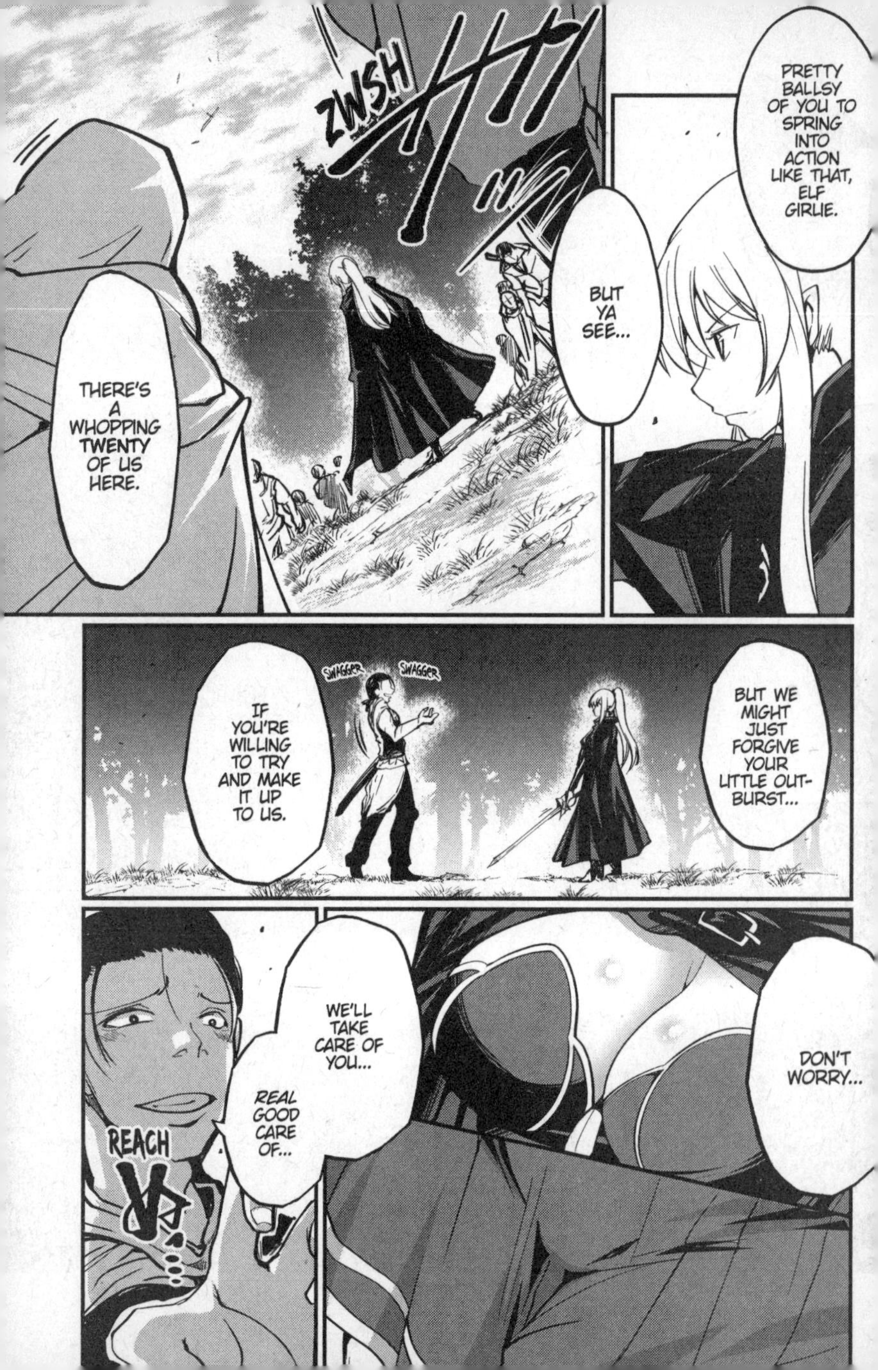
PRETTY BALLSY OF YOU TO SPRING INTO ACTION LIKE THAT, ELF GIRLIE.
BUT YA SEE...
ZWSH
THERE'S A WHOPPING TWENTY OF US HERE.
BUT WE MIGHT JUST FORGIVE YOUR LITTLE OUT-BURST...
SWAGGER
SWAGGER
IF YOU'RE WILLING TO TRY AND MAKE IT UP TO US.
DON'T WORRY...
WE'LL TAKE CARE OF YOU...
REAL GOOD CARE OF...
REACH

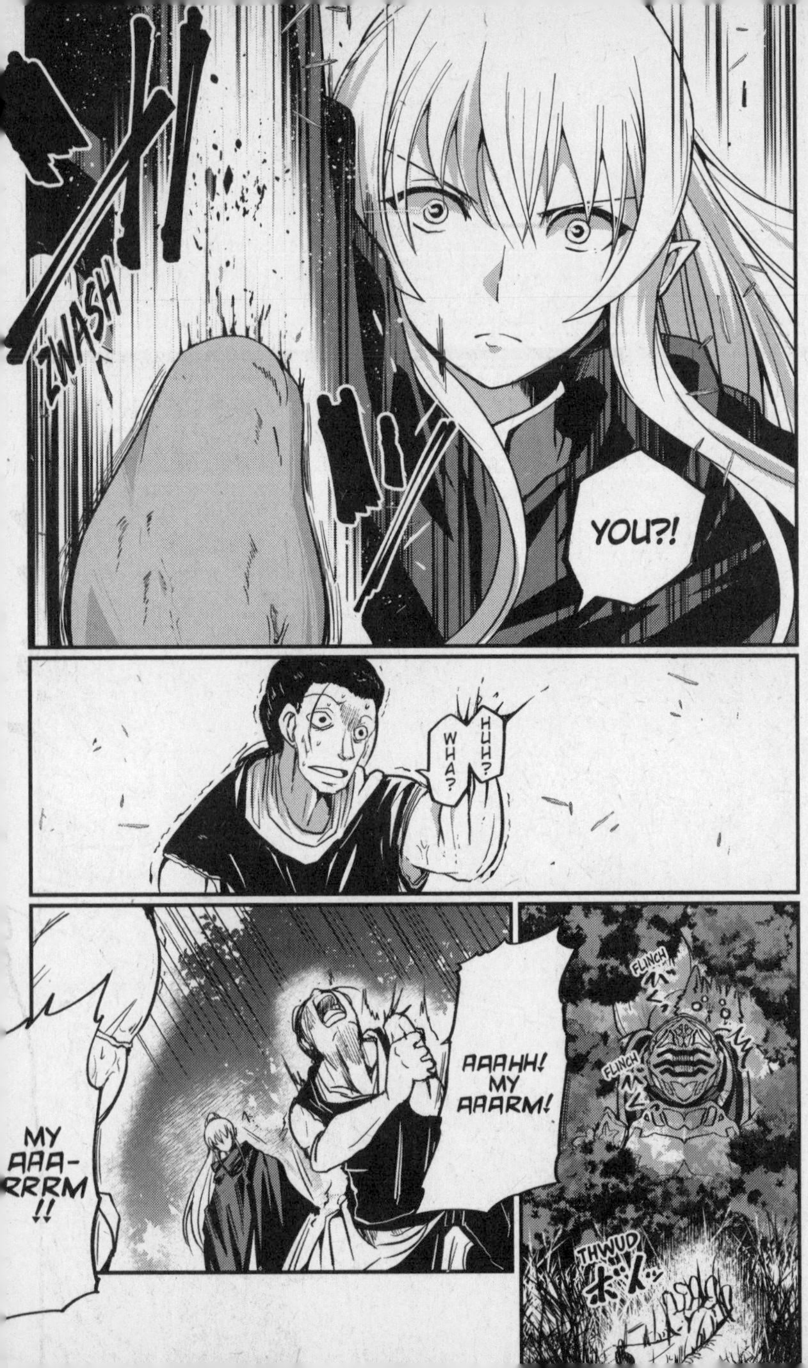
ZWASH
YOU?!
HUH?
WHA?
FLINCH
FLINCH
THWUD
AAAHH! MY AAARM!
MY AAA-RRRM!!

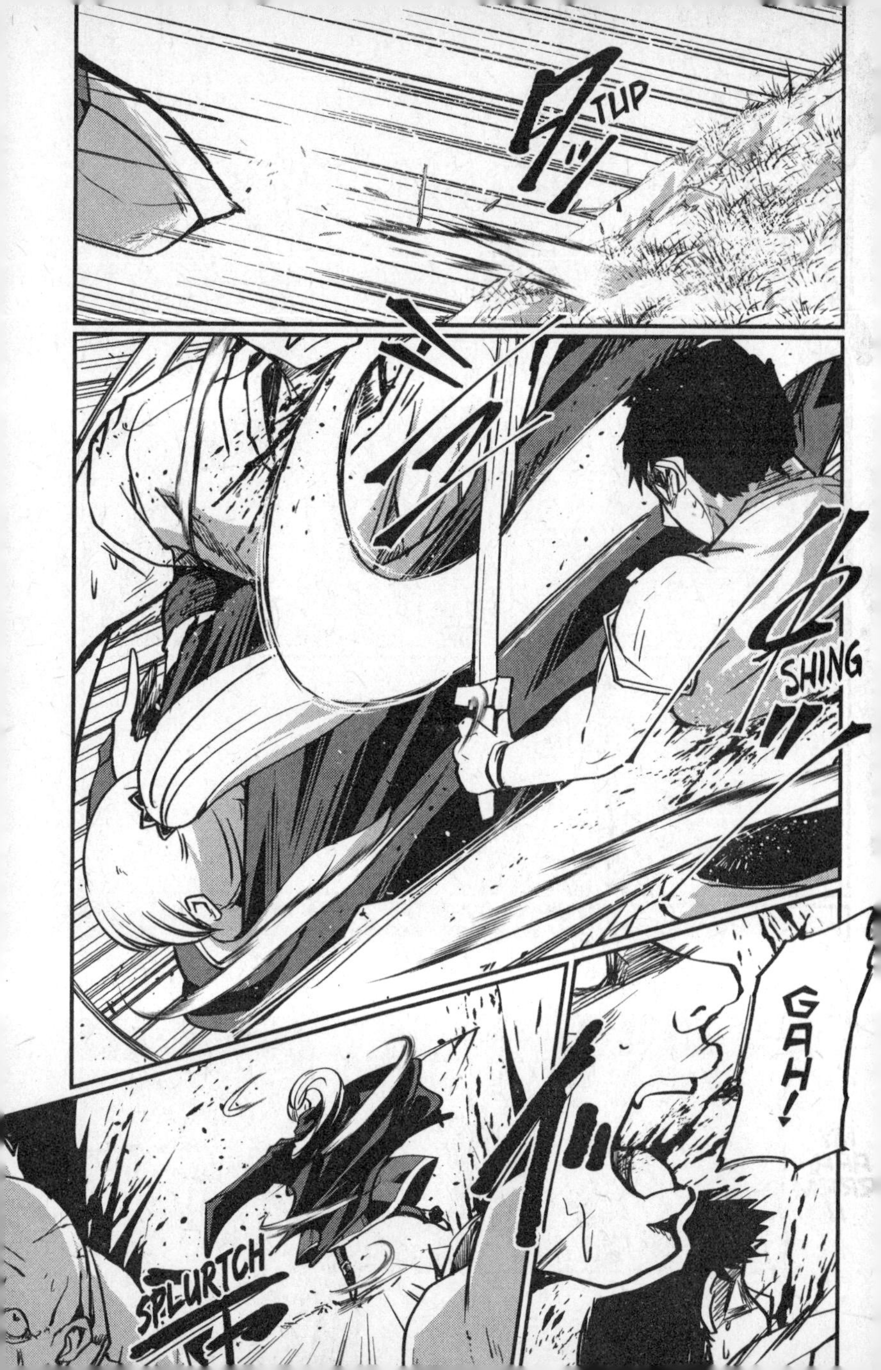
TUP
SHING
GAH!
SPLURTCH

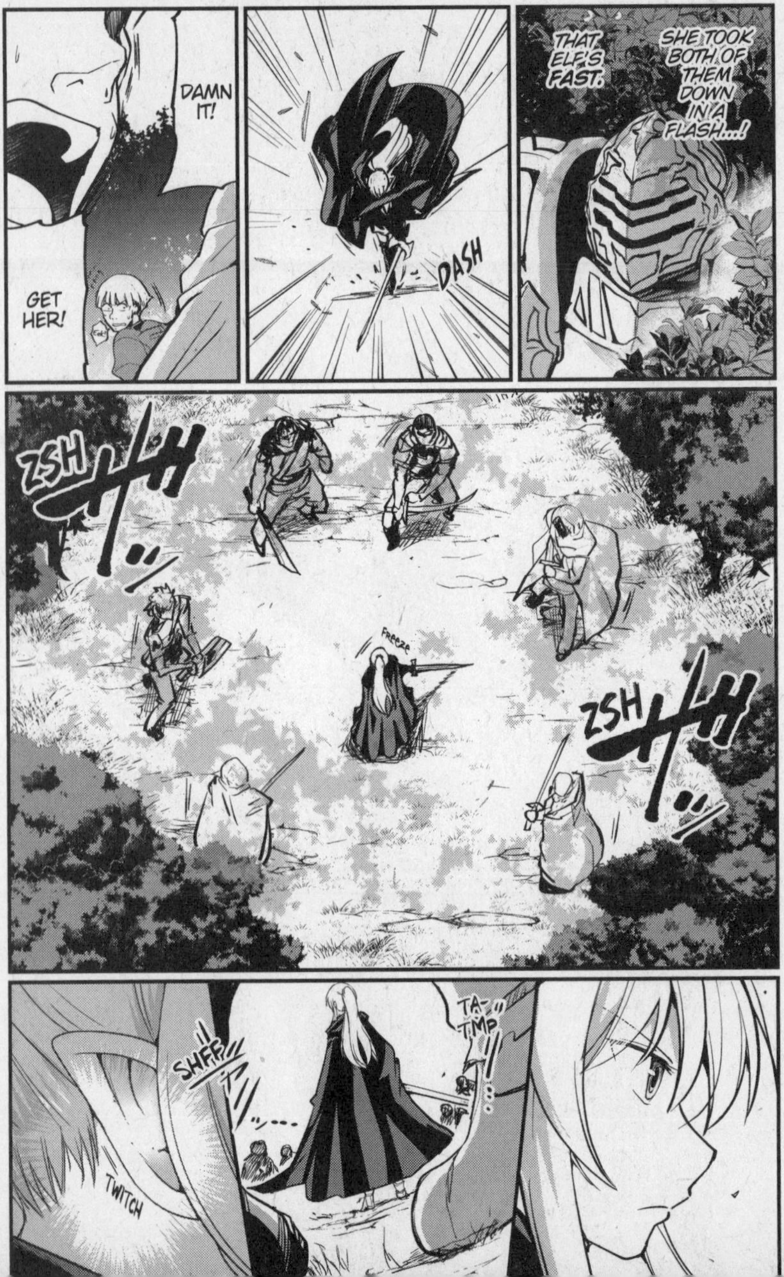
SHE TOOK BOTH OF THEM DOWN IN A FLASH...!
THAT ELF'S FAST.
DASH
DAMN IT!
GET HER!
ZSHHH!!
Freeze
ZSHHH!!
TA-TMP!!...
SHFF!
...
TWITCH

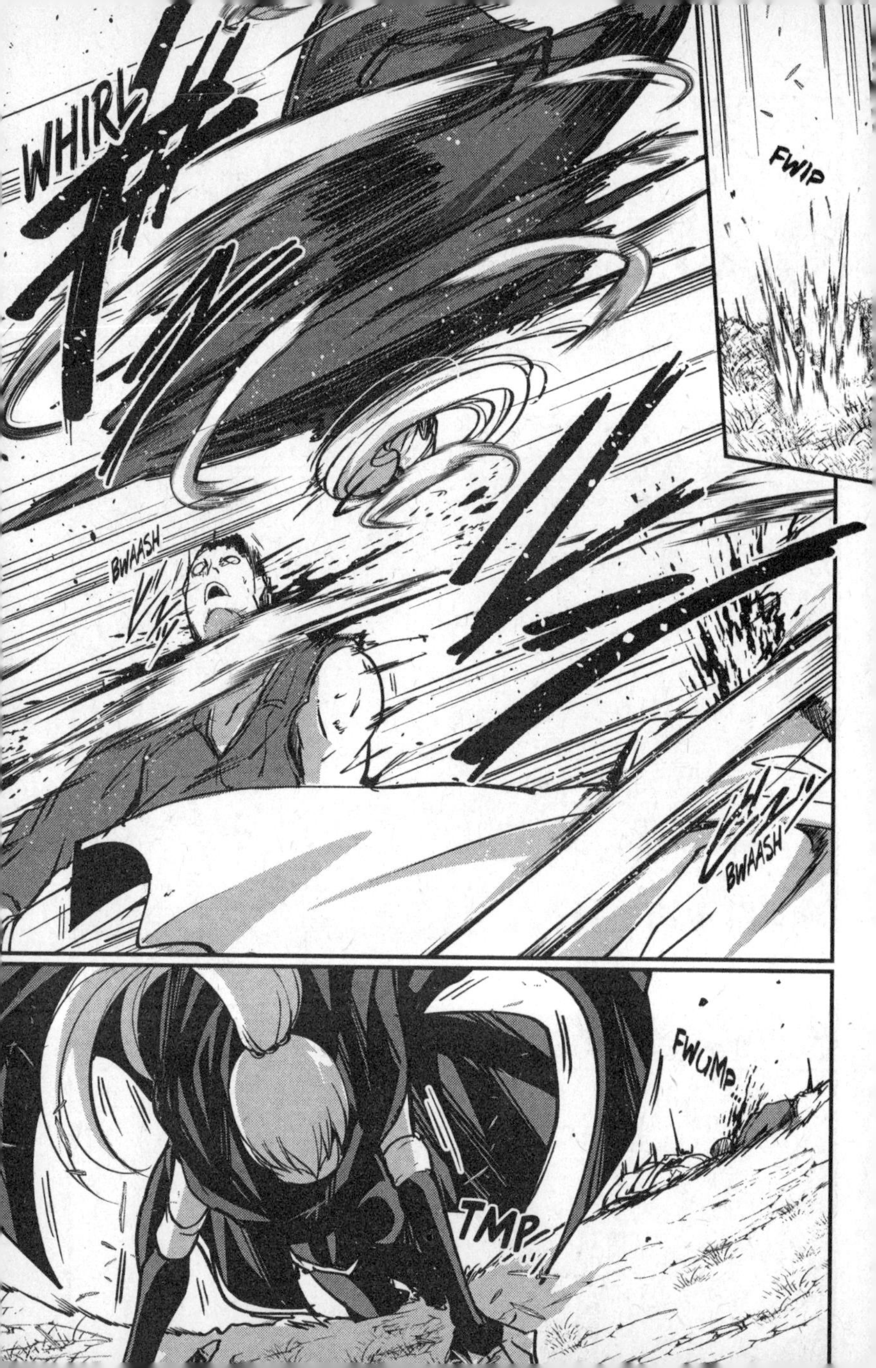
FWIP
WHIRL
BWAASH
BWAASH
FWUMP
TMP

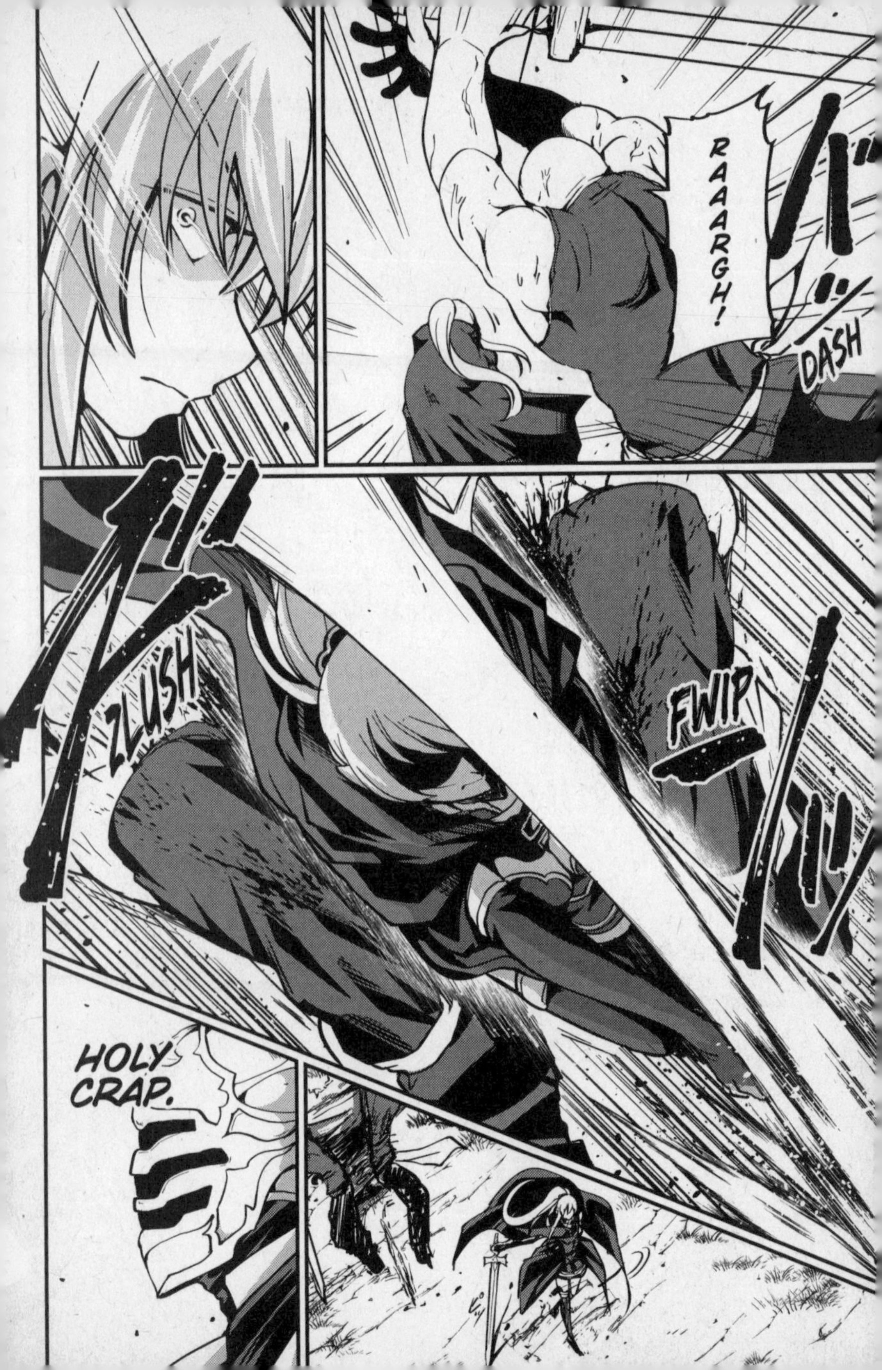
RAAAARGH!
DASH
FWIP
ZLUSH
HOLY CRAP.

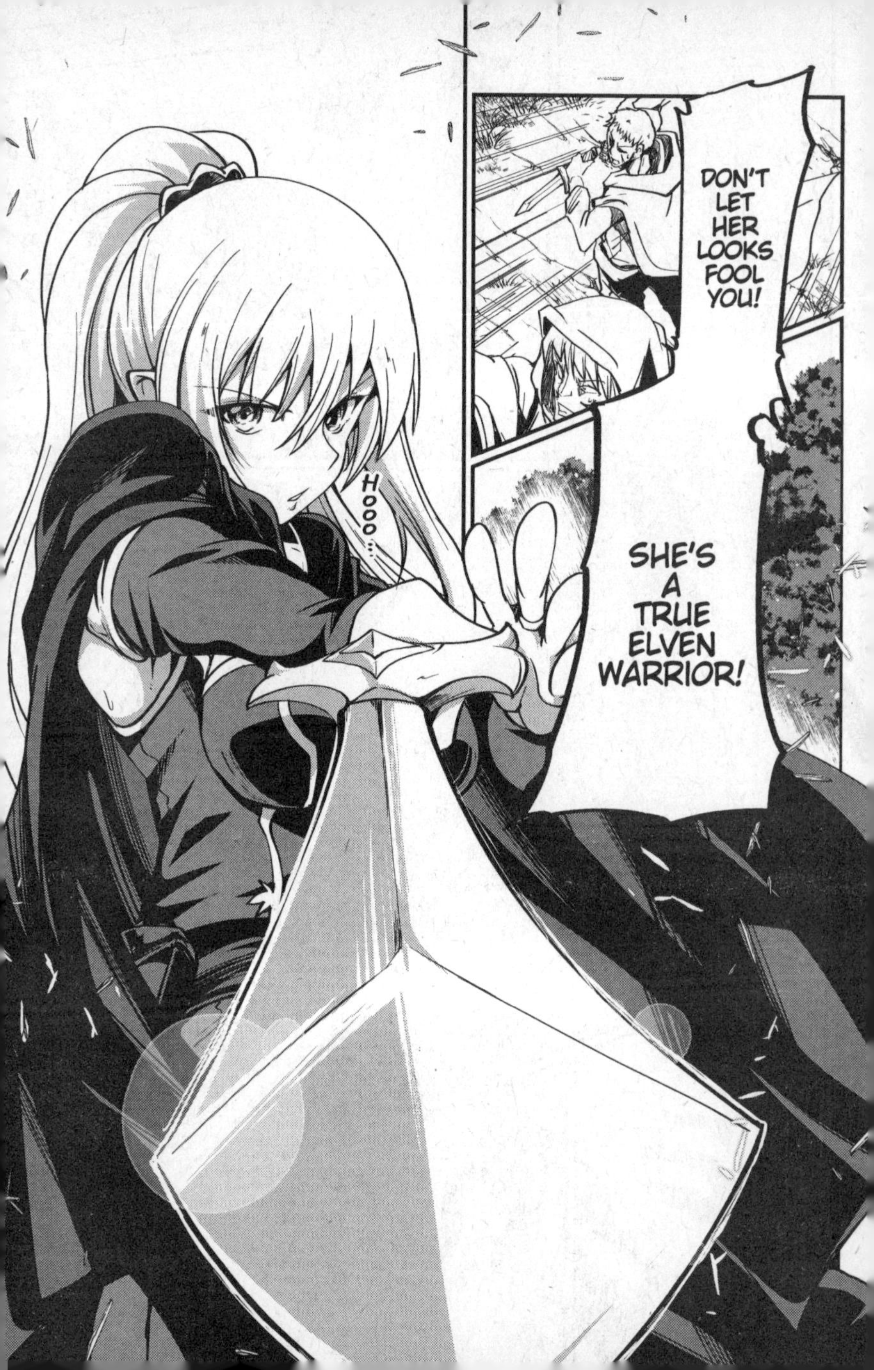
DON'T LET HER LOOKS FOOL YOU!
SHE'S A TRUE ELVEN WARRIOR!
Hooo...

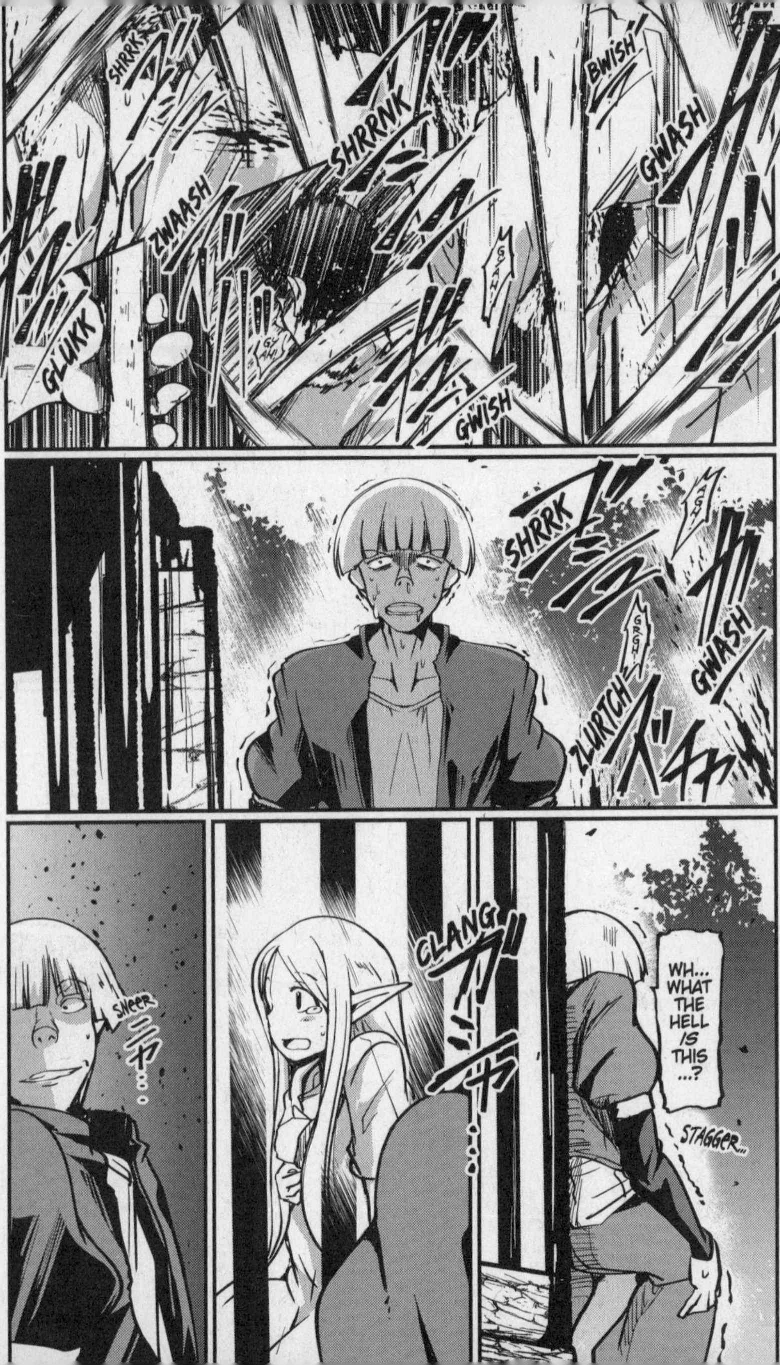
BWISH
GWASH
GYAH!
SHRRNK
SHRRK
ZWAASH
GWISH
GYAH!
GLUKK
AGH!
SHRRK
GWASH
GRGH!
ZLURTCH
WH... WHAT THE HELL IS THIS ...?
STAGGER...
CLANG
SNEER

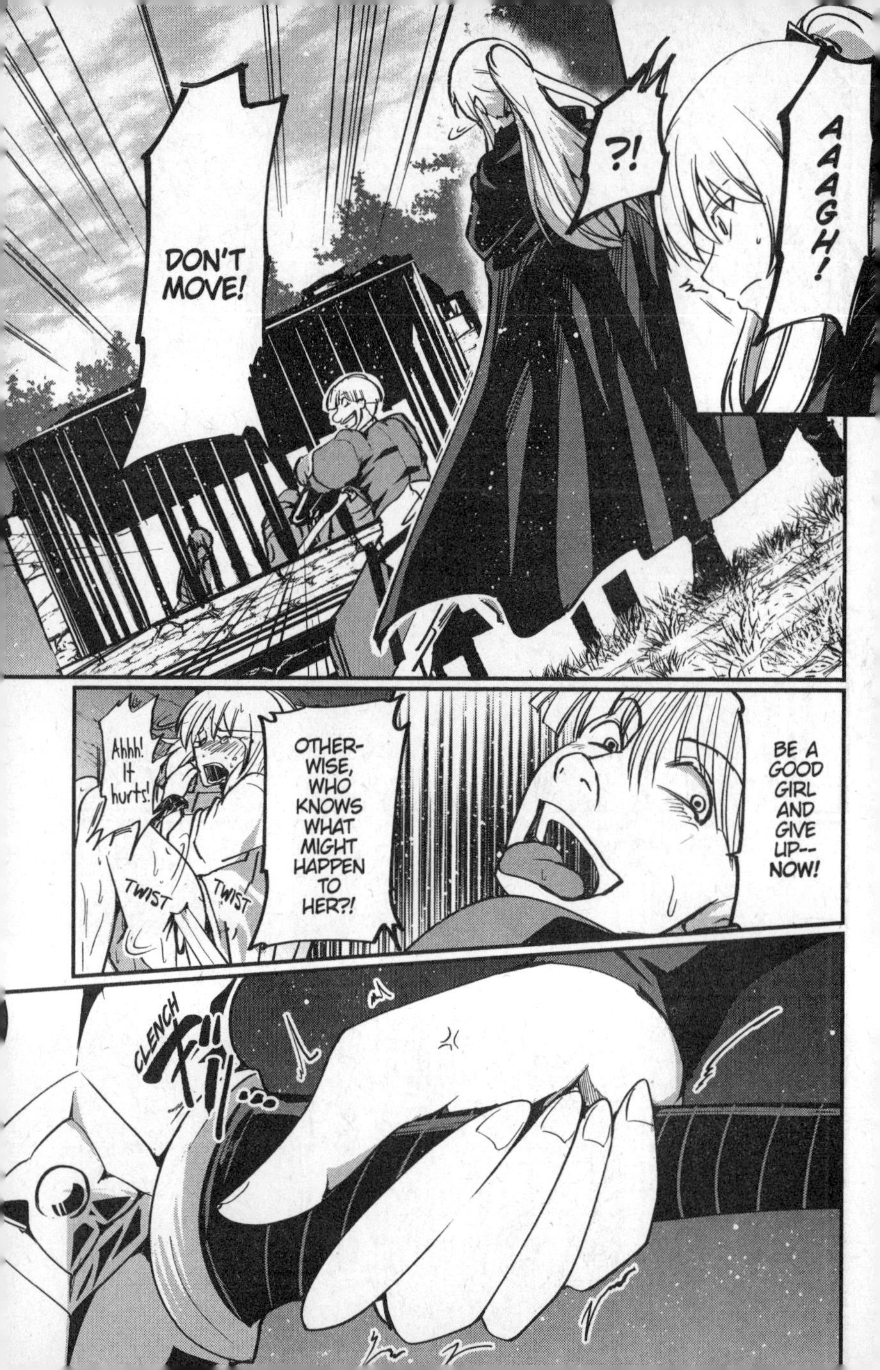
AAAAGH!
?!
DON'T MOVE!
BE A GOOD GIRL AND GIVE UP-- NOW!
OTHER-WISE, WHO KNOWS WHAT MIGHT HAPPEN TO HER?!
Ahhh! It hurts!
TWIST
TWIST
CLENCH

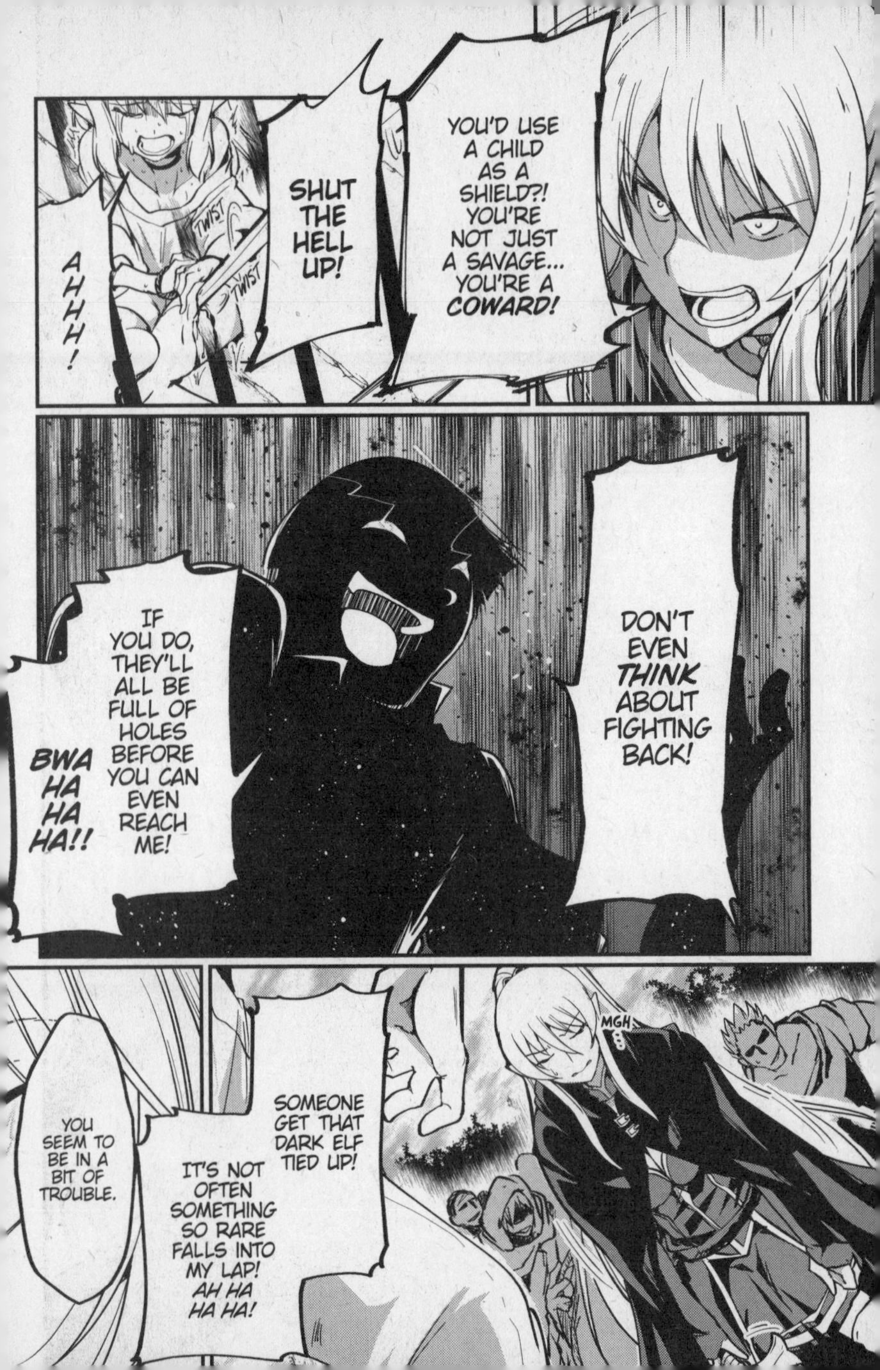
YOU'D USE A CHILD AS A SHIELD?! YOU'RE NOT JUST A SAVAGE... YOU'RE A COWARD!
SHUT THE HELL UP!
TWIST
TWIST
AHHHH!
DON'T EVEN THINK ABOUT FIGHTING BACK!
IF YOU DO, THEY'LL ALL BE FULL OF HOLES BEFORE YOU CAN EVEN REACH ME!
BWA HA HA HA!!
MGH
SOMEONE GET THAT DARK ELF TIED UP!
IT'S NOT OFTEN SOMETHING SO RARE FALLS INTO MY LAP! AH HA HA HA!
YOU SEEM TO BE IN A BIT OF TROUBLE.

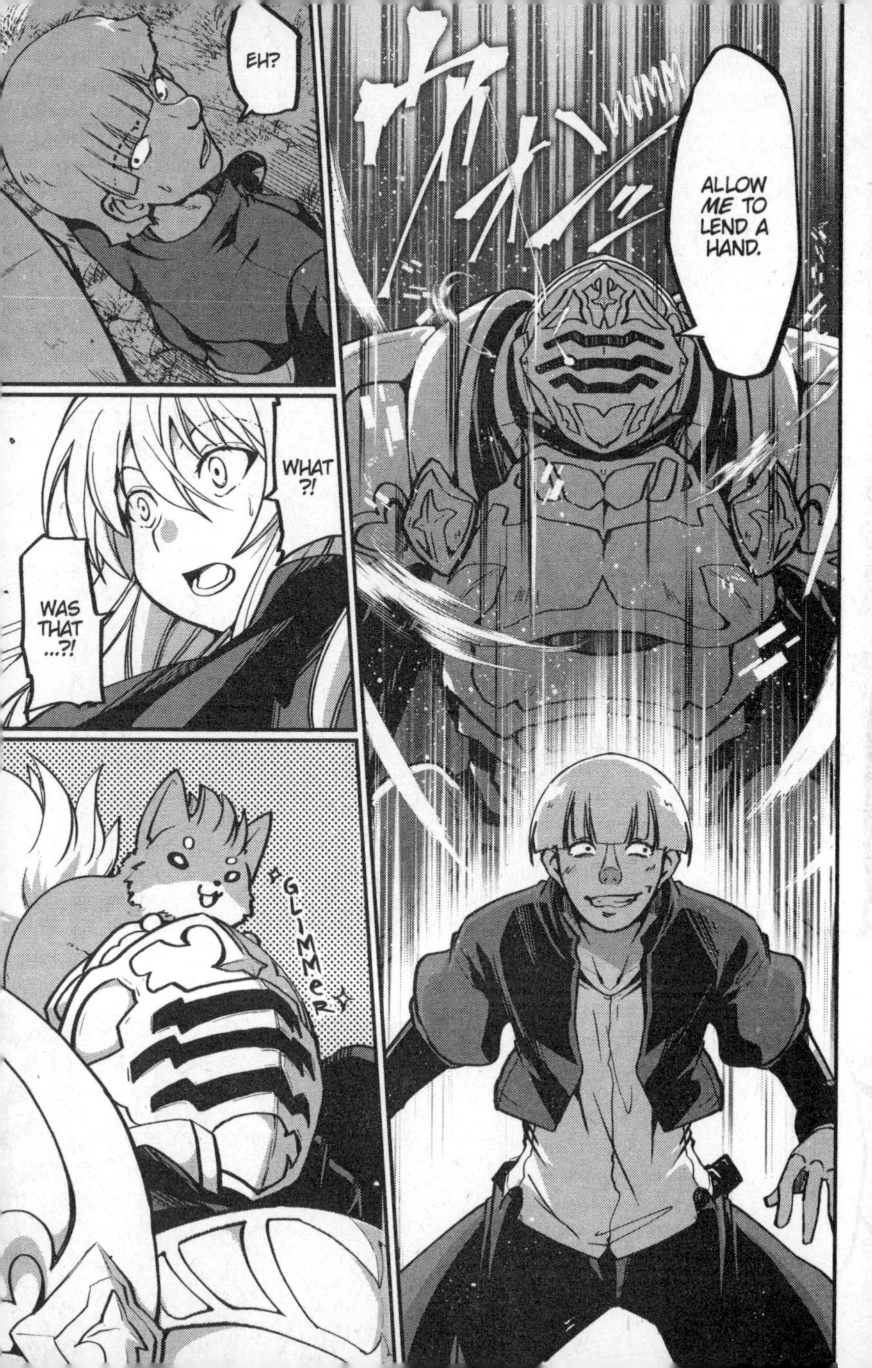
VWMM
ALLOW ME TO LEND A HAND.
EH?
WHAT?!
WAS THAT ...?!
GLIMMER

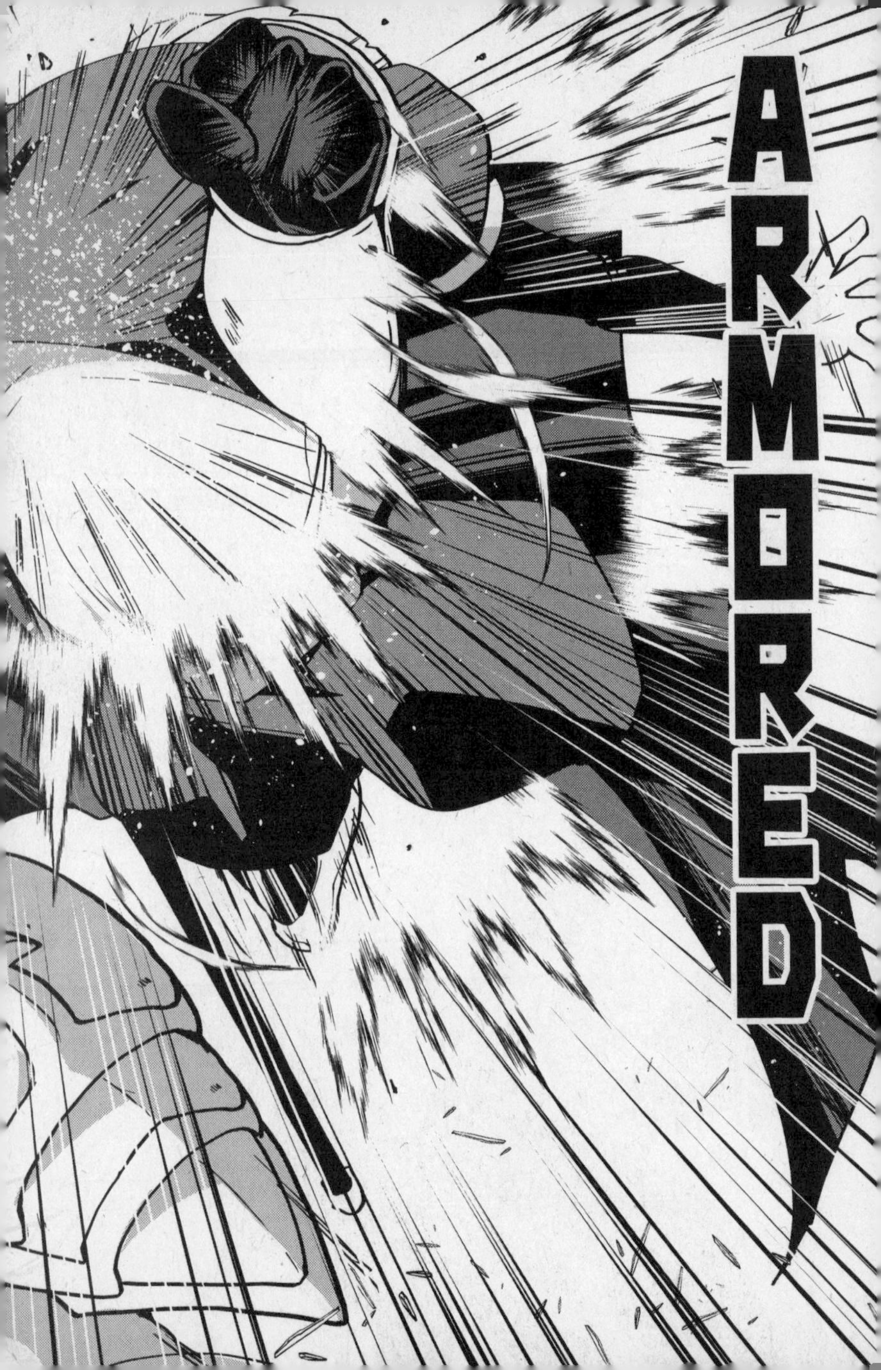
ARMORED

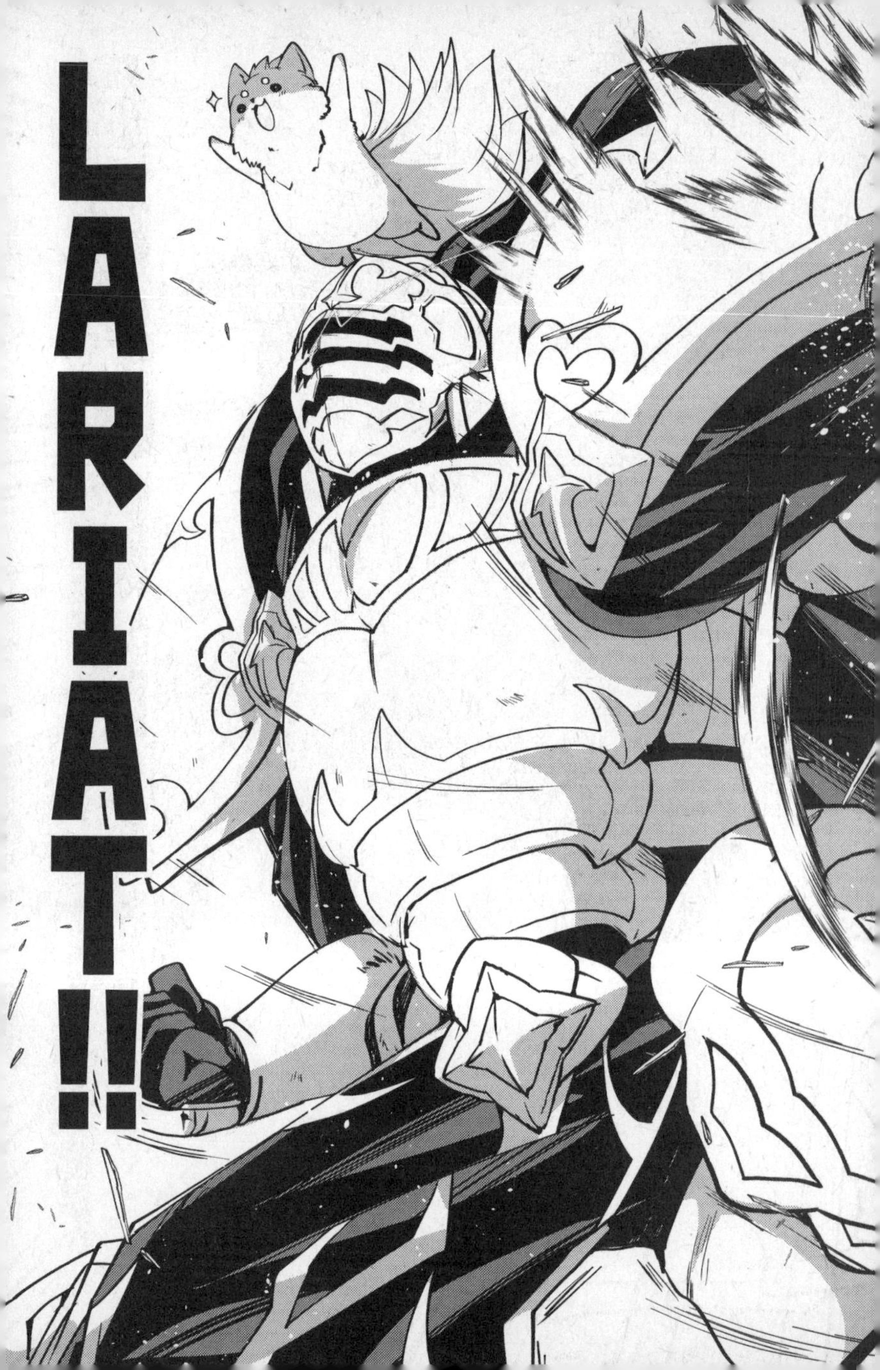
LARIAT!!

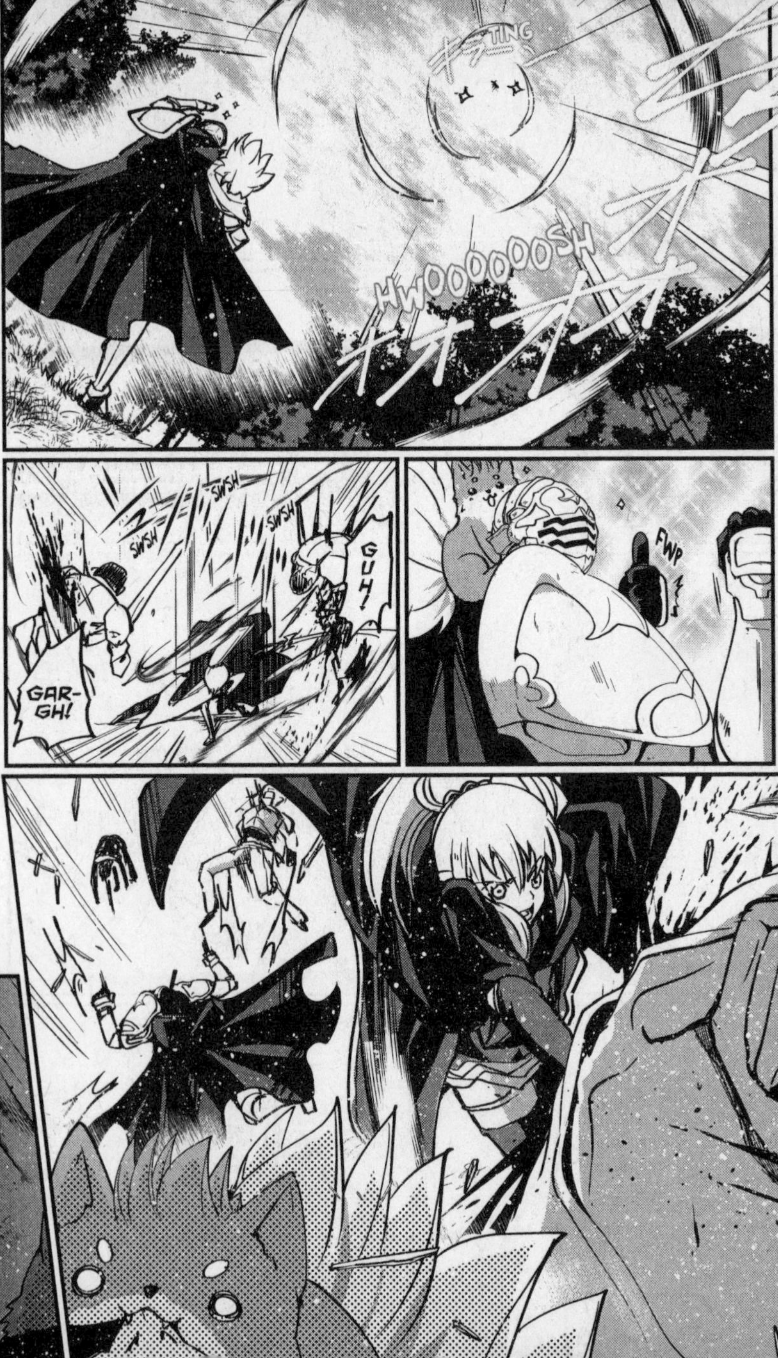
TING
HWOOOOOOSH
FWP
SWSH
SWSH
SWSH
GUH!
GAR-GH!

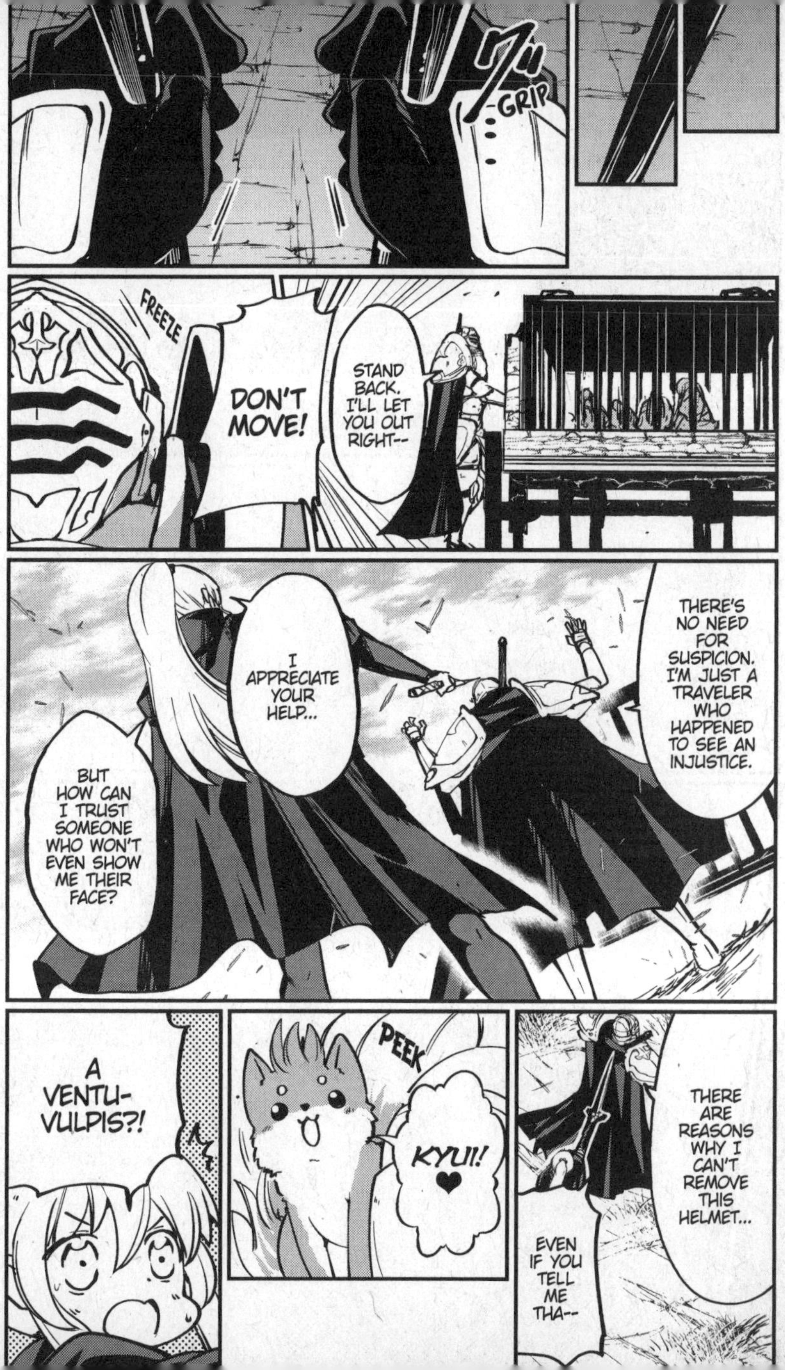
ZU
GRIP
STAND BACK. I'LL LET YOU OUT RIGHT--
FREEZE
DON'T MOVE!
THERE'S NO NEED FOR SUSPICION. I'M JUST A TRAVELER WHO HAPPENED TO SEE AN INJUSTICE.
I APPRECIATE YOUR HELP...
BUT HOW CAN I TRUST SOMEONE WHO WON'T EVEN SHOW ME THEIR FACE?
THERE ARE REASONS WHY I CAN'T REMOVE THIS HELMET...
EVEN IF YOU TELL ME THA--
PEEK
KYUI! ♥
A VENTU-VULPIS?!

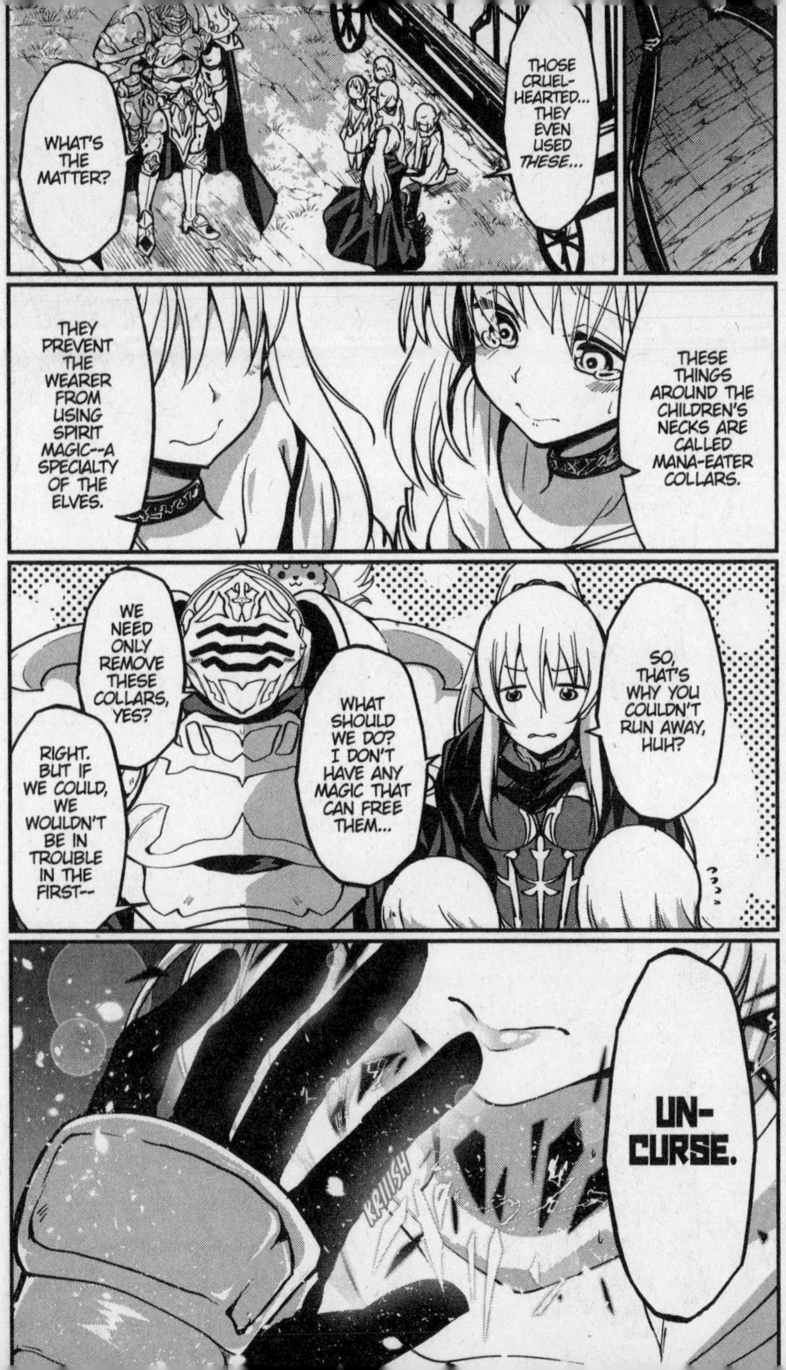
THOSE CRUEL-HEARTED... THEY EVEN USED *THESE*...
WHAT'S THE MATTER?
THESE THINGS AROUND THE CHILDREN'S NECKS ARE CALLED MANA-EATER COLLARS.
THEY PREVENT THE WEARER FROM USING SPIRIT MAGIC--A SPECIALTY OF THE ELVES.
SO, THAT'S WHY YOU COULDN'T RUN AWAY, HUH?
WHAT SHOULD WE DO? I DON'T HAVE ANY MAGIC THAT CAN FREE THEM...
WE NEED ONLY REMOVE THESE COLLARS, YES?
RIGHT. BUT IF WE COULD, WE WOULDN'T BE IN TROUBLE IN THE FIRST--
UN-CURSE.
KRIISH

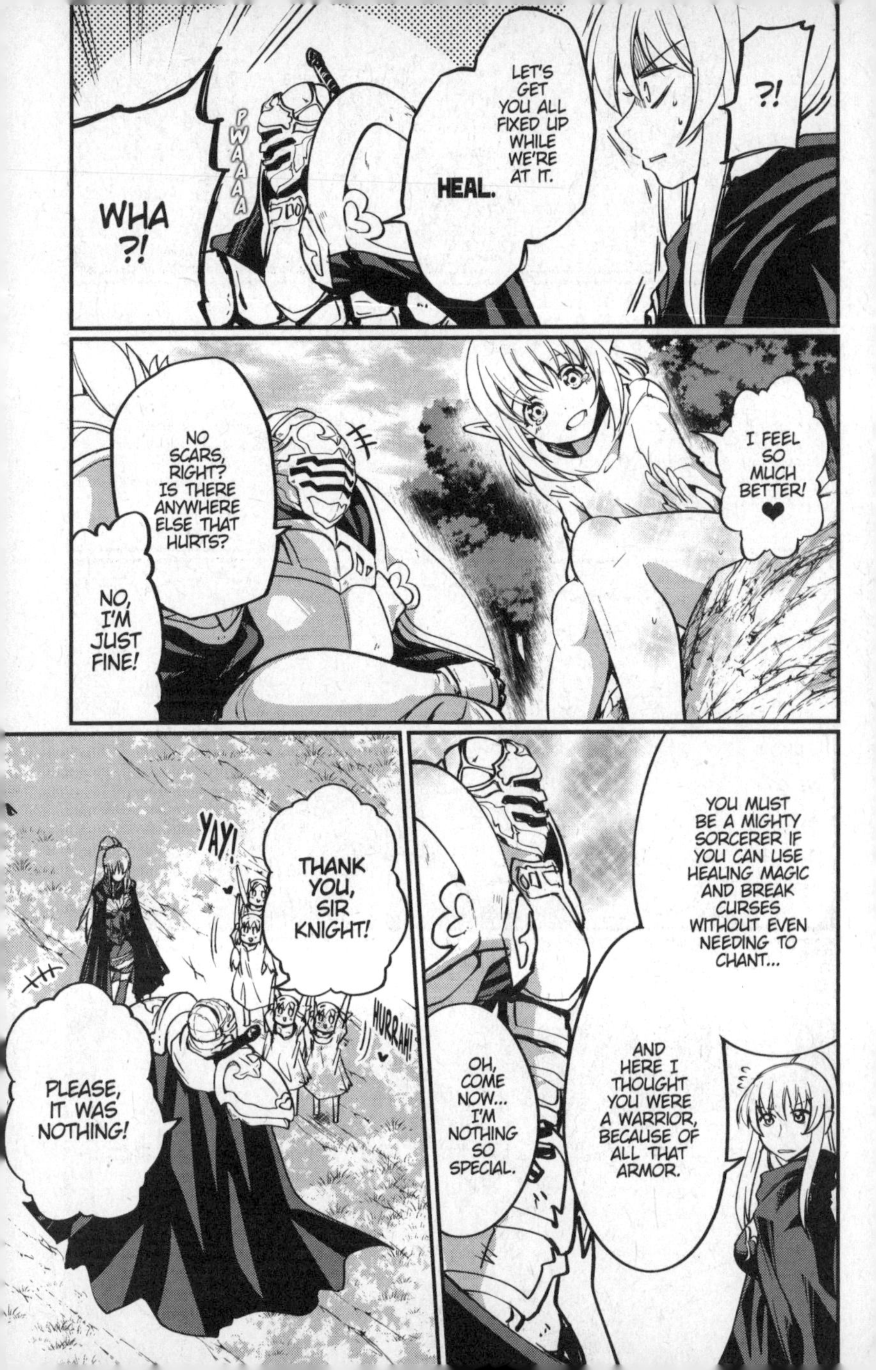
?!
LET'S GET YOU ALL FIXED UP WHILE WE'RE AT IT.
HEAL.
PWAAAA
WHA ?!
I FEEL SO MUCH BETTER! ❤
NO SCARS, RIGHT? IS THERE ANYWHERE ELSE THAT HURTS?
NO, I'M JUST FINE!
YOU MUST BE A MIGHTY SORCERER IF YOU CAN USE HEALING MAGIC AND BREAK CURSES WITHOUT EVEN NEEDING TO CHANT...
AND HERE I THOUGHT YOU WERE A WARRIOR, BECAUSE OF ALL THAT ARMOR.
OH, COME NOW... I'M NOTHING SO SPECIAL.
YAY!
THANK YOU, SIR KNIGHT!
HURRAH!
PLEASE, IT WAS NOTHING!

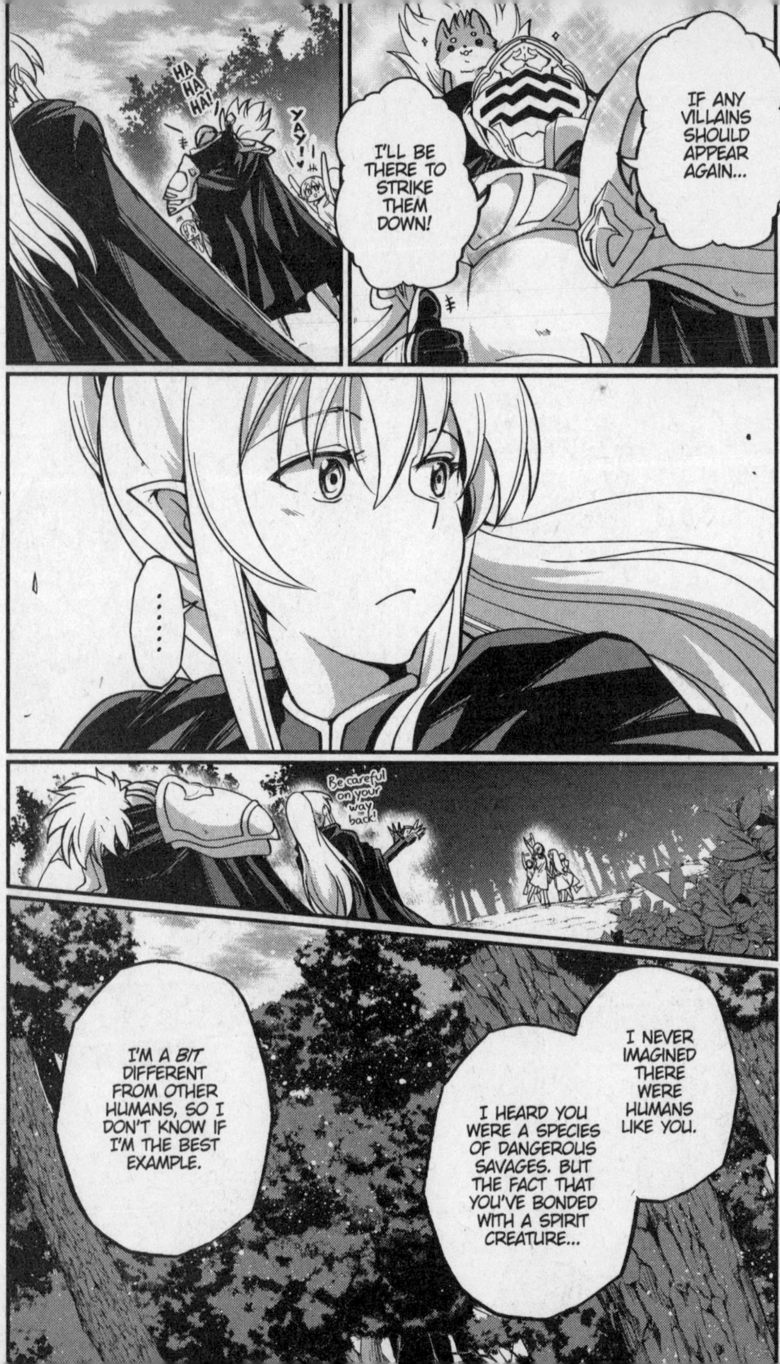
IF ANY VILLAINS SHOULD APPEAR AGAIN...
I'LL BE THERE TO STRIKE THEM DOWN!
HA HA HA!
YAY!
......
Be careful on your way back!
I NEVER IMAGINED THERE WERE HUMANS LIKE YOU.
I HEARD YOU WERE A SPECIES OF DANGEROUS SAVAGES. BUT THE FACT THAT YOU'VE BONDED WITH A SPIRIT CREATURE...
I'M A *BIT* DIFFERENT FROM OTHER HUMANS, SO I DON'T KNOW IF I'M THE BEST EXAMPLE.

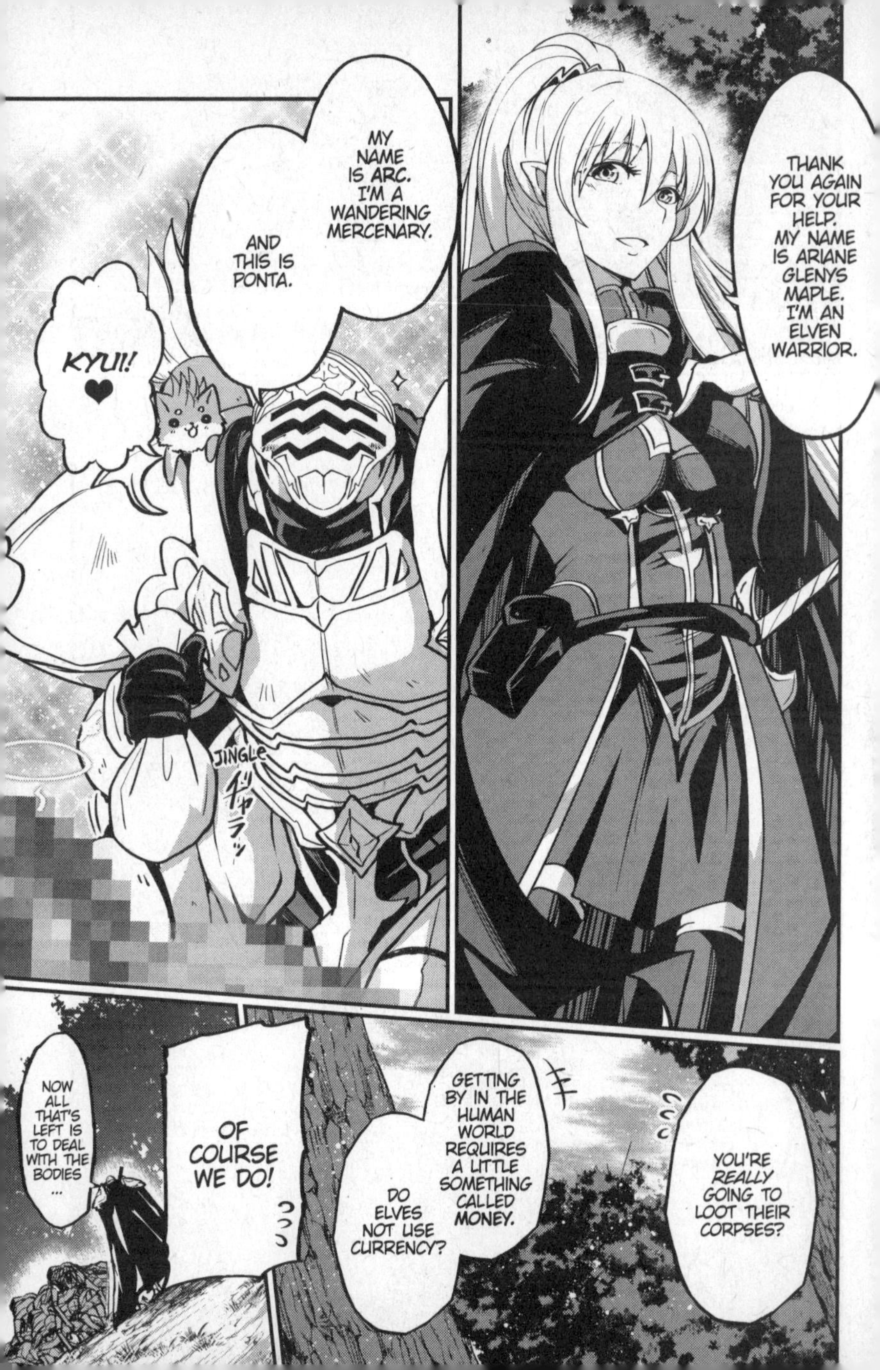
THANK YOU AGAIN FOR YOUR HELP. MY NAME IS ARIANE GLENYS MAPLE. I'M AN ELVEN WARRIOR.
MY NAME IS ARC. I'M A WANDERING MERCENARY.
AND THIS IS PONTA.
KYUI! ❤
JINGLE
YOU'RE *REALLY* GOING TO LOOT THEIR CORPSES?
GETTING BY IN THE HUMAN WORLD REQUIRES A LITTLE SOMETHING CALLED MONEY.
DO ELVES NOT USE CURRENCY?
OF COURSE WE DO!
NOW ALL THAT'S LEFT IS TO DEAL WITH THE BODIES ...

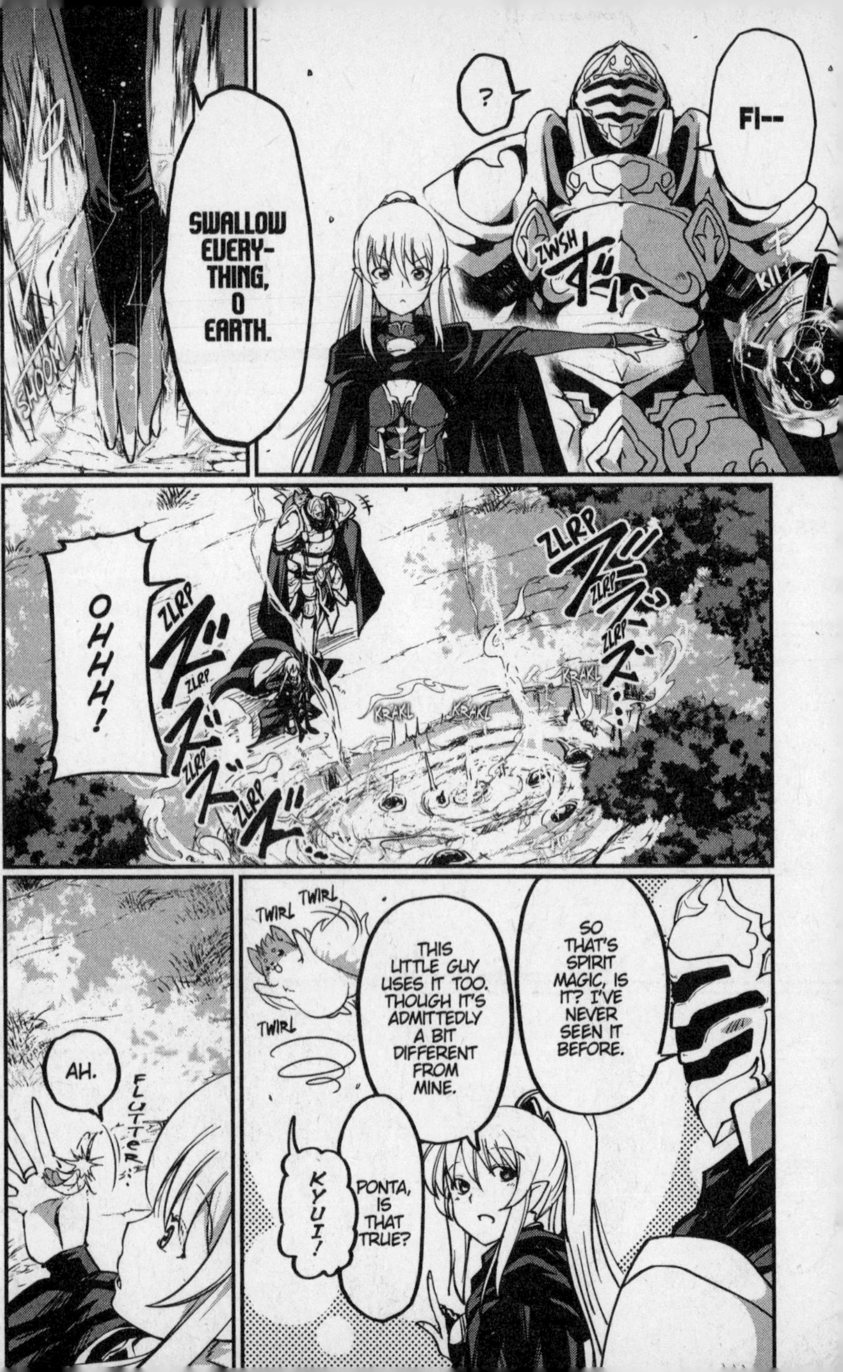
FI--
?
ZWSH
KII
SWALLOW EVERY-THING, O EARTH.
SHOOM
ZLRP
ZLRP
ZLRP
KRAKL
KRAKL
KRAKL
OHHH!
ZLRP
ZLRP
ZLRP
ZLRP
SO THAT'S SPIRIT MAGIC, IS IT? I'VE NEVER SEEN IT BEFORE.
THIS LITTLE GUY USES IT TOO. THOUGH IT'S ADMITTEDLY A BIT DIFFERENT FROM MINE.
TWIRL
TWIRL
TWIRL
PONTA, IS THAT TRUE?
KYUI!
AH.
FLUTTER...

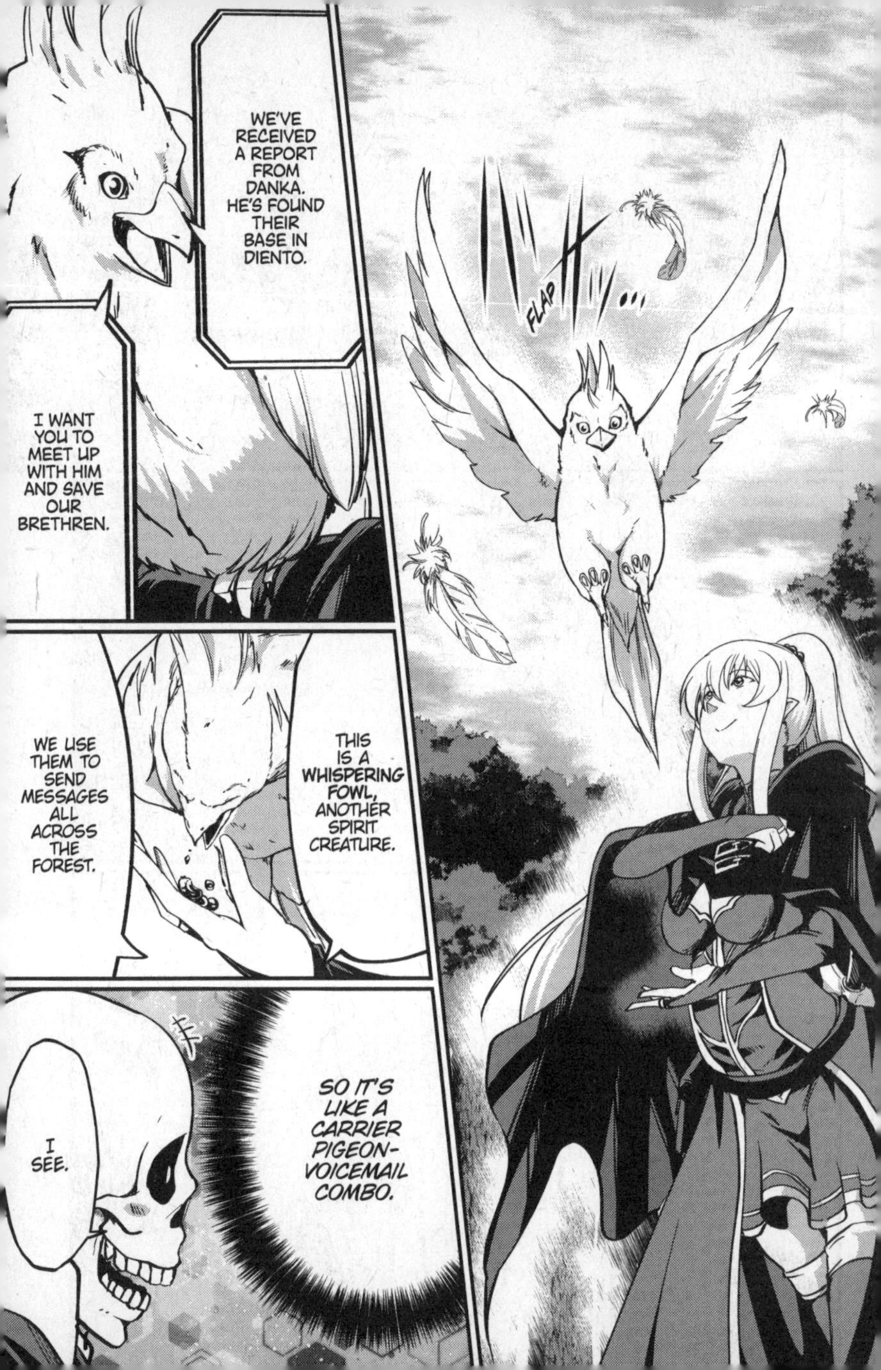
FLAP
WE'VE RECEIVED A REPORT FROM DANKA. HE'S FOUND THEIR BASE IN DIENTO.
I WANT YOU TO MEET UP WITH HIM AND SAVE OUR BRETHREN.
THIS IS A WHISPERING FOWL, ANOTHER SPIRIT CREATURE.
WE USE THEM TO SEND MESSAGES ALL ACROSS THE FOREST.
SO IT'S LIKE A CARRIER PIGEON-VOICEMAIL COMBO.
I SEE.

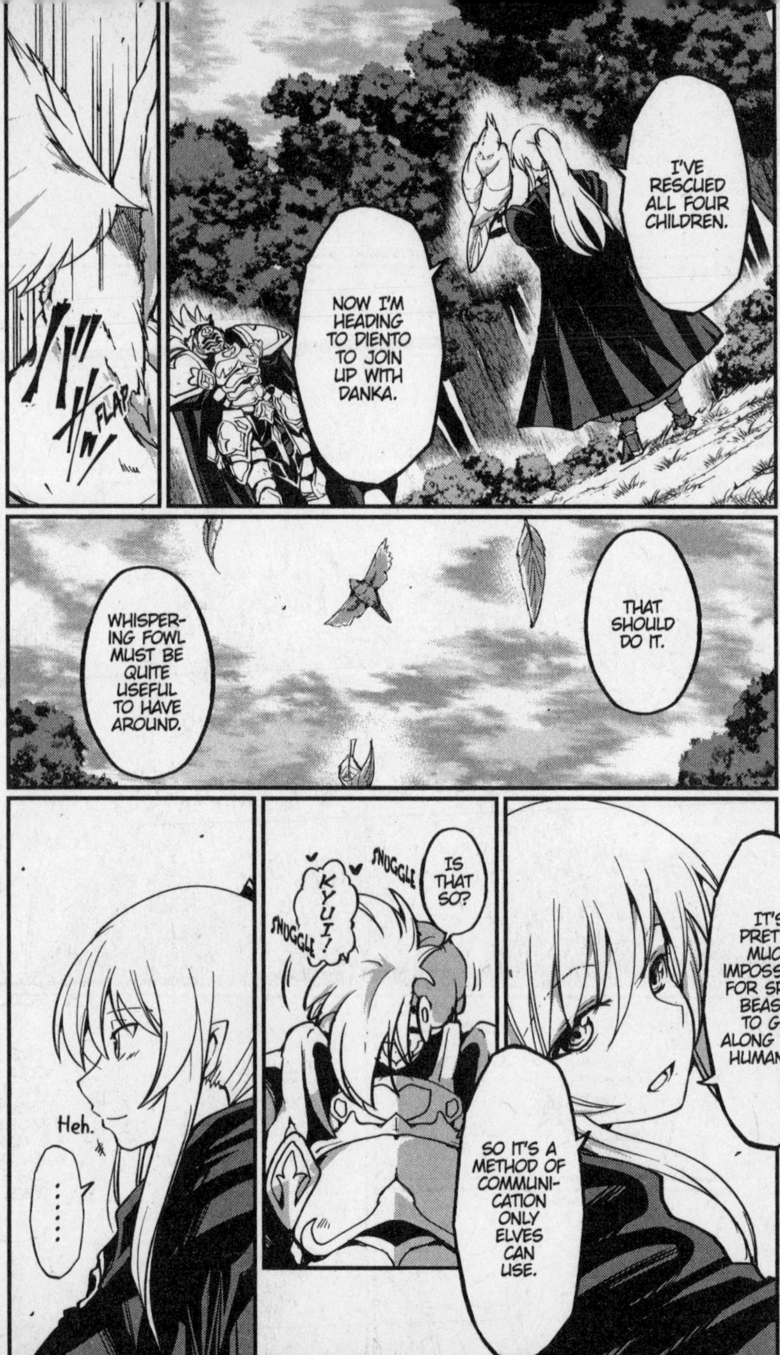
I'VE RESCUED ALL FOUR CHILDREN.
NOW I'M HEADING TO DIENTO TO JOIN UP WITH DANKA.
FLAP
THAT SHOULD DO IT.
WHISPERING-FOWL MUST BE QUITE USEFUL TO HAVE AROUND.
IT'S PRETTY MUCH IMPOSSIBLE FOR SPIRIT BEASTS TO GET ALONG WITH HUMANS...
SO IT'S A METHOD OF COMMUNICATION ONLY ELVES CAN USE.
IS THAT SO?
SNUGGLE
KYUI?!
SNUGGLE
Heh.
......

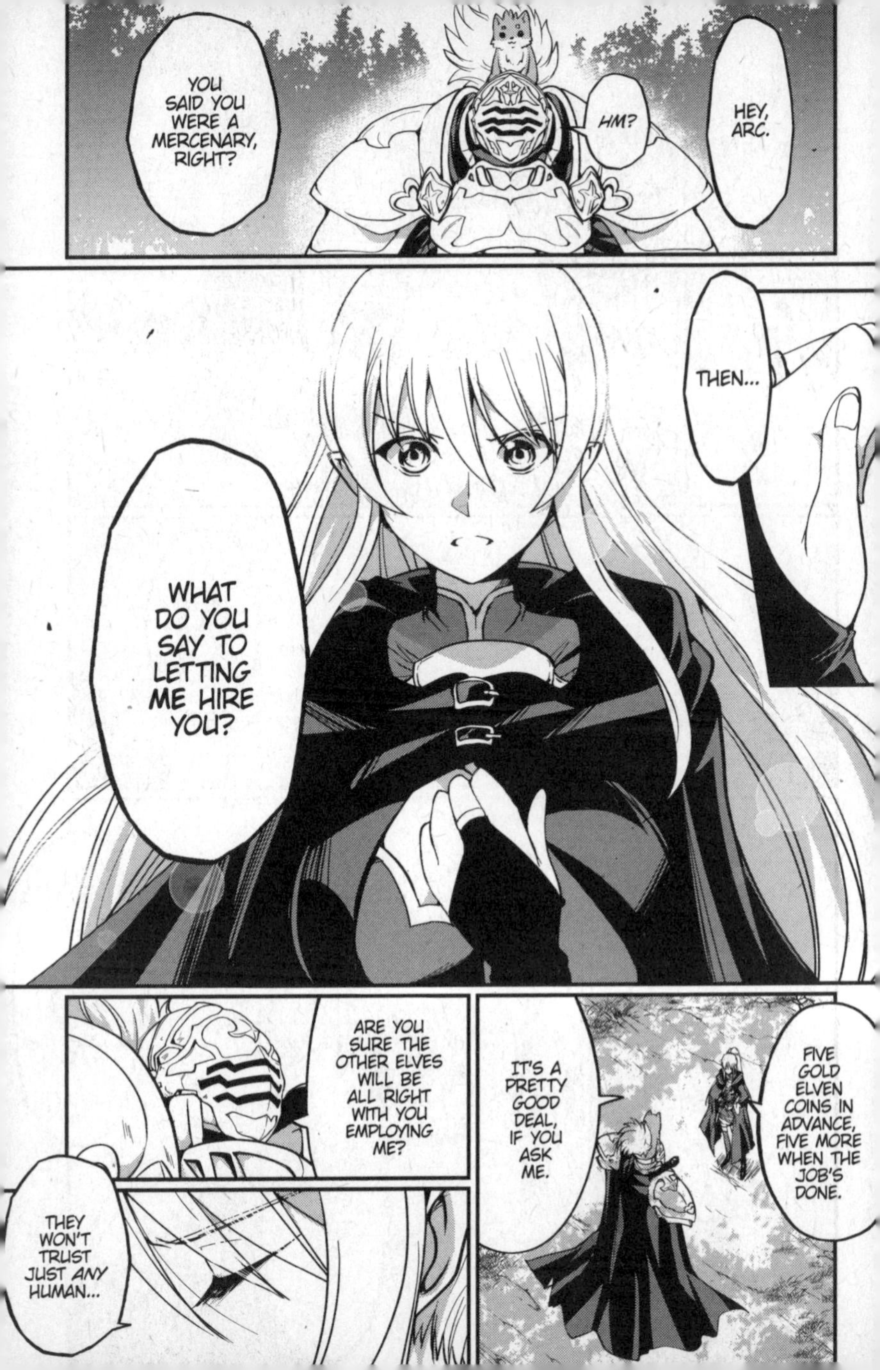
HEY, ARC.
HM?
YOU SAID YOU WERE A MERCENARY, RIGHT?
THEN...
WHAT DO YOU SAY TO LETTING ME HIRE YOU?
FIVE GOLD ELVEN COINS IN ADVANCE, FIVE MORE WHEN THE JOB'S DONE.
IT'S A PRETTY GOOD DEAL, IF YOU ASK ME.
ARE YOU SURE THE OTHER ELVES WILL BE ALL RIGHT WITH YOU EMPLOYING ME?
THEY WON'T TRUST JUST ANY HUMAN...

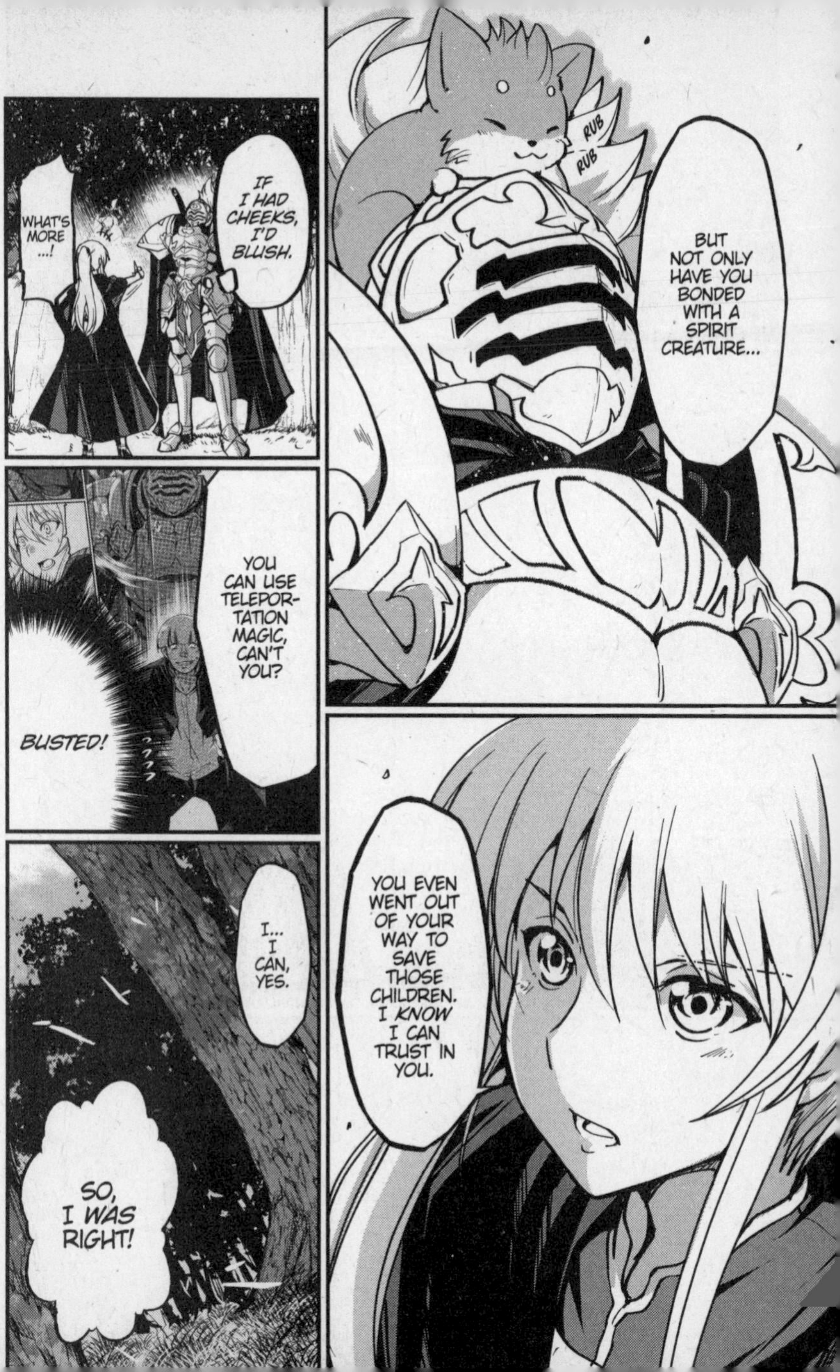
RUB RUB
BUT NOT ONLY HAVE YOU BONDED WITH A SPIRIT CREATURE...
WHAT'S MORE ...!
IF I HAD CHEEKS, I'D BLUSH.
YOU CAN USE TELEPORTATION MAGIC, CAN'T YOU?
BUSTED!
I... I CAN, YES.
SO, I WAS RIGHT!
YOU EVEN WENT OUT OF YOUR WAY TO SAVE THOSE CHILDREN. I KNOW I CAN TRUST IN YOU.

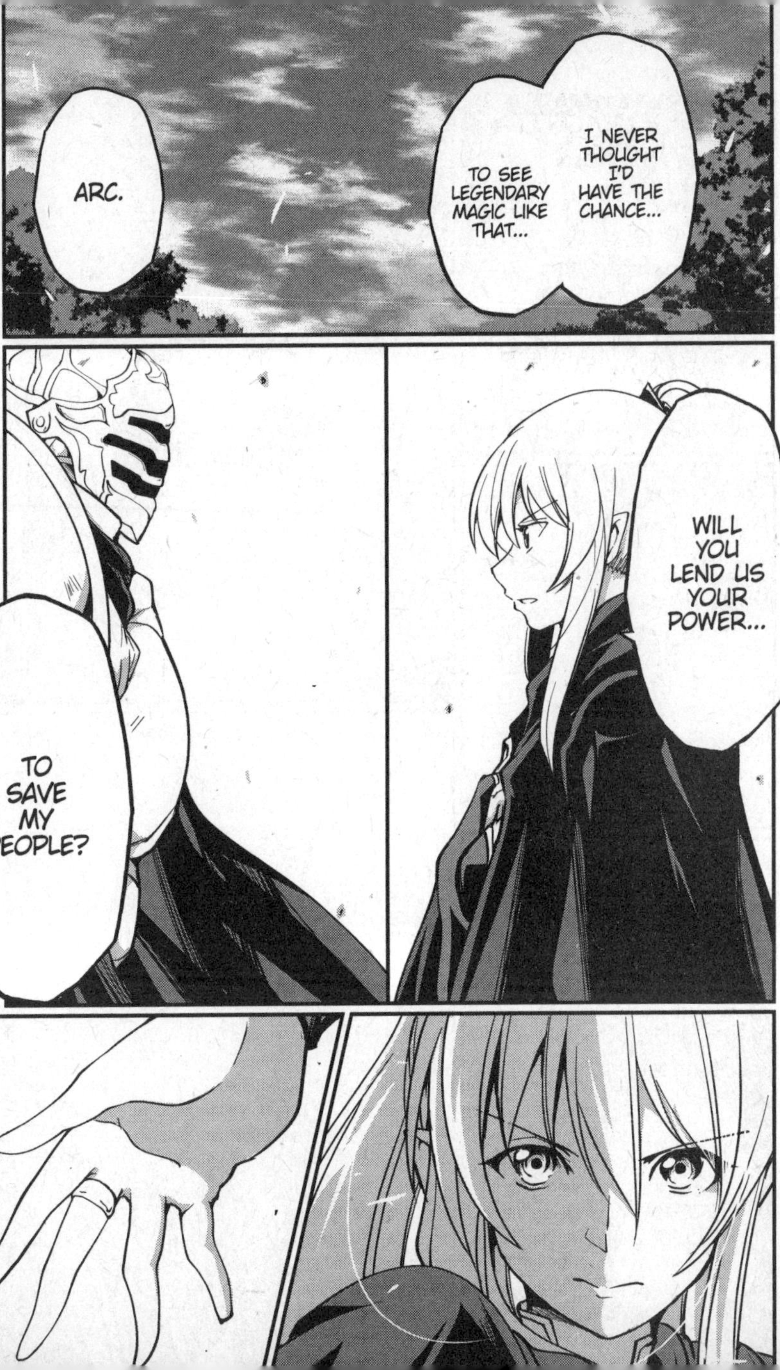
I NEVER THOUGHT I'D HAVE THE CHANCE...
TO SEE LEGENDARY MAGIC LIKE THAT...
ARC.
WILL YOU LEND US YOUR POWER...
TO SAVE MY PEOPLE?

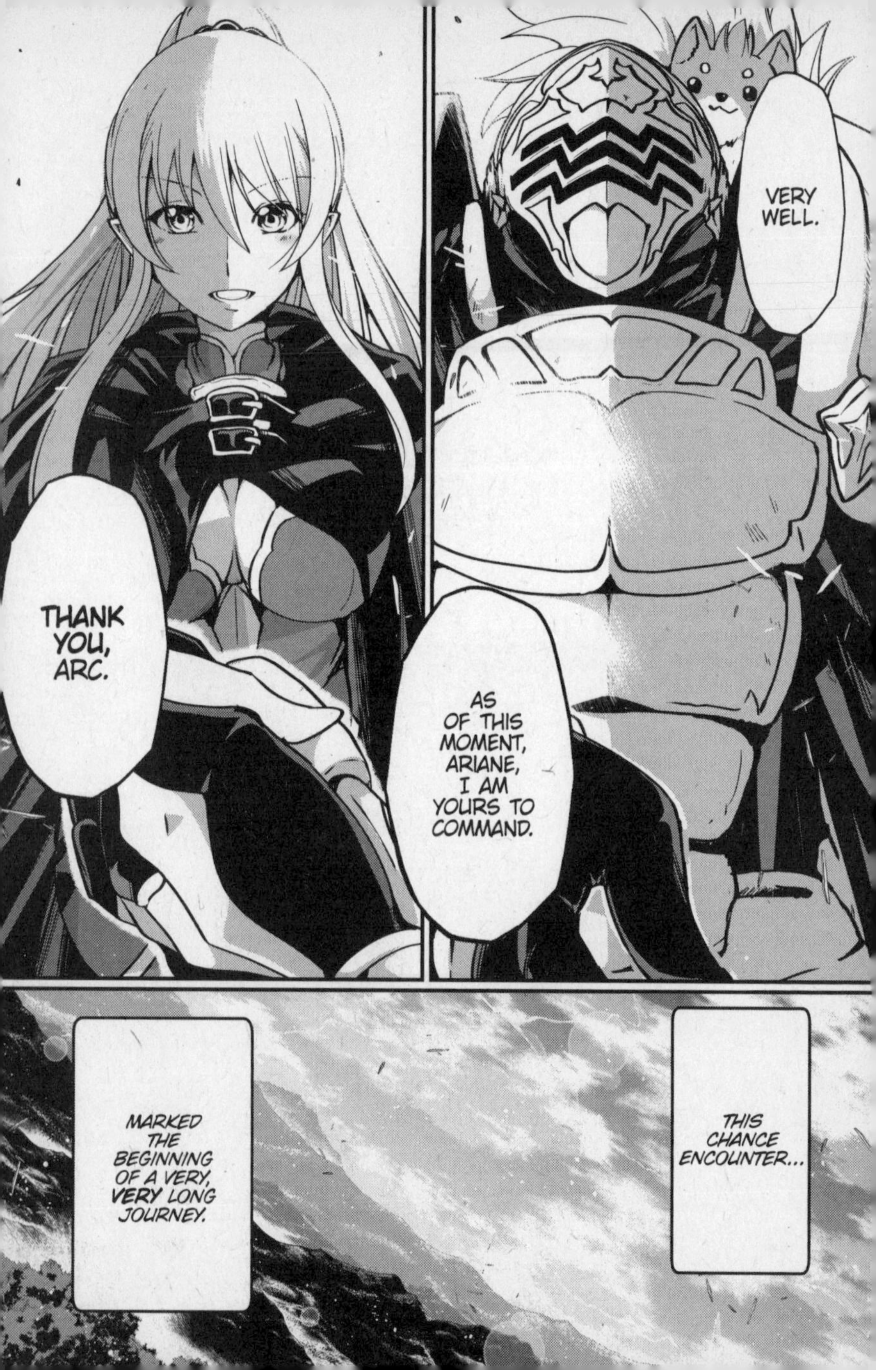
VERY WELL.
AS OF THIS MOMENT, ARIANE, I AM YOURS TO COMMAND.
THANK YOU, ARC.
THIS CHANCE ENCOUNTER...
MARKED THE BEGINNING OF A VERY, **VERY** LONG JOURNEY.

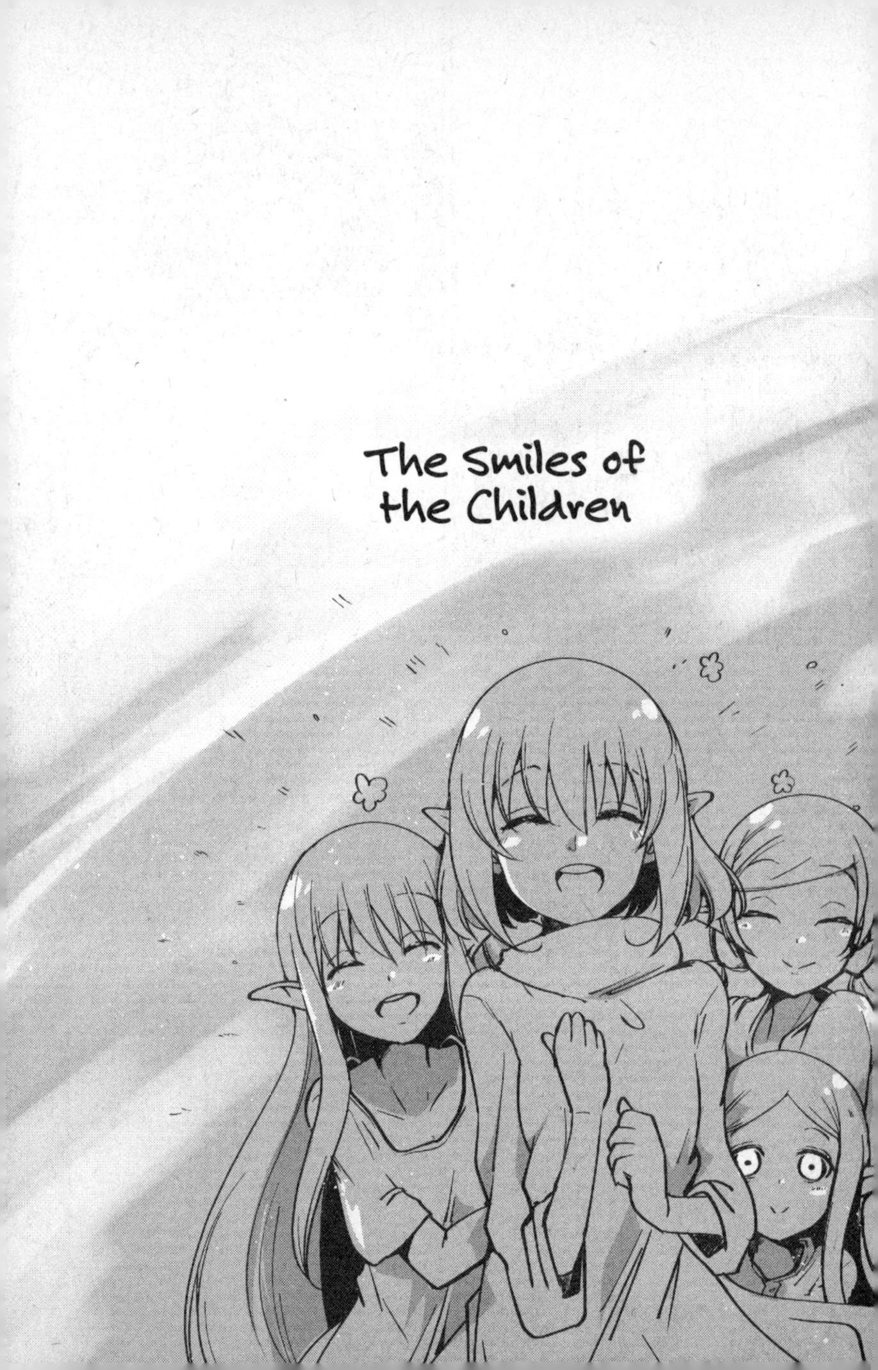
The Smiles of the Children

My Secret with Arc

A young girl from Rata Village had come to pay a visit to the hunter's small workshop. Judging by her small frame, she was probably around thirteen or fourteen years old. Her skin was tanned from all her time out in the sun, and her light brown hair was done up in two pigtails that came down to her shoulders.

"Well, lookie here! It's Marca! Hold on a sec, I'll bring out your family's share."

The hunter gave her a greeting as she entered the shack, then headed into the aging room and reached toward one of the massive chunks of meat strung up there. Marca's blue eyes sparkled as she watched the man work.

This particular chunk of meat was one of many the village hunter had carved from a fang boar. It had reached perfection during the aging process. It had lost a good portion of its water content in the days after he first started, causing it to become much more flavorful and tender.

Because of the massive size of the beast, the workshop was practically bursting at the seams with the spoils of that particular hunt. It was safe to say there was enough here for every household in the village to get their own share, which was why the girl's eyes positively shone with joy.

The man smiled wryly as she gave the same reaction everyone else had when they saw the mountains of meat. He couldn't help but be grateful to the lone knight who'd made this all possible.

It had all started when the girl who stood before him set out to hire a mercenary to act as her escort while she gathered herbs. The person who'd appeared before her wasn't some tactless, run-of-the-mill sword for hire, though--he was a dashing knight covered head to toe in resplendent armor.

It came as no small shock to hear that the man had defeated a fang boar all on his own while protecting his charge. Though fang boars might *look* like enormous bull boars, the danger they posed was beyond compare.

"There ya go, Marca! This ain't all of your share, but it should be more than enough to get ya through for now. Feel free to come back for the rest anytime."

The hunter tied a string around the chunk of meat to make it easier to carry before handing it over to the girl. She staggered a little under the weight, but still flashed him a wide smile as she grappled with it.

"Thank goodness for this, right? You were just saying how you couldn't get any meat around here lately."

"You're tellin' me. Got nothin' but respect for our knight friend from earlier."

The hunter wore a friendly grin as he agreed with Marca. Just like she'd said, the usual small game he would hunt in the nearby forest had up and vanished not too long ago. He hadn't been able to bring home any of his usual haul.

At first, they had thought the fang boar was the culprit--but that wasn't the case. A fearsome monster, much more ferocious than any fang boar, had appeared in the forest.

Though he knew he couldn't do much hunting with that monstrosity on the loose, he depended on trading meat from the game he captured for produce from the village farmers. No meat meant no vegetables for him, so the monster out there devouring his usual quarry was *literally* eating into his livelihood.

But that's when the knight had shown up, the vanquished fang boar in tow. Considering he was generous enough to offer the entire thing to the village with virtually no strings attached, it was easy to understand why the hunter was so grateful to him. He'd only asked for the monster's rune stone and tusks as a reward, and he was even kind enough to give the hunter more work when he requested the beast's fur be put to good use.

"How's that fur pelt workin' out for ya?"

Marca was the one the knight had requested the finished product be delivered to, after all. She fidgeted as the hunter turned his gaze toward her.

"My little sister, Helina, has been using it as an extra blanket on her bed this whole time...even now that spring has come. I haven't had the chance to ask her what she thinks of it yet, though..."

The hunter gave a satisfied nod. "Hahaha! Tell her not to go catchin' a cold from sweatin' too much in her sleep or anythin', ya hear?"

Marca said her thank yous once more before hurrying back home to where her mother and little sister were waiting.

"I'm home! I brought the meat with me, too."

As soon as Marca ducked through the door, Helina bounded happily over. Her eyes stopped on the massive chunk of meat her big sister had brought home.

"Welcome back, Marca! Do you think you could bring it to the kitchen for me?" Marca's mother, Seona, called out to her while fixing up one of their farming tools.

"All right! I'll leave it on one of the shelves in the pantry."

Marca started lugging the meat over to the kitchen, her little sister sticking close by.

"It looks like the governor's soldiers managed to kill the giant monster that appeared in the forest. I heard that not only did it take a hundred men to bring down, but there were actually *two* of them out there..." Seona repeated some of the recent news floating around the village as she watched her daughter go about her business.

Marca thought back to the monster she'd seen Arc take down when they were in the forest together.

It only took Arc one blow to deal with that scary thing, but she's not talking about that *one, is she? I know Arc is strong, but he's not strong enough to beat a monster that took a hundred of the governor's soldiers to finish off all by himself...right?*

After some time lost in thought, Marca realized her mother was staring straight at her.

"Wh-what is it, Mom?"

"Were you listening to me, Marca? From now on, make sure to tell me whenever you're going to the forest. I don't want to go through what happened last time ever again, all right?"

Marca gave a silent nod as she returned her mother's gaze. No matter what, she wouldn't reveal the secret she'd promised to keep with Arc. She swore not to worry her mother any more than she already had, keeping her lips tight and locking away the events of the forest deep inside her.

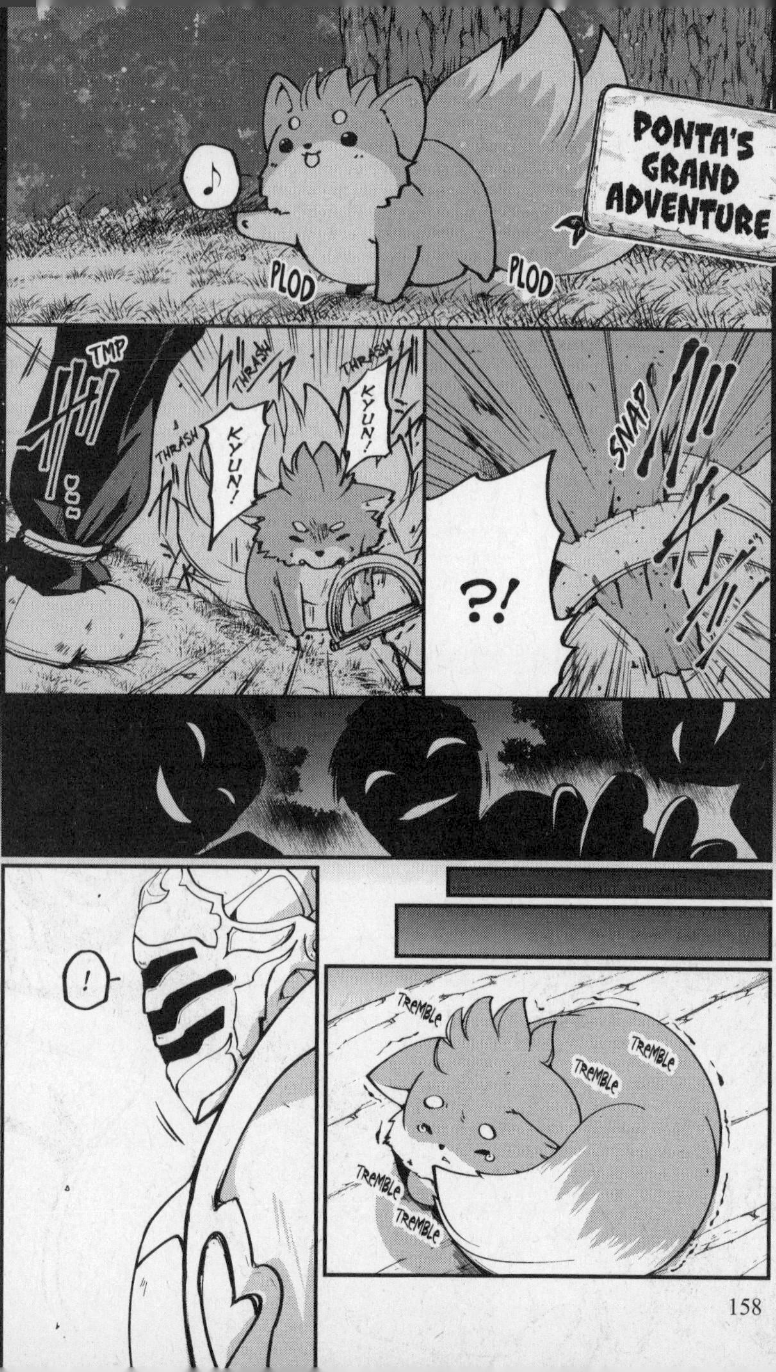
PONTA'S GRAND ADVENTURE
♪
PLOD
PLOD
SNAP
?!
THRASH
KYUN!
KYUN!
THRASH
THRASH
TMP
TREMBLE
TREMBLE
TREMBLE
TREMBLE
TREMBLE
!

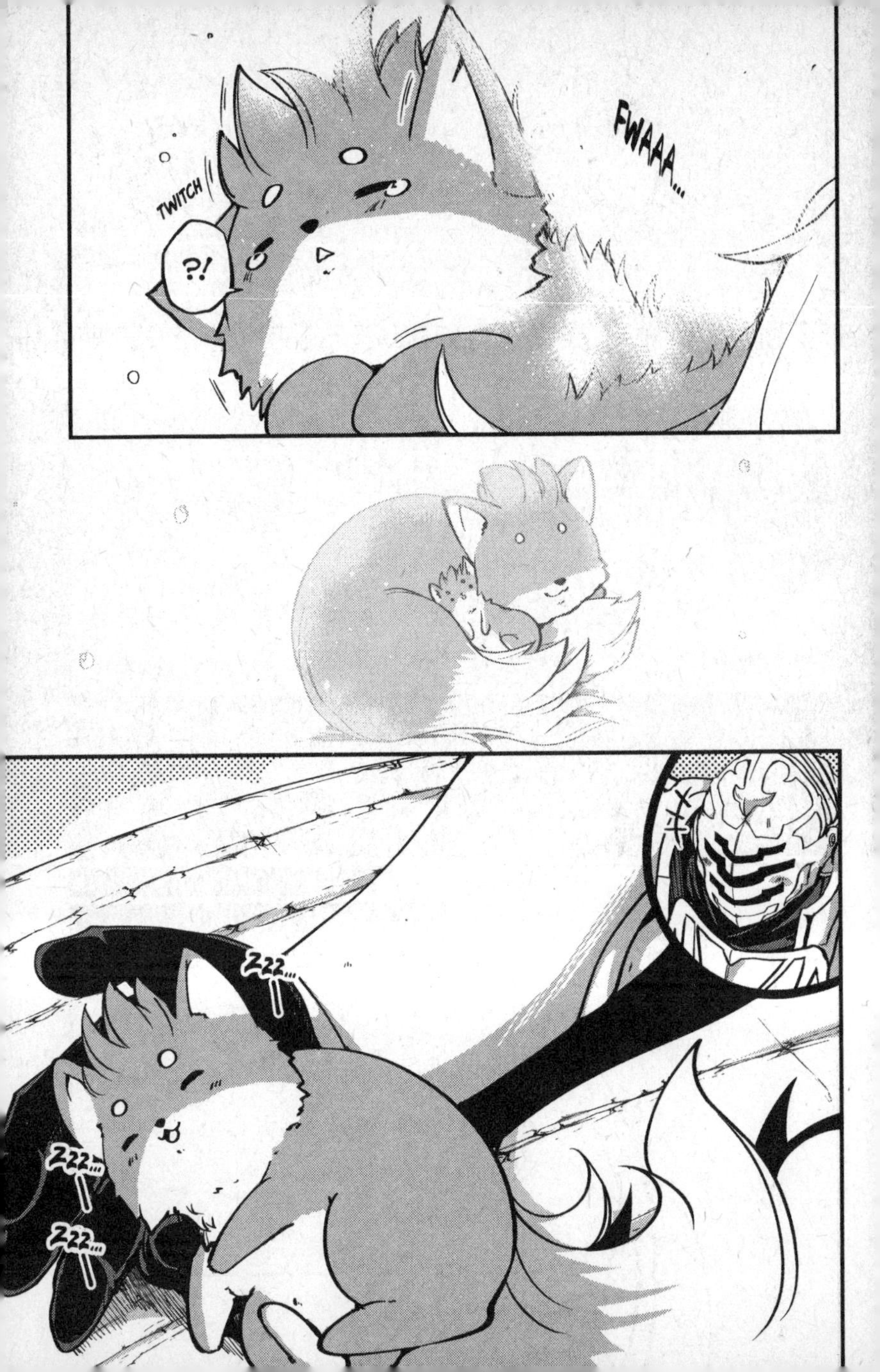
FWAAA...
TWITCH
?!
Zzz...
Zzz...
Zzz...

Thank you for picking up the manga edition of *Skeleton Knight In Another World!* I'm the author who wrote the original light novels, Ennki Hakari.

Being able to see my story come to life in the world of manga is an experience beyond belief, and Akira Sawano-sensei has my utmost gratitude for drawing it.

I think there are plenty of great details you'll only find by comparing the manga with the original story it came from (but maybe that goes without saying). So, if you enjoyed yourself, I'd be happy if you gave the novels a shot as well!

秤 猿鬼
Ennki Hakari

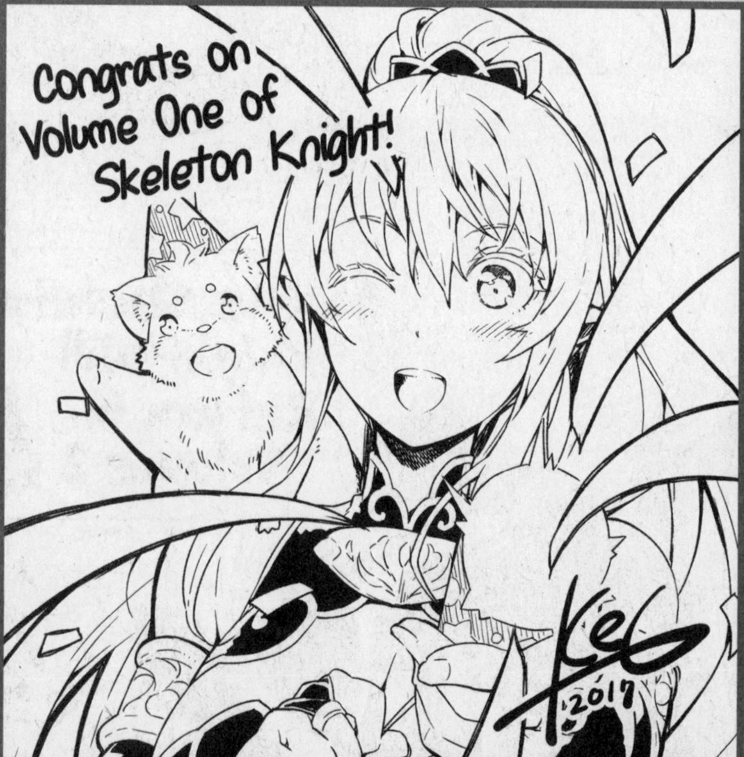
Congrats on Volume One of Skeleton Knight!

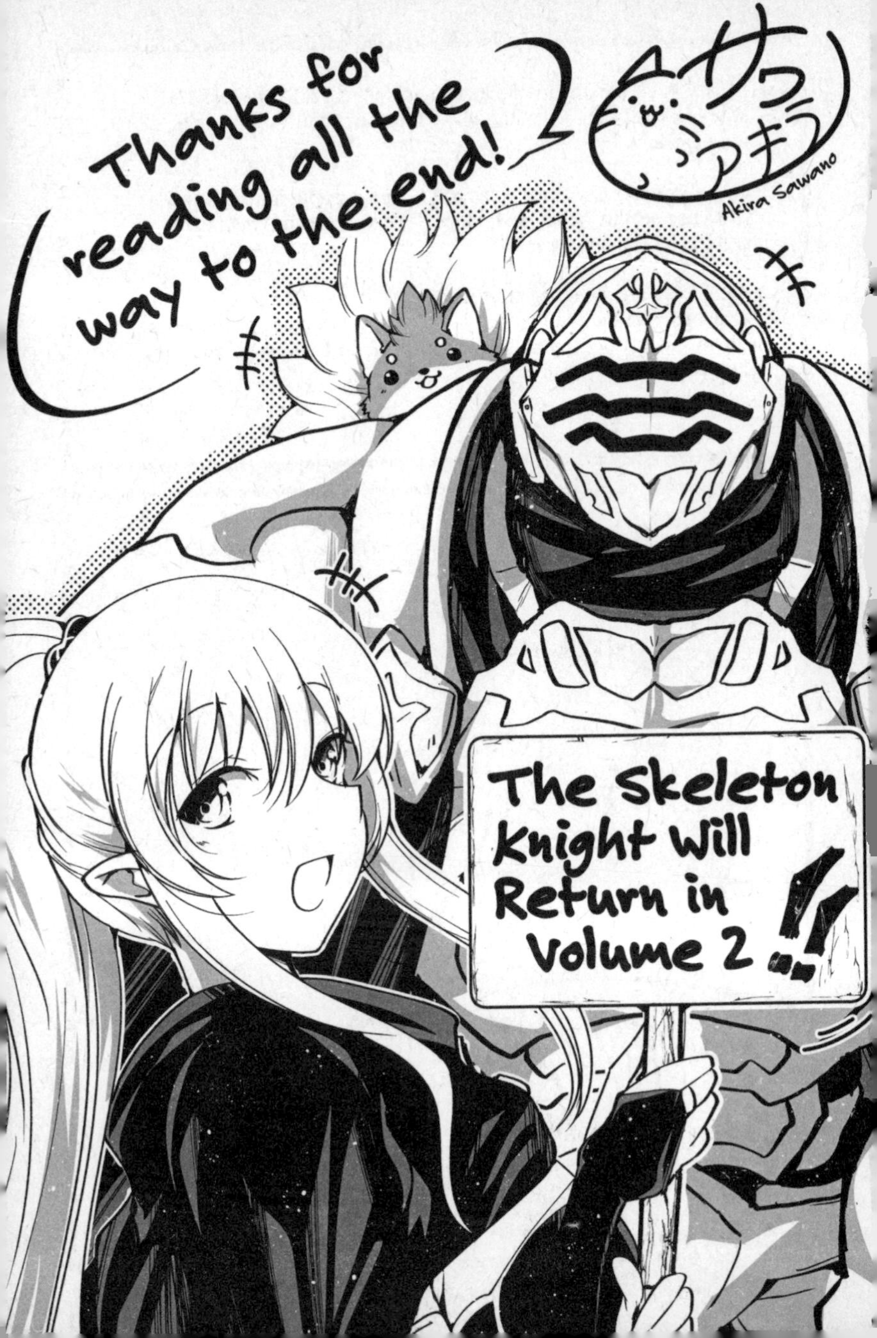

Thanks for reading all the way to the end!
Akira Sawano
The Skeleton Knight Will Return in Volume 2..!!

SEVEN SEAS ENTERTAINMENT PRESENTS

SKELETON KNIGHT IN ANOTHER WORLD

story by ENNKI HAKARI / art by AKIRA SAWANO

VOLUME 1

TRANSLATION
Garrison Denim

ADAPTATION
Peter Adrian Behravesh

LETTERING AND RETOUCH
Meaghan Tucker

COVER DESIGN
KC Fabellon

PROOFREADING
Kurestin Armada
Danielle King

EDITOR
J.P. Sullivan

PRODUCTION MANAGER
Lissa Pattillo

MANAGING EDITOR
Julie Davis

EDITOR-IN-CHIEF
Adam Arnold

PUBLISHER
Jason DeAngelis

GAIKOTSU KISHI-SAMA TADAIMA ISEKAI E ODEKAKE-CHUU VOL. 1

First published in Japan in 2017 by OVERLAP Inc., Ltd., Tokyo.
English translation rights arranged with OVERLAP Inc., Ltd., Tokyo.

Seven Seas press and purchase enquiries can be sent to Marketing Manager Lianne Sentar at press@gomanga.com. Information regarding the distribution and purchase of digital editions is available from Digital Manager CK Russell at digital@gomanga.com.

ISBN: 978-1-64275-065-2

Printed in Canada

First Printing: July 2019

10 9 8 7 6 5 4 3 2 1

FOLLOW US ONLINE: ***www.sevenseasentertainment.com***

READING DIRECTIONS

This book reads from ***right to left***, Japanese style. If this is your first time reading manga, you start reading from the top right panel on each page and take it from there. If you get lost, just follow the numbered diagram here. It may seem backwards at ... Have fun!!

1
2
3
4
5
6
7
8
9

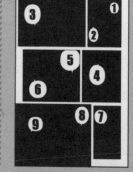